KOREAN YEARBOOK OF INTERNATIONAL LAW

KOREAN YEARBOOK OF INTERNATIONAL LAW

Edited by LEE Jang-Hie

Volume 5
2017

ILCHOKAK
THE KOREAN BRANCH OF THE INTERNATIONAL LAW ASSOCIATION

KOREAN YEARBOOK OF INTERNATIONAL LAW

Copyright © The Korean Branch of the International Law Association 2018
Published by ILCHOKAK

ILCHOKAK Publishing Co., Ltd.
39, Gyeonghuigung-gil, Jongno-gu, Seoul, 03176, Korea
Tel 82-2-733-5430
Fax 82-2-738-5857

First published 2018
Printed in Seoul, Korea
ISSN 2635-8484 85

For subscriptions to this Yearbook, please contact the sole distributor, ILCHOKAK Publishing Co., Ltd.
39, Gyeonghuigung-gil, Jongno-gu, Seoul, 03176, Korea
Tel 82-2-733-5430 Fax 82-2-738-5857   E-mail: ilchokak@hanmail.net

MEMBERS OF EXECUTIVE COUNCIL

SUPPORTING MEMBERS

Northeast Asian History Foundation

Korea Maritime Institute

Korea Institute of Ocean Science & Technology

SHIN & KIM

Law Firm J & C

YOON & YANG LLC

KH Research Center for International Security and Trade

SKKU BK21+ Research Group
on Educational Reform for Cultivating Law Professional
in ICT Global Legal Standards

CONTENTS

EDITOR'S NOTE

With the publication of KYIL Vol.5, the year 2018 will be most remembered by the Korean people for the 2018 *PyeongChang* Winter Olympics. The highlight of the reconciliatory atmosphere between the Republic of Korea and North Korea during the 2018 *PyeongChang* Winter Olympics was meetings between Korean President MOON Jae-In and the high-powered North Korean government delegation.

Nuclear test by the North Korea was the most important issue on the Korean Peninsula in 2017. It seemed very likely that there would be an all-out war between the United States and North Korea on the Korean Peninsula. Efforts in coordinating between denuclearization and peace-regime on the Korean Peninsula seemed to be crucial, though there was no official dialogue between the two nations. In regards to the sixth nuclear test conducted by North Korea on September 9, 2017, U.S. President Donald Trump emphasized "preemptive strike," and having no choice but to "totally destroy" North Korea." The UN Security Council also imposed strong sanctions against North Korea for its nuclear testing and ICBM launch. However, North Korea did not respond to the requests of the international community. North Korea completed its sixth nuclear test in 2017 since the first nuclear test in 2006.

We, Korean people, are very concerned about the prospect of an all-out war on the Korean Peninsula. There has been no dialogue and no contacts between the the Republic of Korea and North Korea since 2008 during the conservative government. Increased military & political tensions escalate the probability of having an all-out-war between two nations.

Fortunately the 2018 *PeyongChang* Winter Olympics was a good opportunity for the Republic of Korea and North Korea to meet and talk. It truly was a miracle on the Korean Peninsula. Since February 2018, dialogues between the Republic of Korea and North Korea have continued. We, Korean

People, expect that the spring of peace will soon be coming to the Korean Peninsula. After the third summit meeting between the Republic of Korea and North Korea, the Panmunjum declaration of April 27, 2018 was signed. Soon thereafter, U.S. President Donald Trump met with North Korean leader Kim Jong-Un on June 12, 2018 in Singapore, for the first summit meeting between the leaders of the two countries. They signed a joint statement, agreeing to security guarantees for North Korea, new peaceful relations, reaffirmed the denuclearization of the Korean Peninsula, return of soldiers' remains, and follow-up negotiations between high-level officials. Immediately following the summit, Trump announced that the US would discontinue "provocative" joint military exercises with the Republic of Korea and would "eventually" withdraw troops stationed in the Republic of Korea.

It is during this critical turning point on the Korean Peninsula that KYIL Vol.5 is being published in 2018.

KYIL consists of five particular parts: Articles, Special Reports, Recent Developments, Contemporary Practice and Judicial Decisions, Treaties/ Agreement concluded by the Republic of Korea regarding international legal issues in Korea.

KYIL Vol.5 extends its deepest appreciations to its editorial staff, colleagues and friends. In particular, we thank Professor LEE Seryon, an Executive Editor of KYIL, for devoting her time for reviewing manuscripts in a professional and precise manner.

I would like to thank the authors who sent us their precious research. I mention with particular gratitude, Professor SUNG Jae-Ho, President of ILA Korean Branch, and Dr. SEO Jin-Woong, the Chief Secretary of ILA Korean branch for their dedication.

KYIL is particularly interested in receiving papers concerning Korean issues in international law for future publications.

LEE Jang-Hie

Editor-in-Chief

Emeritus Professor, Hankuk University of Foreign Studies Law School, Seoul, Korea

ARTICLES

Legal Status of the EEZ and Its Implication for Delimitation of the Areas around Dokdo

LEE Chang-Wee[*]
Professor
University of Seoul, School of Law, Seoul, Korea

Abstract

One of the most controversial issues during the UN Conference on the Law of the Sea was to determine the legal status of the EEZ. The first view envisaged the zone as an extension of the territorial sea, where the coastal states would enjoy sovereignty with certain exceptions. The second view considered the zone to have the high seas status with certain modifications. The third view held that the EEZ was a sui generis zone with its own legal status. The first view was presented by several Latin American States. The second view reflected the concerns of Maritime Powers.

The 1982 UN Convention stipulated broad jurisdiction and sovereign rights of coastal states as well as certain freedoms and duties of other states in the EEZ. Considering the general trend in the UN Conference and the relative articles of the Convention, it would be reasonable to regard the EEZ as a separate functional zone of a sui generis character, situated between the territorial sea and the high seas. It remains to be seen whether an agreement on the issue is reached by accumulation of state practice.

Korea, China and Japan established the EEZ regime in the late 1990s. But they did not agree on the final maritime boundary delimitation. Instead, they concluded three bilateral fisheries agreements establishing several intermediate zones in the overlapping EEZ. As Korea, China and Japan take different stances on the EEZ, conflicts over military activities or marine scientific research in the EEZ make it more difficult for them to delimit maritime boundaries.

Therefore, many agreements have yet to be reached on maritime boundaries relating to the EEZ or legal status of the EEZ among the coastal states in the region. The coastal states should manage and control the EEZ regime under those circumstances.

This paper examines how the EEZ discourse could evolve in Northeast Asia in the future. It will begin with an overview of the legal status of the EEZ, followed by commentary on the EEZ regime in the domestic laws of coastal states concerned, and related issues such as delimitation of the areas around Dokdo. It provides interpretations on the relevant articles of the Convention as well as EEZ-related state practice.

Key Words

UNCLOS, EEZ, boundary delimitation, military activities, MSR

1. INTRODUCTION

Korea, China, and Japan introduced the exclusive economic zone (EEZ) into their domestic laws in 1996 and 1998 and have accordingly instituted various systems relating to the EEZ, such as the utilization of marine resources, protection of the marine environment, and the conduct of marine scientific research. Delimitation of maritime boundaries remains an unfinished business, however, and the EEZ regime has continued to breed conflict and confrontation. Korea and Japan have locked horns over the intermediate zone and marine scientific research,[1] and China's illegal fishing activities have resulted in losses of human life in the course of Korea's crackdown. China and Japan had had similar problems, but they agreed on a joint development system as a stopgap measure.[2] Backlash from the Chinese public, however, has prevented a treaty from being concluded.

Conflict resulting from military activities in the EEZ has also made it difficult for Korea, China, and Japan to delimit maritime boundaries. For example, when Korea and the United States carried out joint military exercise in the Yellow Sea after the artillery barrage on Yeonpyeong Island in 2010, China expressed deep concern over the deployment of the *USS George Washington* in the region. It demonstrates the dangers of neighboring countries failing to agree on the EEZ boundaries, while the maneuver raises once again the question of what kinds of military activities are permissible in the EEZ.[3] Also, the Okinotorishima atoll issue, over which China and Japan were in disagreement at the 19th Meeting of States Parties to the UN Convention on the Law of the Sea (UNCLOS) from June 22 to 26, 2009, originated in marine scientific research in the seas around Okinotorishima. The essence of the issue, however, was that Japan was trying to curb China's build-up of naval forces.[4] Even Korea and China, which have no territorial conflicts over islands, have yet to complete delimitation of maritime boundaries. This was largely due to China's concern over the Ieodo Ocean Research Station. Although Korea and China resumed their negotiation over maritime boundary delimitation in the Yellow Sea in December 2015, the current provisional arrangements regime is expected to last for a while.[5]

These issues can be resolved only when Korea, Japan, and China can refrain from conflict and rivalry over maritime jurisdiction over the EEZ through maritime boundary delimitation. The three nations stand wide apart when it comes to principles governing disputes over jurisdiction or maritime delimitation and the process by which these issues are addressed. They likely will not be able to reach a consensus on these issues for some time. Hence, it is important to understand the other party's position on the EEZ. If the three countries cannot come to an agreement on maritime delimitation in the near future, at least they can seek to minimize conflict by striking deals on a case-by-case basis.

As will be examined in this paper, the EEZ derives from the expansion of fishery zones and changes to the rules concerning continental shelves. Hence, these countries adopted the EEZ regime even before the entry into force of the UNCLOS, calling for sovereign rights to the utilization of marine resources in the EEZ. With the passage of time, however, different countries began to adopt different rules on the EEZ. In some instances, after the UNCLOS took effect, some countries began to push for a comprehensive set of rules encompassing various rights or obligations such as security issues related to the EEZ.[6]

Korea, China, and Japan take different stances on the EEZ. While Japan has viewed the EEZ from an advanced maritime nation's perspective, China has taken a directly opposite approach. Recent disputes in the South China Sea between the United States and China relating to the freedom of navigation as well as the legal status of artificial islands reflect China's position on the EEZ regime.[7] Korea has not taken a clear stance. As can be seen, each of these three countries has accepted and operated the EEZ with dissimilar ideas of what the EEZ is. It is important to understand how these different viewpoints have been translated into domestic laws in Korea, China, and Japan, and to examine how these perspectives have changed in line with the changing maritime order, if we are to discuss the realignment of the Northeast Asian maritime order in the future. If we were to view the EEZ as the high seas—as do advanced nations—we would not need to take maritime delimitation and military activities that seriously. An emphasis on the territoriality of the EEZ, however, could aggravate clashing interests among countries concerned.

The goal of this paper is to examine how the EEZ discourse might evolve in Northeast Asia in the future. It will begin with an overview of the legal status of the EEZ, followed by commentary on the EEZ regime in the domestic laws of coastal states concerned, and related issues such as delimitation of the areas around Dokdo. It provides interpretations on the relevant articles of the Convention as well as EEZ related state practice. Considering recent South China Sea disputes and developments in maritime boundary issues involving China, it would be significant for Korea to understand the context and prospects of the EEZ regime in the region.

2. LEGAL STATUS OF THE EEZ

2-1. CONTEXT

The EEZ, which has become a symbolic regime of modern law of the sea in the name of "creeping jurisdiction," was at first opposed by advanced maritime powers for its broad application area and for the exclusive as well as comprehensive set of rights for coastal states.[8] It is natural that advanced maritime powers objected to limiting the scope of the high seas, where they can enjoy freedom of navigation or unregulated utilization of marine resources. More specifically, the United States and the USSR were concerned about the limited freedom of navigation or flight, and Japan was primarily concerned about the limited use of marine resources.[9]

The conflict over the EEZ between advanced maritime powers and coastal states escalated into a conflict over the legal status of the EEZ, and to this day, after more than 20 years since the UNCLOS went into effect, the conflict remains unresolved. While the EEZ has been introduced domestically by a majority of coastal states, debate over the legal status of the EEZ remains due to different processes by which the EEZ regime is introduced into their domestic legal systems.

The UNCLOS does not clearly stipulate the legal status of the EEZ.[10] Hence, the interpretation of related provisions in the convention becomes important. Each country has a different attitude toward the EEZ depending on their interest, and thus interpretations differ. Hence, it is necessary to iron out differences on key issues related to the EEZ. In particular, a country's implementation of a specific regime is not limited to the UNCLOS but has major implications for interpretation and implementation of norms of international law, and thus it is important to analyze and understand this.[11]

The legal status of the EEZ has invited much controversy from the outset of the UN Conference on the Law of the Sea. While advanced maritime powers, concerned about expanding maritime jurisdiction, tried to emphasize that the EEZ was the high seas, developing countries took the opposite stance.[12] Related provisions in the 1982 UNCLOS stipulated that the EEZ was a sui generis regime and allowed for state jurisdiction and sovereign rights and management of competing claims between coastal states and other states, thus leaving room for dispute, to a degree. The legal status of the EEZ thus depends on how one interprets related provisions in the Convention.[13]

2-2. EEZ as High Seas

Those who deny the territoriality of the EEZ and emphasize it only as the high seas base their argument on the following provisions in the convention. First, according to articles 55 and 57, the EEZ is an area beyond and adjacent to the territorial sea and is thus distinguished from the territorial sea. Second, as per article 56(1) and (3), the coastal state has special sovereign rights and jurisdiction. Third, in the EEZ, according to article 58(1), all states enjoy the freedoms referred to in article 87, which stipulates freedoms of the high seas. Fourth, article 58(2) stipulates that articles 88 to 115 and other pertinent rules of international law apply to the EEZ. Fifth, as per article 86, Part 7 of the UNCLOS applies to contiguous zones, and contiguous zones only extend to 24 nautical miles within an EEZ. Sixth, the principles applied to straits used for international navigation are based on the traditional dichotomy between the territorial sea and the high seas. In particular, articles 35 and 38 mention both—"the EEZ or the high seas." Seventh, article 111 on the right of hot pursuit is based on the traditional dichotomy of territorial sea and high seas. In particular, a coastal state's exercise of the right of hot pursuit in an EEZ is suspended by the pursued vessel's entry into territorial seas.**14**

Looking back on the history of the legislation of article 86, the earlier UN Conference on the Law of the Sea drafts that clearly distinguished between the EEZ and the high seas defined the high seas as "waters that are not part of any one state's EEZ, territorial sea, internal waters, or archipelagic waters."**15** Considering that, it cannot be natural to draw the conclusion that the EEZ and the high seas are identical.

2-3. EEZ as High Seas and Special Zone

A general comparison of the EEZ shows that an argument that mixes the high seas with special zone provides for a more flexible interpretation. In other words, the UNCLOS emphasizes the EEZ as both high seas and a special zone, as shown by these provisions. First, articles 55, 56, and 58 give the coastal state special rights and jurisdiction in the EEZ, and they also give rights and freedoms to third countries in the EEZ. Second, the freedom of navigation on the high seas given to third countries, per article 58(1) and (2), is to be bound by related UNCLOS provisions. Third, article 86 stipulates the principles of applying the high seas provisions in Part 7 without directly giving a definition of the high seas. Instead, article 86 only says that application of Part 7 shall not restrict any country's freedoms in the EEZ. Fourth, as per articles 56(2) and 58(3) the coastal state and third states in their exercise of rights and performance of duties shall have due regard to each other's rights and duties.**16**

2-4. EEZ as Special Zone

Proponents of the EEZ as special zone base their arguments on the following: First, article 55 stipulates that the EEZ, an area beyond and adjacent to the territorial sea, is subject to a special legal regime. Second, articles 33(1) and 78(1) of the UNCLOS, unlike article 24(1) of the

Convention on the Territorial Sea and Contiguous Zone and article 3 of the Convention on the Continental Shelf, do not use the expression "high seas." Third, article 59 of the UNCLOS stipulates that in cases where the UNCLOS does not attribute rights or jurisdiction to the coastal State or to other States within the exclusive economic zone, and a conflict arises between the interests of the coastal State and any other State or States, the conflict should be resolved on the basis of equity and in the light of all the relevant circumstances, taking into account the respective importance of the interests involved to the parties as well as to the international community as a whole.[17]

This view is valid given the UNCLOS provisions, which stipulate that the coastal state, in exercising its rights or performing its duties, should have due regard to other states' rights and duties, and that all states should give due consideration to the coastal state's rights and duties in the EEZ.[18] Furthermore, article 59 is a good guideline for resolving conflicts and disputes over residual rights, and even this alone shows that the EEZ is neither a territorial sea nor high seas but a special zone. Due to sharp differences of opinion between maritime powers and developing states over military activities in the EEZ, how this issue is interpreted and dealt with will be all the more important.

2-5. EVALUATION

Various individual comments were made on the legal status of the EEZ as the UN Conference on the Law of the Sea proceeded. German and USSR academics like Ingo von Munch or S. V. Molodtsov, for example, argued that the EEZ was like the high seas. Munch said the EEZ was not a coastal state's unique zone or part of a coastal state's territorial sea but a functional zone on the high seas. Molodtsov, too, maintained that the EEZ was part of the high seas on the grounds of article 58(2) of the UNCLOS, which stipulates that article 89—which stipulates that no state may validly purport to subject any part of the high seas to its sovereignty—applies to the EEZ.[19] It is worth noting that it was mostly USSR academics like Molodtsov who emphasized that the EEZ was a special zone of the high seas where the coastal state's economic interests come together with the freedoms of the high seas. This was not unrelated to the USSR's emphasis on the freedom to use the sea.

By contrast, Jean-Pierre Quéneude saw the EEZ not as territorial sea or high seas, but as secondary waters or intermediate waters,[20] and Nakamura said the EEZ was a mixed zone or a composite zone.[21] René Jean Dupuy claimed that the EEZ was an economic sovereignty zone, keying in on the coastal state's authority in the EEZ,[22] and Yamamoto called it a zone where, unlike the territorial sea, functional sovereignty or jurisdiction is exercised based on the adjacency or contiguity to the coastal state's territory.[23]

Tommy T. B. Koh, citing the process of negotiations concerning EEZ-related provisions of the UNCLOS, said the EEZ had already been established as a special zone.[24] In the Japanese version of a UNCLOS commentary, Oda, like Koh, explained that the EEZ was a special zone.[25]

Generally speaking, it would be acceptable to interpret the EEZ as a special zone with its own characteristics. While the freedom of navigation and communications in the EEZ is supposed to be identical to the freedoms in the high seas as stipulated by the UNCLOS, such freedoms in the EEZ should be balanced out with the rights and jurisdiction of the coastal state. Hence, the logic that the EEZ is a special zone becomes all the more convincing.

3. THE EEZ REGIME IN NORTHEAST ASIA

3-1. KOREA

When the EEZ regime was being discussed at the UN Conference on the Law of the Sea, Korea did not actively offer its thoughts.[26] At the time, developing countries were expressing full support for the EEZ regime, while maritime powers were objecting to it. It would have been natural for Korea, which was not too far removed from being a developing country, to endorse the EEZ regime. Korea had already established the quintessential maritime policy of a developing nation in 1952 by boldly broadening its maritime jurisdiction under the Peace Line declaration.[27]

Korea, however, did not endorse the EEZ regime for a number of reasons. The foremost reason was Korea's vested interest as a distant water fishing nation. At the time, Korea was heavily reliant on overseas fishing, including distant water fishing, and thus it had no choice but to take a lukewarm attitude to the EEZ regime.[28]

The next major reason was the difficulty of maritime boundary delimitation with China and Japan if Korea had declared its EEZ. Maritime boundary delimitation with Japan would have been particularly difficult, as Dokdo would have been the most sensitive issue. Hence, Korea probably decided that maintaining the status quo was more beneficial.[29] Besides, Japan and China were not actively seeking to introduce the EEZ, either.

This all changed when the UNCLOS entered into force in 1994. Korea was compelled to work the new global order of the law of the sea into its domestic law. Specifically, the UNCLOS stipulated that effective management of the natural resources and the preservation of the marine environment were to be carried out through the EEZ regime, and that in enclosed or semi-enclosed seas like in Northeast Asia, the spirit of the UNCLOS should be materialized through regional cooperation.[30] Moreover, all Northeast Asian states had already declared their EEZs or were moving toward turning their 200-nautical mile fishing zones into EEZs. Thus Korea could no longer turn a blind eye to these developments.[31] As of July 1996, 121 states had declared 200-nautical mile jurisdictional waters: 95 states declared their EEZs, 15 states declared 200-nautical mile fishing zones, and 11 claimed 200-nautical mile territorial sea.[32]

In August 1996, the Korean government promulgated the "EEZ Act." The EEZ Act was made because Korea had ratified the UNCLOS in January 1996. As a follow-on measure, it was positively introducing the new international maritime order into domestic law by defining the scope of the EEZ and establishing the structure of sovereign rights and jurisdiction in the EEZ.[33] The EEZ Act faithfully reflected EEZ-related provisions laid out in the UNCLOS.

One issue that remains unresolved externally with respect to the operation of the EEZ is maritime boundary delimitation with neighboring states. As regards the boundary delimitation issue, article 2 (2) of the Korean EEZ Act stipulates that maritime boundaries with neighboring countries shall be delimited upon mutual agreement based on international law. In other words, Korea made it clear that it respects international law in negotiations with China and Japan.

In addition to the "EEZ Act," Korea enacted the "Act on Exercising Sovereign Rights Regarding Foreigners' Fishing in the EEZ" in 1996. This act was aimed at efficiently responding to the fishing environment in waters surrounding the Korean Peninsula and at regulating foreigners' fishing activities to conserve and manage fish resources in the EEZ.[34] This act has efficiently regulated foreigners' fishing operations in Korea's EEZ over the past years.

Regarding domestic operation of the EEZ, an important issue besides marine resources management is the exercise of the right of marine environment and marine scientific research. In 1977, Korea enacted the "Prevention of Marine Pollution Act," which stipulated in detail all the necessary steps for protecting and preserving the marine environment.[35] The "Prevention of Marine Pollution Act" was abolished on January 19, 2007, and the "Marine Environment Management Act" was enacted and implemented, establishing a new marine environmental protection regime.[36]

With respect to marine scientific research, Korea established the "Marine Scientific Research Act" in 1995, prior to the introduction of the

EEZ, thus accepting domestically those UNCLOS provisions related to marine scientific research. This act was amended with minor changes in 2013.

In March 2017, the Korean government revised the 1996 "EEZ Act" to include the continental shelf regime into it. As a result, the title of the law has changed into the "EEZ and Continental Shelf Act."

3-2. CHINA

When the UN Conference on the Law of the Sea was discussing the EEZ regime, China endorsed it wholeheartedly. As with other Third World countries, China's basic maritime policy was to limit advanced maritime powers' freedoms in the seas by broadening its maritime jurisdiction. Accordingly, China denied the EEZ as the high seas, claimed its jurisdictional rights to the EEZ, and asserted the superiority of jurisdiction.[37] China's argument was that, if the coastal state's jurisdiction in the EEZ was not recognized actively, it would make it difficult for the coastal state to maintain security or adequately exercise its rights or jurisdiction over marine resources and thus make it impossible for the coastal state to respond effectively to advanced nations' plundering of resources. China's position was clearly reflected in the "Working Paper on Sea Area within the Limits of National Jurisdiction" that it submitted to the committee for the peaceful use of the seabed in July 1973.[38]

Some parts of China's argument on the EEZ, however, indicate that China's interpretation of the coastal state's rights was excessively broad. One case in point is that China said that no country's normal navigation or overflight in the EEZ shall be hindered. China did not explain in detail what "normal" navigation and overflight meant. This part offers crucial guidance on military activities in the EEZ, but regarding this, Jeanette Greenfield pointed out that China clearly did not approve of military use of the EEZ.[39] Another point worth noting is that, as with the case of the continental shelf, China excluded certain principles of boundary delimitation in the EEZ. In that vein, China claimed as a principle of maritime boundary delimitation equitable principles when declaring the EEZ regime.[40]

In this context, China's EEZ was formally institutionalized, along with the continental shelf, by the "EEZ and Continental Shelf Act" enacted on June 26, 1998. China's "EEZ and Continental Shelf Act" stipulates the declaration of the EEZ, boundary delimitation and China's exercise of sovereign rights and jurisdiction, and the application and implementation of related laws.[41] China's "EEZ and Continental Shelf Act" was basically composed of related provisions in the UNCLOS, and it contains more provisions and details than do the corresponding laws of Korea and Japan. The Chinese law does not seem to deviate much from the standards set by the UNCLOS. However, the law does interpret to the coastal state's advantage those UNCLOS provisions that are ambiguous or fail to offer specific standards. For example, article 14, which stipulates that EEZ-related provisions in the law do not affect the historical rights of the PRC, leaves room for debate externally.[42] That is because countries normally do not work historical rights into their domestic law and claim those rights externally.

Also worth noting is that the law stipulates equitable principles with respect to maritime boundary delimitation.[43] A policy that China invariably stood by at the third UN Conference on the Law of the Sea was reiterated in China's domestic legislation.

The law stipulates foreign countries' freedom of navigation and overflight along with their freedom of laying submarine cables and pipelines, and that was meant to show respect for foreign countries' rights. The law, however, also makes it mandatory for foreign countries to receive the Chinese government's or a relevant organ's authority before laying submarine cables and pipelines without distinguishing between the EEZ and the continental shelf. That could be interpreted as China's intent to manage foreign countries' activities to a certain extent.[44]

Worth noting are those provisions that stipulate China's jurisdiction over marine scientific research in the EEZ and the continental shelf. China's marine scientific research is detailed in domestic legislation on marine scientific research—specifically, "regulations on managing foreign-related marine scientific research."[45]

3-3. JAPAN

Japan has traditionally supported the freedom of the seas, from an advanced maritime power's perspective. Accordingly, Japan's state policy has been "narrow territorial sea, broad high seas" and has actively opposed the extension of maritime jurisdiction. Hence, of the four conventions adopted at the Geneva Conference on the Law of the Sea, Japan acceded to only the territorial sea and the contiguous zone convention and the high seas convention and did not join the continental shelf convention and the convention on fishing and conservation of the living resources of the high seas.[46] Japan was of the belief that the latter two conventions violated its interests in the seas.

Japan's position remained unchanged at the Third UN Conference on the Law of the Sea. In particular, with respect to the introduction of the EEZ regime, Japan remained the only country that had vocally opposed it since the regime began to be discussed at the Caracas session in 1974. For that reason, Japan was called "Mr. Except One"— the one country that remained opposed to the EEZ.[47] Between 1976 and 1977, when the United States and the USSR each declared their 200-nautical mile fishing zones, Japan responded by quickly legislating the territorial sea law and the provisional law on fishing zones in 1977. By doing so, Japan established its 12-nautical mile territorial sea and its 200-nautical mile fishing zone. When the UNCLOS took effect and a majority of countries eventually supported the EEZ regime, Japan went with the trend and declared its EEZ in 1996. Japan declared its continental shelf and EEZ through the legislation of the "EEZ and Continental Shelf Law."

Japan's EEZ and Continental Shelf Law allows for Japan to exercise sovereign rights and other types of jurisdiction in the continental shelf, which includes the 200-nautical mile EEZ and its seabed, in accordance with the EEZ and continental shelf provisions of the UNCLOS. This law, along with the law on the territorial sea and the contiguous zones, is a basic law that regulates the legal structure of state sovereignty over Japan's surrounding seas.[48]

Like Korea's EEZ Act, Japan's EEZ and Continental Shelf Law complies with related principles of international law. What makes it different from the Korean law, however, is that it regulates the EEZ and continental shelf with a single law. While Korea enacted the "Submarine Mineral Resources Development Act" in 1970, Japan introduced the continental shelf regime relatively late. Worth noting, though, is that Japan has been more flexible toward changes in the new maritime order since the 1980s.[49] The Japanese government has a single law for both the continental shelf and the EEZ because of similarities and a certain level of overlap between the two regimes.

Japan ensured that fishing in the EEZ was regulated by streamlining the "Act on Exercise of Sovereign Rights to Fishing and Others in the EEZ" and the "Act on Conservation and Management of Marine Living Resources." The use of the sea related to the EEZ, such as the preservation of the marine environment or marine scientific research, is regulated by other laws. For example, Japan has a law for preventing marine pollution, called "Act on Prevention of Marine Pollution and Disaster in the Sea."

Unlike Korea and China, Japan does not have a separate set of laws for marine scientific research. Instead, the "Guidelines on Marine Scientific Research in Areas under National Jurisdiction of Japan" established in 1996 are being implemented in relation to article 3(1).[50] Thus these guidelines are considered as Japan's support for a flexible interpretation— one echoing advanced maritime powers' preference for free marine scientific research.

4. SOVEREIGN RIGHTS, JURISDICTION AND MILITARY ACTIVITIES

4-1. LEGAL IMPLICATIONS

Unlike the territorial sea, the EEZ is not part of the coastal state's territory. Moreover, the EEZ is based on the 200-nautical mile distance concept. As such, it is not as territorial as the continental shelf, which is a natural extension of the territorial land.

The coastal state's rights in the EEZ are different in nature and effect from territorial sovereignty. The coastal state is entitled to exercise, to a certain extent, limited sovereign rights or jurisdiction in the EEZ. Sovereign rights have come to bear the meaning of rights that the coastal state has to explore and exploit continental shelf resources, as stipulated by article 2 of the Convention on the Continental Shelf. Accordingly, this means the coastal state's exercise of rights to achieve certain ends in specific zones, and it is different from territorial sovereignty.[51]

Of course, the coastal state's sovereign rights derive from exclusivity against third states, as they include authority regulating foreign countries within the scope of its objectives. Accordingly, while sovereign rights given to the coastal state in the EEZ are limited to specific objectives but are exclusive, the concept of EEZ does connote, to a certain extent, factors of territorialization. If each state adopts an EEZ regime that further strengthens the coastal state's rights or authority in the EEZ than is prescribed by the UNCLOS, territorialization may be further cemented. The coastal state, however, is directly limited, in that it is bound to have due regard to foreign countries' rights and duties in the EEZ and to comply with the UNCLOS.[52] In addition, foreign countries are entitled to keep exercising their freedoms of navigation and overflight in a coastal state's EEZ, and thus the coastal state's exclusivity in the EEZ is bound to be limited.

Jurisdiction in the EEZ, in the meantime, indicates the level of authority the coastal state can exercise, and compared to sovereign rights, it is watered down to some extent. The coastal sate, for example, has the duty to give appropriate notices and warnings on constructing and using artificial islands, installations, and structures, and they cannot be a hindrance to the use of international navigation routes.[53] Moreover, the coastal state's executive jurisdiction and judicial jurisdiction are limited to a certain extent with regard to the protection and preservation of the marine environment, and in some cases, it competes with the flag state's jurisdiction.[54] In conclusion, understanding of the legal characteristics of the EEZ through the interpretations of sovereign rights or jurisdiction may be complemented by the accumulation of state practice.

4-2. Maritime Powers vs. Costal States

Korea, China, and Japan have three distinct positions on the EEZ. China has endorsed broadened maritime jurisdiction, reflecting the positions of developing countries. As such, China has been vocal about the EEZ and has worked its position on the EEZ into its domestic law. Article 14 of the EEZ and Continental Shelf Act prescribed the exclusion of the impact on historical rights – an indication that China had in mind sensitive issues like the Gulf of Tonkin and islands in the East China and South China Seas, even though it did not directly mention territorial issues. This sheds light on why China has made excessive claims about straight baselines that deviate from international law standards.

In the meantime, Japan's position reflects the quintessential view of advanced maritime powers. Japan objected to the institutionalization of the EEZ to the end because of its interests in distant water fishing. Once the EEZ regime was established, however, Japan accepted it and used to its own advantage. When the maritime delimitation issue stalled, for example, it proposed intermediate zones to Korea and China as a stopgap measure and concluded new fisheries agreements with both countries, and that can be viewed as part of Japan's positive maritime policy.

What, then, is Korea's situation? The most unique point about Korea is that, unlike China and Japan, it has failed to take a clear stance. When the EEZ was under discussion at the 3rd UN Conference on the Law of the Sea, Korea was not able to voice its stance, the reasons for which were mentioned earlier. Once the UN Conference decided to introduce the EEZ regime, though, Korea was relatively quick to take steps to accommodate the EEZ regime. It has taken a series of legislative measures on the regulation of foreigners' fishing operations, and on marine scientific research, and marine environmental protection.

Korea, China, and Japan have distinctive laws on the EEZ for a number of reasons. While Korea enacted a single law on the EEZ, China and Japan both have one law to govern the EEZ and the continental shelf. While Korea had already introduced the continental shelf through its submarine mineral resources development act, Japan and China had accepted the continental shelf as customary law, without a positive law. In their EEZ laws, Korea and Japan simply stipulated the declaration and scope of the EEZ, boundary delimitation, and the application of relevant laws. China, on the other hand, prescribed these points in greater detail and added a few more issues, resulting in 16 articles.

Korea, China, and Japan regulate marine environmental protection and marine scientific research through separate laws. In particular, all three nations have established individual laws containing detailed prescriptions on marine environmental protection. Besides instituting basic laws on marine environmental protection, such as marine environment management act, marine environmental protection law, and act on the prevention of marine pollution and disaster in the sea, Korea, China, and Japan also prescribe marine environmental protection in other maritime affairs and environmental laws. Laws on maritime environmental protection issues should constantly be streamlined domestically by continually analyzing those issues in various related international treaties in the works at the IMO, in addition to the London Convention and MARPOL73/78.

Worth noting is that, unlike Korea and China, Japan regulates marine scientific research, not through the law but through guidelines. This reflects Japan's position on marine scientific research as an advanced maritime power. China, on the other hand, has over-emphasized its discretionary authority on marine scientific research, and this has posed problems. Since 2004, China has triggered a conflict with Japan over marine scientific research in the waters around Okinotorishima, and this owed to China's rigorous stance on marine scientific research. China's position was that, because Japan's claim that the waters around Okinotorishima were under its jurisdiction was in itself wrong, China was thus free to carry out marine scientific research without receiving Japan's permission. Sino-Japanese conflict over marine scientific research is now directly related to jurisdiction and maritime delimitation, and it remains a major cause of conflict to this day.

4-3. Military Activities in the EEZ

Military activities in the EEZ have long been a controversial issue since the early 1980s. Some coastal States claim that other States cannot conduct military activities, including naval exercises and military surveys, in their EEZs without their consent. They have sought to apply restrictions on navigation and overflight in this zone. Maritime powers strongly opposed this enhanced jurisdiction over activities carried out therein.

China and the United States represent the two groups respectively. In 2001 and again in 2009, China's continuing challenges to U.S. military activities in its EEZ led to dangerous confrontations. China has also objected to hydrographic surveys undertaken by U.S. vessels in the zone. Similar issues were raised during the joint military exercise of Korea and the United States after North Korea's shelling of Yeonpyeong Island in November 2010. The *USS George Washington*, one of the largest U.S. aircraft carriers, was mobilized in the joint military exercise that was carried out over four days starting from November 28. China expressed its serious concern over the deployment of the aircraft carrier, claiming that the military exercise in the Yellow Sea where the maritime boundary between Korea and China was not delimited, was against the spirit of the EEZ regime under the international law of the sea.[55] As there is a wide gap between the viewpoints of the two groups, conflicts over the military activities in the EEZ are not expected to be settled in the near future. This kind of conflict should be understood in the context of the maritime policy implementation in the long run.

Article 58 of the UNCLOS was intended to preserve the right to conduct military activities in the EEZ. It can be argued that there is no agreement on what limitations there are on States when conducting military activities in the EEZ. Also, it can be said that the "due regard" obligation imposes a limit on user States to consult and negotiate with the coastal States.

As was mentioned earlier, Jeanette Greenfield's interpretation is that China regulates military activities in the EEZ, and it has become another cause of conflict between China and Japan over Okinotorishima, in addition to marine scientific research. China is rising as a maritime power and has built up its maritime defense capabilities vis-à-vis the United States and Japan in the East China Sea and the Pacific Ocean. As such, it has designated the distance from Japan's Southwest Islands to Taiwan as the First Island Chain, and the route from the Ogasawara Islands to Mariana, Guam, and Palau as the Second Island Chain. Okinotorishima is located in the middle of these two Island Chains, and thus Sino-Japanese conflict over Okinotorishima is not likely to be resolved easily. China also views Ieodo as part of the First Island Chain, and that could be a hurdle to ROK-China maritime delimitation.[56]

4-4. PEACEFUL USES OF THE SEAS AND SOUTH CHINA SEA DISPUTES

There are several provisions regarding the notion of peaceful uses of the seas in the UNCLOS. First of all, regarding the high seas, Article 88 stipulates that the high seas shall be reserved for peaceful purposes.

This provision did not exist in the 1958 Convention on the High Seas. And it also applies to the EEZ in so far as it is not incompatible with Part V.[57] In Part XI, the same rule has been stipulated as peaceful uses of the deep sea-bed.[58] Furthermore in Part XIII, it states that marine scientific research shall be conducted for peaceful purposes.[59] It is notable that article 246 states that coastal States shall agree to other States' or international organization's marine scientific research in their EEZ or on their continental shelf when the research is for peaceful purposes. Because marine scientific research is different from military surveys or research, its peaceful purpose is an essential element.

These articles established the fundamental principle that the high seas and the EEZ shall be used peacefully. However there was no clarification during the 3rd Law of the Sea Conference of what exactly was the notion of peaceful uses of the seas. Especially because coastal States' exercise of sovereign rights or jurisdiction in the EEZ restricts other States' freedom of the high seas, it is causing a big controversy.

This problem can be examined in relation to other provisions of the UNCLOS. For example, by interpreting Part XVI as a general principle regarding peaceful uses of the seas, one can examine whether military activities in the EEZ are similar to those stated in article 56 or in article 58. Article 301 stipulates that in exercising their rights and performing their duties under this Convention, States Parties shall refrain from any threat or use of force against the territorial integrity or political independence of any State, or in any other manner inconsistent with the principles of international law embodied in the UN Charter. According to this provision, military activities in the high seas are allowed, as long as they do not violate international principles such as "prohibition of armed attacks" stated in the UN Charter, let alone freedom of navigation thereof.

In this context, it can be said that China's claims to the South China Sea disputes are groundless from the perspective of international law.[60] China is not entitled to claim its territorial sea around the artificial islands established in the low tide elevations in the South China Sea. They cannot prohibit ordinary navigation or innocent passage of warships around their artificial islands.

5. DELIMINATION OF THE AREAS AROUND DOKDO

Korea and Japan concluded bilateral fisheries agreement in 1999, establishing two intermediate/provisional zones in the East Sea and in the East China Sea respectively. The two countries agreed to shelve delicate issues on maritime boundary delimitation during transitional period. Conclusion of the fisheries agreement led to the question of whether Korea and Japan can tackle boundary delimitation first despite the enduring territoriality issue, or whether the two countries should delimit a boundary after settling the territorial dispute first. Considering that territorial disputes are generally long drawn-out battles, it would be reasonable to leave territorial claims to Dokdo for the time being and discuss boundary delimitation first.

A review of state practice shows that several states tend to interpret the definition of the island as broadly as possible to extend their maritime jurisdiction. However, all points considered, it would be natural for the time being to describe Dokdo as rocks, as stipulated in Paragraph 3, article 121 of the LOSC.

For Japan, the interpretation of Paragraph 3, article 121 is probably a more complicated issue because of its rather numerous uninhabited islands and rocks in the adjacent waters which can be used as basepoints of EEZs or continental shelves. For example, it could be said that Okinotorishima in the Pacific cannot have an EEZ or continental shelf of its own if viewed in the light of that paragraph.

As regards Dokdo, it could theoretically be given full effect or half effect by recognizing its status not as rocks as stipulated in Paragraph 3, article 121 of the LOSC, but as an island. As long as the tug-of-war over Dokdo continues, however, the very possibility of a Korea-Japan agreement on who should have the right to claim the islet as the basepoint would seem remote. For this reason, it would be rational to view Dokdo as rocks as defined in that paragraph and not recognize its basepoint effect at all or otherwise recognize it only to a limited extent. To Korea, the ideal scenario would be to disregard Dokdo and fix the median line between Ullungdo and Okinoshima as the boundary. Doing so would mean the boundary line will lie 18 miles away from Dokdo toward Japan.

Besides the method of delimiting boundary line, some Japanese scholars as well as Korean scholars suggest establishing kind of enclaves around Dokdo. But, in any case, this proposal would bear an equivalent meaning to the downsizing of the "intermediate zone" created under the current fisheries agreement.

It is a formidable task to resolve delimitation issues rationally in a short period of time when each coastal state's positions are entangled. At this juncture, it would be worth recalling the fundamental meaning of maritime delimitation *per se* to the coastal states in Northeast Asia. The significance of maritime delimitation in the enclosed or semi-enclosed seas, namely those of Northeast Asia, ultimately lies in the establishment of a rational maritime order through the efficient allocation of jurisdiction or maritime resources. The question that arises here is whether states must go as far as seeking maritime boundary delimitations at the risk of stirring up territorial controversies, which can never bring satisfactory outcomes to all the coastal states involved, if it is possible to establish a sound maritime order without clear-cut delimitations. In short, realistically, it would be optimal for the states involved to come up with a means by which to efficiently exploit and utilize maritime resources while at the same time settling territorial disputes over islands in a roundabout way.

Anyway, Korea and Japan have no choice but to settle delimitation issues within the framework of international law, based on cooperation and mutual concessions. As professor Tadao Kuribayashi pointed out, international boundaries are not only territorial by nature but also multi-functional: they are preserved or altered by a combination of historical, geographical, cultural, political, and economic factors.[61] If we focus our attention on the territorial aspects of maritime boundary, it would be almost impossible to settle boundary issue between Korea and Japan.

6. CONCLUDING REMARKS

All in all, these issues have to be resolved among Korea, China, and Japan through negotiations, with their positions on the EEZ serving as the basis of the talks. Domestic legislation and policies can serve as guidelines for understanding each of these countries' positions on the EEZ. Korea, which has to maximize its interests in the face of China and Japan, should compare the three nations' stances well and make a good judgment call.

By placing importance on strict management of resources or protection of the marine environment like Japan, the sensitive intermediate zone issue might be resolved with ease. If maritime boundary delimitation issues cannot be resolved in the short term with legal logic, Korea could at least attach more importance on the functional characteristics of the EEZ and more strictly manage fishery and environmental issues. Should Korea's policy remain as ambiguous as it has been, the territoriality of the EEZ will be emphasized, and that, in turn, could escalate into serious maritime conflicts in areas where boundaries have yet to be delimited.

Likewise, with military activities in the EEZ, while a country may not permit active military activities in the name of marine environmental protection, its grounds for opposing navigation and passage will likely be weak. China's concern over maritime issues with Korea largely stems from military reasons. If we understand that, the problem can be easily solved. While it is understandable why Korea had to take a middle-of-the-road approach between China and Japan, at least juridically speaking, it need not take an ambiguous attitude any longer.

Many States have used the high seas for military uses as long as they do not conflict with the Nuclear Test-Ban Treaty or the Seabed Arms

Control Treaty. This is consistent with international law and state practice. However because the EEZ is not owned by all States, not all military actions should be admitted. But when military activities are viewed in the light of freedom to use the high seas, it is reasonable to note that the coastal States do not possess the right to strictly regulate other States' military activities in the EEZ. Therefore, the question of whether to allow military activities in the EEZ shall be evaluated by the specific conducts and characteristics of the activities.

While a blanket statement cannot be made by this author, Korea has perceived and managed the EEZ from the viewpoint of endorsing the freedom of the seas, partially or depending on the field. In the twenty-first century, when a new maritime legal regime has been established due to extended maritime jurisdiction, the freedom of the seas will only be limited further. The importance of rational resource management and marine environmental protection, which the EEZ regime promotes, has become an important legal value that no maritime power can deny. This is a self-evident fact, without going having to go so far as to recognize the territoriality of the EEZ. It is now time for Korea to attach importance to these aspects as it operates the EEZ as a responsible maritime state.

Notes

* Email: chalee@uos.ac.kr   This article has been written, with changes and updates, based on the paper, "The EEZ Regime in Northeast Asia," which was published in the 28(1) The Korean Journal of Defense Analysis(2016). The Author is deeply grateful to the Korea Institute for Defense Analyses for its permission to republish it.

1. Kim Charn-kiu, "Dispute over Ocean Currents Survey: Japan is Deluded," *Segye Ilbo,* July 5, 2006.

2. Kim Chran-kiu, "Solution for Developing East China Sea Resources," *Segye Ilbo,* July 14, 2008.

3. Jerome A. Cohen and Jon M. Van Dyke, "Limits of Tolerance," *South China Morning Post*, December 7, 2010.

4. Gong Ying-Chun, "China's Position on Uninhabited Islands: Responses According to Domestic Law and International Position," *Study on China's Maritime Policy and Law* (Ocean Policy Research Foundation, 2006) [in Japanese], 69–70; Proposal for the Inclusion of a Supplementary Item in the Agenda of the 19th Meeting of States Parties, SPLOS/196.

5. The ROK Ministry of Foreign Affairs, "ROK-China 1st Official Talks for Delimitation of Maritime boundaries held," [in Korean] Press Release, December 22, 2015.

6. For example, countries like Maldives regulate the passage of vessels through their EEZs, pursuant to their maritime waters laws. South Africa clearly stipulates its exercise of the right of self-defense in its EEZ. For an analysis of other key coastal states' EEZ institutions. See Lee Chang-Wee et al., *Study of Key Coastal States' Laws for Integrated Management of EEZs*, 2007.

7. *The Economist*, October 27, 2015, "An American Warship Sails through Disputed Waters in the South China Sea."

8. R. R. Churchill and A. V. Lowe, *The Law of the Sea*, 3rd ed. (Yonkers, NY: Juris, 1999), 160–61.

9. When the establishment of the EEZ became an undeniable trend in the early days of the UNCLOS, the United States and the USSR gave up objecting to it and affected a policy switchover to accommodate the EEZ domestically. That was because they foresaw that the freedom of navigation in EEZs would be maintained, and that the right of innocent passage in straits for international navigation would be established. See John F. Murphy, *The United States and the Rule of Law in International Affairs* (Cambridge: Cambridge University Press, 2004), 229–234; and Kuribayashi Tadao, *Development of the Law of the Sea and Japan* 3, *One Hundred Years of Japan and International Law* [in Japanese] (2001), 10–11.

10. UNCLOS, Article 55.

11. R. R. Churchill, "The Impact of State Practice on the Jurisdictional Framework Contained in the LOS Convention," in *Stability and Change in the Law of the Sea: the Role of the LOS Convention*, ed. Alex G. Oude Elferink (Leiden: Martinus Nijhoff Publishers, 2005), 91–96.

12. David Joseph Attard, *The Exclusive Economic Zone in International Law* (New York, NY: Oxford University Press, 1987), 61–62.

13. By stipulating "specific legal regime of the exclusive economic zone," Article 55 of the UNCLOS gave way to a dispute over the legal characteristics of the EEZ, specifically over the high seas and specific legal regime. The difference between the two positions, however, is how the legal characteristics of the EEZ are formed--like the glass half empty, half full example. See Barbara Kwiatkowska, *The 200 Mile Exclusive Economic Zone in the New Law of the Sea* (Leiden: Martinus Nijhoff Publishers, 1989), 230.

14. *Ibid.*, 231.

15. Satya N. Nandan C.B.E & Shabtai Rosenne, *United Nations Convention on the Law of the Sea 1982 A Commentary*, 3 vols. (Leiden: Martinus Nijhoff Publishers, 1995), 59–71.

16. Barbara Kwiatkowska, *The 200-Mile Exclusive Economic Zone*, 232.

17. *Ibid.*, 232–33.

18. UNCLOS, Articles 56(2) and 58(3).

19. Mizukami Chiyuki, "Exclusive Economic Zone," *New Order of the Law of the Sea*, ed. Hayashi Hisashige (Tokyo: Toshinto, 1993) [in Japanese], 138–39.

20. Mizukami Chiyuki, *Exclusive Economic Zone* (Tokyo: Yushinto-Kobubsha, 2005) [in Japanese], 58–59.

21. Nakamura Ko, "Legal Nature of the Exclusive Economic Zone," in *Basic Issues of International Law (Jurisprudence Class)*, ed. Uchida Terasawa [in Japanese] (1986), 137.

22. René Jean Dupuy and Daniel Vignes, *Traité du Nouveau Droit de la MER*, (Paris, Brussels, Montreal: Economica, 1985), 255.

23. Yamamoto Soji, "200-Nautical Mile Economic Zone," *Jurist*, No. 647, September 1, 1977, 37–38.

24. Tommy T. B. Koh, "The Exclusive Economic Zone," in *Law of the Sea*, ed. Hugo Caminos (Aldershot: Dartmouth Publishing Co., 2001), 31–33.

25. This part is written, with changes and updates, based on a part of the article, "Legal Status of the EEZ and Relevant State Practice," [in Korean] *Maritime Law Studies* 21, No.2 (2009). For Japan's perspective, see Oda Shigeru, *Commentary on the International Law of the Sea* 1 (Tokyo: Yuhikaku, 1985) [in Japanese], 188–92.

26. Satya N. Nandan and Shabtai Rosenne, *United Nations Convention on the Law of the*

Sea 1982: A Commentary, 2 vols. (Dordrecht: Martinus Nijhoff Publishers, 1993), 491–510.

27. On January 18, 1952, President Rhee Syngman promulgated the "Declaration on Sovereignty in the ROK's Adjacent Waters." This was a preemptive measure taken before the peace treaty with Japan was to go into effect, so as to gear up for the abolition of Japan's MacArthur line. For more on the peace line declaration, see Ji Cheol-keun, *Peace Line* (Seoul: Beomusa, 1979) [in Korean]. For Japan's perspective, see Oda Shigeru, *Searching for the Origin of the Law of the Sea* [in Japanese] (Tokyo: Yushinto, 1989).

28. Choi Jong-hwa, *Modern International Law of the Sea* [in Korean] (Seoul: Sejong Publishing House, 2000), 334–35.

29. Choi Jong-hwa, *International Law of the Sea Lecture* [in Korean] (Seoul: Taehwa Publishing House, 1998), 107–08; and Kim Young-koo, *The ROK and International Law of the Sea* [in Korean] (Seoul: Hyosung Publishing House, 1999), 406–08.

30. UNCLOS, Article 55.

31. In Northeast Asia, the former USSR declared a 200-nautical mile fishing zone in 1977, and in 1984, it turned it into an EEZ through a decree. In 1998, Russia changed it into a federal law, declaring it as an EEZ. In response to the USSR's declaration of a fishing zone, Japan declared its own 200-mile fishing zone, and in 1996, it turned it into an EEZ. Ratifying the UNCLOS in May 1996, China declared its own EEZ and continental shelf. North Korea had already declared its EEZ in 1977. See Lee Chang-Wee, "Extension of State Jurisdiction by Korea and Japan," [in Korean] *Korean Journal of International Law* 41, No. 2 (1996): 163–76.

32. National Assembly Unification and Foreign Affairs Committee, "Report on EEZ Bill Review," [in Korean] July 1996, 3.

33. The EEZ Act is composed of five articles and supplementary provisions. Article 1 is on setting an EEZ. Article 2 stipulates the scope of an EEZ and setting its borders. Article 3 deals with Korea's rights in its EEZ. Article 4 addresses foreign countries' rights and obligations, and Article 5 discusses the exercise of rights. Notice No. 13382 in the ROK official gazette, August 8, 1996, 4–5.

34. This law comprises 26 articles and supplementary provisions. Articles 1 through 4 stipulate the purpose, definition, and scope of the law. Articles 5 through 13 address specific standards and conditions for permitting foreign entities' fishing in Korea's EEZ. Articles 14 through 26 discuss the sedentary fish species and the protection of and penalties related to anadromous fish species. For more details, see National Assembly Unification and Foreign Affairs Committee, "Report on EEZ Bill Review" and "Report on EEZ Bill Evaluation," [in Korean] July 1996.

35. This law was enacted primarily with the goal of implementing domestically

the Convention on the Prevention of Maritime Pollution by Dumping of Wastes and Other Matter (also known as the London Convention of 1972) and the International Convention for the Prevention of Pollution from Ships (MARPOL73/78). See Law of the Sea Forum, *Commentary on UNCLOS II* (Seoul: Jiinbooks, 2010) [in Korean], 403.

36. Park Su-jin and Mok Jin-yong, *Key New Institutions of Marine Environment Management Act: Evaluation and Tasks for Legislation,* [in Korean] Korea Maritime Institute, 2009, 8–17.

37. Jeanette Greenfield, *China's Practice in the Law of the Sea* (Oxford: Clarendon Press, 1992), 88–89.

38. See Sec.2, *Working Paper on Sea Area within the Limits of National Jurisdiction,* July 16, 1973.

39. Jeanette Greenfield, *China's Practice in the Law of the Sea*, 92.

40. Lee Chang-Wee, "Thoughts on China's Policy of Creeping Jurisdiction," [in Korean] *Maritime Law Studies*, Vol. 20, No. 3, 2008, 91–98.

41. EEZ and Continental Shelf Act, Articles 2, 3, 4, 6–11.

42. Yann-Huei Song and Zou Keyuan, "Maritime Legislation of Mainland China and Taiwan: Developments, Comparison, Implications, and Potential Challenges for the United States," *Ocean Development and International Law* 31, No. 4, 2000, 318.

43. EEZ and Continental Shelf Act, Article 2.

44. EEZ and Continental Shelf Act, Article 11.

45. Regulations on the Management of the Foreign-Related Marine Scientific Research. For China's perspective, see Zou Keyuan, *China's Marine Legal System and the Law of the Sea* (Leiden/Boston: Martinus Nijhoff Publishers, 2005), 289–311.

46. Nakamura Ko, "UN Convention on the Law of the Sea and Basic Maritime Law," *Jurist* September 1996 [in Japanese], 34–35.

47. Kuribayashi Tadao, *Modern International Law* (Tokyo: Keio University Press, 1999) [in Japanese], 291–92; and ROK Ministry of Foreign Affairs and Trade, *Study of Relationship between the Exclusive Economic Zones and the Continental Shelf in relation to Boundaries* [in Korean], 2000, 40–41.

48. Article 1 of Japan's EEZ and Continental Shelf Law established an EEZ that extends up to 200 nautical miles. As per Article 76 of the UNCLOS, Article 2 distinguishes between continental shelves that extend up to 200-nautical mile line, which overlap with the EEZ, and those that extend beyond the 200-nautical mile line. Article 3 (1) states that related laws shall be applied to issues related to the EEZ and the continental shelf. Article 3 (2) stipulates that Japanese law shall apply to artificial islands, installations, and structures. Article 3 (3) stipulates that enforcement decrees may adjust the application of the law.

49. Law of the Sea Forum, *Study of Key Coastal States' Laws for Integrated Management of the EEZ* (Daejeon: Ad Power, 2007) [in Korean], 14–17.

50. Kanehara Atsuko, "Marine Scientific Research in the Waters Where Claims of the Exclusive Economic Zone Overlap between Japan and the Republic of Korea-Incidents between the Two States in 2006," *The Japanese Annual of International Law* 49, 2006, 104–105.

51. For commentary and discussion on how the continental shelf convention came to stipulate sovereign rights, see Myres S. McDougal and William T. Burke, *The Public Order of the Oceans: A Contemporary International Law of the Sea* (New Haven, CT: New Haven Press and Martinus Nijhoff Publishers, 1987), 693–724.

52. UNCLOS, Article 56 (2).

53. UNCLOS, Article 60 (3) (7).

54. UNCLOS, Articles 217 and 218.

55. Jerome A. Cohen and Jon M. Van Dyke, "Limits of Tolerance," *South China Morning Post*, December 7, 2010.

56. Gao Zhi-guo, "Ieodo and Okinotorishima," *Development of the International Law of the Sea* [in Chinese], 2007, 1–9.

57. UNCLOS, Article 58 (2).

58. UNCLOS, Article 141. Tadao Kuribayashi, "Spatial Structure of Boundary in International Law," *International Law and Municipal Law: A Tribute to 60th Anniversary of Soji Yamamoto's Birth*, 1991[in Japanese], 295.

59. UNCLOS, Article 240 (a).

60. *The Economist*, October 17, 2015, "Who Rules the Waves?: China No Longer Accepts that America Should be Asia-Pacific's Dominant Naval Power."

61. Tadao Kuribayashi, "Spatial Structure of Boundary in International Law," *International Law and Municipal Law: A Tribute to 60th Anniversary of Soji Yamamoto's Birth*, 1991[in Japanese], 295.

The Protection of Migrant Workers in the Republic of Korea and Accession to the International Convention on the Protection of the Rights of All Migrant Workers and Members of their Families

LEE Whiejin
Visiting Professor, Gyeongsang National University, Jinju, Korea
Former Ambassador to Papua New Guinea

Abstract

Having joined major international human rights treaties, the Korean government has been under pressure from NGOs, trade unions and liberal groups of lawyers and professionals to accede to the International Convention on the Protection of the Rights of all Migrant Workers and Members of their Families. Korea has been sympathetic with the protection of rights of migrant workers as a nation which had sent its own workers overseas in the 1960s and 70s and endeavors to make amendments to the laws and system to be consistent with international standard.

Human rights treaties have the same effect as the domestic laws according to the article 6, paragraph 1 of the Constitution of the Republic of Korea. Thus, the Korean government has applied and enforced the treaties which it ratified or acceded to. Accession to the Convention has to wait until the consistency of the provisions of the domestic laws with the Convention has been made.

This article examines the main contents of the Convention and makes the comparison with domestic laws and court rulings. At the present Korea's accession to the Convention won't be easy under the current circumstances where no migrant-receiving states have joined the Convention. As more migrant workers reside in Korea and other migrant-receiving states join the Convention, it is expected that the Korean government will give serious consideration to the Convention.

Key Words

International Human Rights Treaties, Migrant Workers Convention, Domestic Law, Trade Union

1. INTRODUCTION

The Korean government has been pressured by NGOs, liberal groups of lawyers and professionals, and labor organizations to join the International Convention on the Protection of the Rights of all Migrant Workers and Members of their Families (hereinafter referred to as "International Migrant Workers Convention" or "the Convention") which came into effect in 2003.[1] As a country which once sent its own migrant workers abroad in the 1960s and 70s to Germany and the Middle East to earn foreign currency, Korea is sympathetic with the position of migrant workers in Korea, making amendment to the relevant domestic legislation to be more in line with the international agreements. Korea acceded to seven major international human rights treaties, symbolizing its status as a treaty-abiding nation. In accordance with the requirement in the treaties, the Korean government has faithfully submitted its position documents and reported to the concerned treaty committee.

These human rights treaties have been in force since being ratified or acceded to by Korea, in accordance with its constitution, article 6 para 1 of which stipulates that treaties duly concluded and promulgated under the constitution and the generally recognized rules of international law shall have the same effect as the domestic laws. The constitution as the supreme legal framework encapsulates principles of law like equality before the law. Under the guidance of the constitution, laws and decrees have been enacted to implement more in detail relevant provisions relating to the treatment of workers and relations between employers and employees.

On the other hand, human rights treaties have provided for the status of workers and especially the International Migrant Workers Convention elaborates upon the rights of migrant workers and their status equivalent to the national workers. Migrant workers in Korea have been treated better as the legislations have been amended to gear up to international treaties and the recommendations of the relevant human rights treaties committee have been accommodated.

This paper above all examines labor-related contents and principles of the Convention and a comparative study will be made between the domestic law and the Convention to see any conflict or discrepancy. The jurisprudence of courts making interpretation of relevant laws to be more consistent with the Convention will be taken into account. The required changes, if any, to the domestic legislation in joining the Convention will be sought mainly in the area of labor relations and social security.

2. LABOR-RELATED CONTENTS OF THE CONVENTION

The Convention[2] is wide-ranging and comprehensive in its coverage of protection of migrant workers. It applies to all migrant workers, both documented/regular and undocumented/irregular workers. The Convention is based upon the principle of equality or rather the principle of non-discrimination. It provides for the human rights enjoyed by migrant workers irrespective of their stay status.

Parts III, IV and V are concerned with the rights and protection of migrant workers in respect of the labor relations. Part III provides for the basic protection of all migrant workers and their families. Article 25 stipulates national treatment, prohibiting discrimination against migrant workers in respect of conditions of work and terms of employment. The right to take part in and join meetings and activities of trade unions and other associations is provided in article 26, and equal treatment with respect to social security shall be provided by article 27.

Part IV contains articles on the rights of migrant workers and families documented or in regular situations. According to article 40 migrant workers and their families shall have the right to form associations and trade unions. Article 43 stipulates that migrant workers enjoy access to educational, vocational, housing, and social services equal to those provided to the nationals of the state of employment. Articles 49 and 51 guarantee the right of residence during the period of remunerated activities, and therefore migrant workers shall not lose their authorization of residence by the termination of their remunerated activity prior to the expiration of their work permits or similar authorizations. It is provided in article 52 that the migrant workers shall have right freely to choose their remunerated activity, subject to some restrictions or conditions. Article 54 provides for the national treatment to migrant workers in respect of protection against dismissal and unemployment benefits.

2-1. THE PRINCIPLE OF NON-DISCRIMINATION

The principle of non-discrimination is embodied in the Convention. Article 7 in Part II describes the principle as a basic rule, underlying the whole contents of the Convention. The principle of non-discrimination goes beyond the simple principle of equality.[3] Non-discrimination obliges the state to establish a system guaranteeing the equality and makes a more active intervention to prevent any possible inequality. Article 7 stipulates under the rubric of Part II (non-discrimination with respect to rights): "States Parties undertake, in accordance with the international instruments concerning human rights, to respect and to ensure to all migrant workers and members of their families within their territory or subject to their jurisdiction the rights provided for in the present Convention without distinction of any kind as to sex, race, colour, language, religion or conviction, political or other opinion, national, ethnic or social origin, nationality, age, economic position, property, marital status, birth or other status." This principle is typical, common clause in human rights treaties. This Convention as part of a set of international human rights conventions places the principle of non-discrimination before the main contents of the Convention. The principle applies to all migrant workers inclusive of irregular workers and family members. As it states in this clause: "… in accordance with the international instrument concerning human rights …" principles in human rights will apply in the interpretation of the Convention."The kind of discrimination is not confined to the illustration in this clause, for example including sex and race.

The Korean constitution, in article 11 para.1, states that all citizens shall be equal before the law and there shall be no discrimination in political, economic, social, cultural life on account of sex, religion or social status. It signifies the principle of equality and right to equality. The principle of equality is natural, inalienable basic right of liberty which is enjoyed by all people including migrant workers. This right is not bestowed by the government, endowed to individuals as a natural right from birth.

Stemming from this principle of equality and non-discrimination, individual right of equality is stated in other clauses of the constitution relating to education, labor, and family etc. Article 31, para.1 provides for the right to equitable education in accordance with capacities, offering equal opportunities to all people. Article 32, para.4 mentions non-discrimination against female workers, providing that female workers receive special protection and shall not be subject to unjust discrimination in respect of employment, wage and working conditions.

The Korean constitution ensures basic rights to all its nationals as its main subject. As for the treatment and status of foreigners article 6, para.2 states the principle of reciprocity, providing that foreigners are treated according to international law and treaties. Nevertheless, general opinion of scholars and jurisprudence of courts is that human rights like natural right of liberty, different from social and economic rights will be granted to foreigners. But political right entitling people to participating in the formation of government and political assembly excludes foreigners in the decision making process. Generally human rights and freedom will not burden governments financially and legislatively. In this way foreigners enjoy rights in the realm of liberty and freedom.

2-2. BASIC LABOR RIGHTS OF MIGRANT WORKERS

Issues relating to major labor relations are non-discrimination in the conditions of work and employment, the extent of granting of three basic labor rights,[4] and vocational guidance and training service in labor market.

Article 25 of the Convention is typical in the individual labor relations. This article provides equal treatment regarding conditions of work and applies to irregular or undocumented migrant workers[5] in addition to regular workers. As a result of the non-discrimination principle, migrant workers shall not be treated less favorably than the nationals of the state of employment as provided in article 25.[6] The clause makes distinction between conditions of work and terms of employment. It is provided that conditions of work include remuneration, overtime etc, while terms of employment refers to minimum age of employment and restriction on work. Articles 54 and 55 in Part IV make provisions for migrant workers documented or in regular situations, which are similar to articles 25 and 27 for all migrant workers. Article 54 provides migrant workers with equality of treatment with nationals of the state of employment in respect of protection against dismissal, unemployment benefits, access to public work schemes intended to combat unemployment, and access to alternative employment in the event of loss of work or termination of other remunerated activity. Likewise, article 55 states that migrant workers shall be entitled to equality of treatment with nationals of the state of employment in the exercise of that remunerated activity.

The principle of nationals treatment in the Convention is considered as comparatively progressive in comparison with other international standards. Nationals treatment clauses ensure rights of migrant workers in the state of employment as well as the employer, providing wider scope of application than ILO standards.[7]

3. THE PROTECTION OF MIGRANT WORKERS IN KOREA

Non-discrimination principle is stipulated in the constitution and other laws of Korea. With respect to conditions of work, Labor Standards Act provides for equal treatment in article 6[8] and the Act on the Employment of Migrant Workers, in article 22, states that employers shall not give unjustifiable discriminatory treatment to migrant workers. The Act on the Employment of Migrant Workers does not contain any penality clause in breach of discrimination based upon nationality, while Labor Standards Act provides for penality in that case.

The vocational training program which was once in the throes of great controversy around the breach of non-discrimination on conditions of work was abolished in December 2006, while the case was considered by the Constitutional Court. The Commission on Migrant Manpower Policy held on July 27, 2005 took a decision that the migrant manpower scheme would be changed to the employment permission system from Jan. 1, 2007 onward. The Constitutional Court declared the vocational training program unconstitutional. In the opinion of the Court the main reason was that article 4, article 8 para.1 and article 17 of Labor Ministry regulation on the protection and supervision of migrant vocational trainees breached the right of equality.[9] Furthermore, the Court held that although limiting the right to enjoy equal conditions of work for work of equivalent value belongs to the realm of legislation pursuant to article 5 of Labor Standards Act and article 4 of UN International Covenant on Economic, Social and Cultural Rights, migrant vocational training was provided for by the Labor Ministry regulation named "guideline on the protection and supervision of migrant vocational trainees," in breach of the principle of statutory reservation.

Another controversial issue is concerned with the termination of the employment relationship in article 25 para.1(a) which might come to the surface while being applied to all migrant workers, especially in irregular situations. Whether the termination of employment relationship would not lead to the deprival of residential right subject to certain limitations brings about different interpretation. Apparently the Convention provides for non-discrimination between documented and undocumented workers as regards conditions of work. The condition of workers in irregular situations impacts upon the status of residence and labor contract itself. The Supreme Court of Korea also ruled that employment entitlement is needed to work legally in Korea, and a party is entitled to suspend the employment contract made with unauthorized migrant workers.[10]

The right of collective bargaining and association is provided in articles 26[11] and 40[12] of the Convention, the difference being article 26 for all migrant workers and article 40 for documented workers. Migrant workers are in principle entitled to enjoy three basic labor rights. Documented and regular workers are granted the right to form association and trade union, which will be excepted to the undocumented and irregular workers, whose right will be limited to the right to take part in meetings and activities of trade unions and of any other associations and join trade union and association. The distinction between the two in the way of excluding the right to form trade union for undocumented workers is criticized as it will fall short of the existing international human rights treaties like International Human Rights Covenants A and B and ILO Convention 87,[13] which recognize the right to formation of trade union for all workers.[14] Article 12[15] (freedom of assembly and association) of the Charter of Fundamental Rights of the European Union provides for the right to form and join trade union for everyone as a freedom of assembly and association. It is noteworthy to separate the freedom of assembly and association and the collective bargaining and action in the EU Charter of Fundamental Rights. The freedom of assembly and association is stated under the title II-Freedoms as part of right of liberty. On the other hand the collective bargaining and action is provided in the title IV-Solidarity in article 28.[16] Despite a slight difference of the character of the right, three basic labor rights are in the realm of fundamental right of liberty, in the sense that those rights will not take on the nature of social right as a right to request social service from state, but have the nature of right of liberty formulated based upon contract of employment.[17]

Turning to Korean legislation and jurisprudence, the Korean constitution stipulates three basic labor rights in article 33 paragraph 1. Article 5 of Trade Union and Labor Relations Adjustment Act provides for the right to form and join a trade union. But the Act on the Employment of Migrant Workers contains no clause on basic labor rights for migrant workers. Nevertheless, there is no doubt about the eligibility of documented workers for basic labor rights in the opinion of scholars and court jurisprudence. It is natural to recognize such rights to migrant workers, who are treated similarly to national workers based upon the employment permission system. Controversy arises around whether the right to form trade union will be allowed to the undocumented workers. Opinion has been split between Labor Ministry (whose name was changed to the Ministry of Employment and Labor in 2010) and Labor Union, and judgments of lower courts have been disparate. The Labor Ministry, considering that undocumented migrant workers are not the subject of three basic labor rights aimed at improving work conditions, remanded the document of application.[18] In the court proceedings, the lower court and higher court have been split in their opinions. The court of 1st instance has concurred with the decision of the Ministry of Labor, considering that undocumented workers are not in the category of workers permitted to join trade union in the Trade Union and Labor Relations Adjustment Act.[19] The court of appeals, Seoul High Court, reversing the decision of lower court, ruled that in view of the objective of Trade Union and

Labor Relations Adjustment Act undocumented workers should be in the category of workers entitled to establish trade union, as they live on salary, wage and other equivalent income in return for their service.[20] The Supreme Court, concurring with the decision of the court of 2nd instance, has ruled that Immigration Act providing for the regulation of migrant workers aims merely to prohibit the factual act of employment of foreigners without work entitlement, yet it hardly purports to prohibit the legal effects of various rights in the work-related laws of foreign workers without employment entitlement resulting from de facto work or already obtained in the capacity of workers in work relations. Therefore, employees working and living on wages are thought to be in the category of workers under the Trade Union and Labor Relations Adjustment Act irrespective of the nationality or employment entitlement. In this regard, migrant workers without work permit are allowed to form and join trade union.[21]

As the Convention does not recognize the right to form trade union for undocumented workers, no gap or discrepancy between the Convention and Korean legislation exists, irrespective of granting three basic labor rights to undocumented workers. The Convention is denounced as falling short of other human rights treaties in recognizing the right to form trade union only to documented workers.

4. PROTECTION IN THE AREA OF LABOR LAW

4-1. STATUS OF MIGRANT WORKERS IN THE LABOR MARKET

The Convention, in articles 43[22] and 45,[23] provides for rights to educational institutions and services, vocational guidance, placement services and vocational training of documented workers and members of their families, enabling them to enjoy equality of treatment with nationals of the state of employment.

It appears that related domestic legislation, the Employment Security

Act, does not explicitly exclude migrant workers from the vocational guidance and placement services,[24] nor does it confine its application to national job seekers. The article 2 of Employment Security Act[25] provides for the equality of treatment and has not illustrated the element of nationality in the factors of non-discrimination. The clause leaves some room for disparate interpretation on whether nationality will be taken into account in consideration of non-discrimination. The Supreme Court has handed down its ruling that vocational guidance business toward migrant workers be covered by the Employment Security Act, considering discrimination elements as an illustration.[26] In the judgment of the Supreme Court no distinction is to be made between nationals and migrant workers as regards the application of the clause on the permission of vocational guidance business charging fee in the Employment Security Act. By this interpretation no discrepancy is found between the Convention and domestic legislation.

Vocational training and retraining facilities and institutions in article 43 para.1(c) of the Convention is related to domestic legislations like Employment Insurance Act, Industrial Accident Compensation Insurance Act, and Act on the Development of Vocational Skills of Workers etc. In principle migrant workers are not covered by the Employment Insurance Act. To be more specific, the category of non-professional employment or visitor employment visa is not covered by Employment Insurance Act, except that the applicant wishes to join the employment insurance as provided for in article 10 of Employment Insurance Act and its enforcement decree, article 3 para.2(1). Migrant workers who are not covered by the Employment Insurance Act are not entitled to receive job capabilities development training in the Employment Insurance Act. The exclusion in principle in domestic legislation of migrant workers from the vocational training and retraining of the Convention, allowing such service only in exceptional cases, exhibits a degree of conflict with the provisions of the Convention.

Migrant workers are currently insured against and compensated for industrial accident damage irrespective of their stay status under article 6 of Industrial Accident Compensation Insurance Act which covers all business or workplace employing workers referred to in the Labor Standards Act.[27] The ruling of Supreme Court extends the application of Industrial Accident Compensation Insurance Act to undocumented workers.[28] The Ministry of Employment and Labor operates job capabilities development training programs for industrial workers. Under the Industrial Accident Compensation Insurance Act, articles 92 and 94, the Ministry of Employment and Labor runs programs to establish and operate facilities for job rehabilitation. It has been argued whether migrant workers who are victims of industrial accidents are eligible for vocational training service. For the access to vocational training and retraining facilities and institutions in article 43 para.1(c), migrant workers enjoy the equality of treatment with nationals of the state of employment. Korea's related laws contain no clause to exclude documented migrant workers from the access to training and retraining service, as related laws apply to workers or those who are willing to work, or insured persons. The reality was that migrant workers were not qualified for access to job retraining facilities in the event of industrial accidents. With regard to the complaint submitted by migrant workers, the National Human Rights Commission made a recommendation to improve retraining selection system not to exclude migrant workers.[29] As a result the access application qualification was recognized to migrant workers. About the issue of job training expense subsidy the Supreme Court excluded migrant workers from the object of training expense subsidy for lack of any explicit clause.[30] It seems unjustifiable not to treat national and foreign workers equally in respect of retraining including retraining expense subsidy. In view of the nature of work and industrial accident, no ground for distinction may be justified. The Convention, in Part IV for workers documented or in a regular situation, provides for access to vocational training facilities. Granting access to retraining for documented migrant workers meets the requirement for accession to the Convention. It won't be hard to narrow down the gap between the practice and required conditions.

The Convention in articles 52[31] and 53[32] provides for the right of migrant workers and their members of families to freely choose the remunerated activity. Migrant workers enjoy the right to freely choose their remunerated activity subject to restrictions and conditions under article 52 para.1. To a certain extent the sovereignty of a state is limited by allowing a freedom of choosing remunerated activity to migrant workers. Hereby the limitations on freedom of remunerated activity appear in three ways. First, some categories of employment, functions, services or activities where this is necessary in the interests of the state as provided in article 52 para.2(a) will be restricted for migrant workers. This category may include public service, national security, defense service, high-tech industry, depending upon domestic legislation and policy. Second, in accordance with article 52 para.3 of the Convention the extent of freedom to choose the remunerated activity extends over the passage of employment time. For the starting 2 years the freedom of remunerated activity is restricted and thereafter extends subject to the condition of preferential treatment for nationals.[33] After 5 years no restriction on the choice of remunerated activity is imposed. Third, the principle of national preference treatment restricts the access of migrant workers to an area of certain work. It is common that national employment policy is oriented toward employing its own nationals and quasi-nationals preferentially. European Union member states adopt and carry out the policy of employing its own nationals or EU member states nationals more preferentially than nationals of other foreign states. For this reason the national preferential treatment policy results in restrictions on the employment of foreigners staying legally in the state. The interpretation of R. Cholewinski is that article 52 para.3 of the Convention on time limitation is recommendatory,[34] and then the interpretation will further restrict the freedom of choice of remunerated activities.

In Korea foreigners' remunerated activities are strictly limited by the Immigration Act, which provides that foreigners are required to get relevant visas to work and are not allowed to work outside the designated workplace. Thus the freedom of remunerated activities for foreign workers is in principle denied with limited exceptions. The Act on the Employment of Foreign Workers, in article 25, allows workplace transfer only in exceptional cases, in which foreign workers cease to work due to suspension or closure of business, or for other reasons not attributable to foreign workers. This restriction is in conflict with article 52 of the Convention. Article 25 para.4 of the Act limits the number of application for workplace transfer up to three times. In addition, paragraph 3 of article 25 provides that foreign workers are required to leave the state unless no permission is granted for workplace transfer within 3 months after its application or no application is made within 1 month after the expiry of work contract.

Under normal circumstances foreigners are allowed to work for three years, with extension of another two years in case employers make requests under the Act on the Employment of Foreign Workers, articles 18 and 18 bis. The restriction of work period, continuous work in the designated workplace, work period extension to be applied for by employers and other limitations on foreign workers subject foreign workers to employers, prone to worsen the work conditions and causing, for example, forced or illegal work.[35] Controversy arose around the possible violation of human rights treaties Korea ratified or acceded to. The Committee on Economic, Social and Cultural Rights, in its concluding observation, recommended that particular attention be paid to the fact that the three-month period stipulated for workplace transfer is highly insufficient. This is especially true in the current economic situation. In which migrant workers often have little choice but to accept jobs with unfavorable work conditions just to retain a regular work status.[36] The recommendation is based upon article 6 of International Covenant on Economic, Social and Cultural Rights, providing for the right to freely choose or accept work similar to article 51 of Migrant Workers Convention. Pursuant to ILO Convention No. 111 (Employment and Occupation Discrimination) which Korea ratified on December 4, 1998, the Committee of Experts on the Application of Conventions and Recommendations (CEACR) observed that the suggested amendment would have the aim of providing a direct basis for migrant workers to request a workplace transfer in case of discrimination or abuse, as compared to the current legislation which construes the workplace transfer as a consequence of the cancellation of the employers' permit rather than as a measure to assist migrant workers whose rights have been violated.[37] About the constitutionality of the limitation of workplace transfer to three times provided for in article 25 para.4 of the Act on the Employment of Foreign Workers, the Korean Constitutional Court ruled that in consideration of the objective of the Act on the Employment of Foreign Workers which is to protect the employment opportunity of national workers by limiting unreasonable workplace transfer of foreign workers and to achieve balanced development of national economy by facilitating smooth demand and supply of manpower through effective employment control it is not interpreted to be unreasonable and arbitrary to limit the workplace transfer of foreign workers to three times and therefore would not prejudice the freedom of job choice.[38] The Act on the Employment of Foreign Workers, providing that the extension of work contract beyond two years is left to the employer, is in conflict with the Migrant Workers Convention and ILO No. 143.[39] The amendment of the Act is necessary to be in tune with the Convention, allowing free choice of remunerated activities for migrant workers who work beyond two years.

4-2. Economic and Social Rights of Migrant Workers

Article 27[40] of the Convention is a principal clause on the social security of migrant workers. It is not clear whether this clause is applied to undocumented migrant workers even though it is provided under Part III for all migrant workers and members of their families.[41] As regards social security, migrant workers and their families are entitled to national treatment subject to fulfillment of domestic legislation and treaties.

Whether foreigners will be subject of domestic legal regime is at issue, and especially among basic rights the social right is arguable apart from the right of liberty which is enjoyed by foreigners without restrictions as natural, inalienable right. The general opinion of scholars and court jurisprudence is that the social right does not apply to foreigners except provided for under the principle of reciprocity. The constitution, in article 6 para.2, implies reciprocity, ensuring the status of foreigners in accordance with international law and treaties. The principle of reciprocity is stipulated in article 8 of Framework Act on Social Security and article 3 of Foreigner's Land Acquisition Act. In consideration of the Constitution and domestic laws the social right is recognized to foreigners with limitation on the basis of reciprocity. Furthermore, if necessity arises to ensure the dignity and happiness of foreigners as human beings, minimum social security provision extends to foreigners. The extent of social security benefit depends on the budgetary apportionment.

Under article 28[42] of the Convention migrant workers and members of their families have the right to receive emergency medical care irrespective of stay or employment status. The principle of non-discrimination in medical care is provided for in the Emergency Service Act and in case patients can not pay for medical expenses, government will pay in advance and the expense be reimbursed by the beneficiary patients. In emergency, medical care can be provided to migrant workers including irregular workers suffering financial difficulties. In reality the reimbursement system itself is difficult to be utilized due to budgetary constraint of government and inactive response of medical agency in making use of reimbursement system. Despite this reality domestic legislation corresponds to the Convention in respect of medical service.

Children of migrant workers have the right to education irrespective of stay or employment status pursuant to article 30[43] of the Convention. The access to education is granted on the basis of equality of treatment to nationals of the state. Korean Elementary and Secondary Education Act, in article 19 para.2 of the enforcement decree of the Act, provides for education for children of migrant workers which is limited to the primary education, while Korean nationals are entitled to 6 years of primary education and 3 years of lower secondary education. In this regard, conflict occurs between domestic laws and the Convention, though not serious.

Article 29[44] of the Convention strives to remove any possible statelessness of children of migrant workers born in the state of employment. In case of children whose parents are both foreigners, children are required to obtain stay entitlement within 90 days after birth as provided for in the Immigration Act. After obtaining consular authentication on birth of children from the concerned diplomatic office in Korea, birth certificate will be submitted to the immigration office for foreigner registration and stay permission. The children of undocumented migrant workers are faced with obstacles, for reasons that irregular status is to be notified to the immigration authorities as required by article 84 para. 1 of the Immigration Act.

5. CONCLUSION

Some gap or discrepancy between the Convention and domestic legislations has been noticed above. On the surface plugging the gap seems not to be daunting under the current circumstances, as Korea has ratified or acceded to various international human rights treaties and domestic legislations have been amended to be more in conformity with the provisions of treaties. Court jurisprudence has been progressive and active in recognizing the basic right of the constitution for migrant workers. To a certain degree, foreigners are subjects of basic economic, social rights, in addition to the basic right of liberty.

Nevertheless, there are still hurdles and gap which will take some time to remove. Sovereignty of a state is geared to the protection and treatment of its own nationals. Still, many advanced, liberal and open states are reluctant to be open-armed toward joining the Convention.[45]

For the present, many migrant workers are engaged in diverse manufacturing industries in Korea. NGOs have voiced their opinion strongly and put pressure upon the government to accede to the Convention. The Korean government has taken gradual steps to accept the demand from diverse sectors of society.

In response to the request for accession to the Convention made by migrant-sending states, The Korean government has expressed its views at the Universal Periodic Review meeting of the UN Human Rights Council held in May 2008, stating that conflicts between the Convention and domestic laws should be sorted out to accede to the Convention, but the government would do its utmost to protect the health, safety, employment and other human rights of migrant workers.[46]

Under the current circumstances where no migrant-receiving states have ratified or acceded to the Convention, the Korean government's position seems to be practical and reasonable. Up till now it has made amendment to the relevant laws and systems to protect migrant workers, reflecting the international human rights treaties. As more migrant workers reside in Korea and other migrant-receiving states join the Convention, it is expected that the Korean government will give serious consideration to the Convention.

Notes

1. The Convention was adopted on December 18, 1990 and entered into force on July 1, 2003 after reaching the threshold of 20 ratifying states. As of January 2018, the number of state parties is 51. Korea has not signed the Convention. Thus far states that have ratified the Convention are primarily migrant-sending ones like the Philippines and Mexico. The Convention is a main vehicle to look after their citizens abroad. No states in western Europe or North America, or other migrant-receiving states have ratified the Convention.
https://treaties.un.org/Pages/ViewDetails.aspx?src=IND&mtdsg_no=IV-13&chapter=4&lang=en

2. The Convention consists of preamble and main text of 93 articles. The Convention provides for wide-ranging contents more in detail than ILO Conventions or European Union Charter. The primary objective of the Convention is to foster respect for migrant workers' human rights.

3. Non-discrimination is considered as a special kind of equality in comparison with the principle of equality which represents the equality before the law. The upshot of the non-discrimination in the Convention is to prohibit discrimination as part of a principle of individual equality going beyond the principle of general equality, suggesting a solution for the integration of multi-cultural society. Jinwan Park, "A Discourse on the constitutionality of rights in the Migrant Workers Convention," World Constitution Research, Vol. 16, No. 2, 2010, p.157.

4. The three basic labor rights comprise the right to organize trade unions (the right of association), collective bargaining and collective action.

5. Irregular or undocumented migrant workers refer to workers who enter or reside in a state without permission of sojourn. L.S. Bosniak, "Human rights, state sovereignty and the protection of undocumented migrants under the international migrant workers convention," International Migration Review, 1991, p.742.

6. Article 25 provides:
   1. Migrant workers shall enjoy treatment not less favourable than that which applies to nationals of the State of employment in respect of remuneration and:
      (a) Other conditions of work, that is to say, overtime, hours of work, weekly rest, holidays with pay, safety, health, termination of the employment relationship and any other conditions of work which, according to national law and practice, are covered by these terms;
      (b) Other terms of employment, that is to say, minimum age of employment, restriction on work and any other matters which, according to national law and practice, are considered a term of employment.

2. It shall not be lawful to derogate in private contracts of employment from the principle of equality of treatment referred to in paragraph 1 of the present article.

3. States Parties shall take all appropriate measures to ensure that migrant workers are not deprived of any rights derived from this principle by reason of any irregularity in their stay or employment. In particular, employers shall not be relieved of any legal or contractual obligations, nor shall their obligations be limited in any manner by reason of such irregularity.

7. ILO standards provide state of employment with equal treatment only. For example ILO Convention No. 97(Migration for Employment) article 6 states that "Each Member … apply … treatment no less favourable than … its own nationals …" Hongyup Choi, "UN Migrant Workers Convention and Labor Law of Korea," Yeongnam Law Journal, Vol. 31, Oct. 2010, p.519.

8. Article 6 of Labor Standards Act provides that an employer shall neither discriminate against workers on the basis of gender, nor take discriminatory treatment in relation to terms and conditions of employment on the ground of nationality, religion, or social status.

9. Constitutional Court ruling, Aug. 30, 2007. 2004Hun-Ma670. "Considering that migrant vocational trainees have been in identical labor relationship providing de facto labor service and receiving wage in the form of allowance, it is unreasonable not to apply the provisions of Labor Standards Act to migrant vocational trainees. In recognizing that vocational training firms meet the conditions required in the Small- and Medium-sized Business Service directive and are alloted vocational training manpower suitable for the size of vocational training firms, satisfying the law-abiding capabilities of employers and endowed with work supervisory capabilities and other conditions relating to the observance of Labor Standards Act, under these circumstances excluding the application of some provisions of Labor Standards Act would be arbitrary and discriminatory."

10. Supreme Court of Korea ruling, Sep. 15, 1995. 94Nu12067.

11. Article 26 of the Convention provides:

1. States Parties recognize the right of migrant workers and members of their families:

   (a) To take part in meetings and activities of trade unions and of any other associations established in accordance with law, with a view to protecting their economic, social, cultural and other interests, subject only to the rules of the organization concerned;

   (b) To join freely any trade union and any such association as aforesaid, subject only to the rules of the organization concerned;

   (c) To seek the aid and assistance of any trade union and of any such association as aforesaid.

2. No restrictions may be placed on the exercise of these rights other than those that are prescribed by law and which are necessary in a democratic society in the interests of national security, public order (ordre public) or the protection of the rights and freedoms of others.

12. Article 40 of the Convention provides:

1. Migrant workers and members of their families shall have the right to form associations and trade unions in the State of employment for the promotion and protection of their economic, social, cultural and other interests.

2. No restrictions may be placed on the exercise of this right other than those that are prescribed by law and are necessary in a democratic society in the interests of national security, public order (ordre public) or the protection of the rights and freedoms of others.

13. ILO Convention No. 87 concerning Freedom of Association and Protection of the Right to Organize.

14. Hongyup Choi, *op. cit.*, pp. 522-523.

15. Article 12 of the Charter of Fundamental Rights of the European Union states:

1. Everyone has the right to freedom of peaceful assembly and to freedom of association at all levels, in particular in political, trade union and civic matters, which implies the right of everyone to form and to join trade unions for the protection of his or her interests.

2. Political parties at Union level contribute to expressing the political will of the citizens of the Union.

16. Article 28 of EU Charter of Fundamental Rights (Right of collective bargaining and action) states:

Workers and employers, or their respective organisations, have, in accordance with Union law and national laws and practices, the right to negotiate and conclude collective agreements at the appropriate levels and, in cases of conflicts of interest, to take collective action to defend their interests, including strike action.

17. Constitutional Court considers basic labor rights as "right of liberty with the function of social protection" or "right of liberty with character of social right," having opportunity to exercise influence over the labor conditions. Constitutional Court ruling, Feb. 27, 1998. 94Hun-Ba13.26, 95Hun-Ba44(Combined). It is an eclectic position. Jinwan Park, *op. cit.*, p.162; Kwangsung Kim, "Remedial measures on related laws for protecting foreign worker's rights," The Journal of Labor Law, Vol. 23, Dec., 2011, p.191.

18. The Labor Ministry has not considered the association in the category of trade union within the meaning of Trade Union Act stating as follows: "The plaintiff is considered an association composed of illegal migrant workers not entitled to join trade union, for reasons that two(one chairman and one auditing supervisor) out of three executives are confirmed to be illegal and undocumented, and plaintiff has not responded positively to request for list of association members for purpose of affirming employment eligibility of association members, and the objective of association statute includes objection to search for and measure against illegal stay. The decision was arrived at in consideration of main and supplementary documents submitted for the establishment of trade union."

19. Seoul Administrative Court has ruled: "Considering that undocumented workers, having no entitlement to stay in Korea, are strictly prohibited to be employed under the Immigration Act, having no legal status to maintain and improve work conditions and enhance their position, presupposing the continuous legal work relations, they are hardly thought to be in the category of workers permitted to join trade union under the Article 2 paragraph 4(d)." Seoul Administrative Court ruling, Feb. 7, 2006. 2005Gu-Hap18266.

20. Seoul High Court ruling, Feb. 1, 2007. 2006Nu6774.

21. Supreme Court ruling, June 25, 2015. 2007Du4995. The Supreme Court adjudicated on 25 June, 2015 that those who provided labor and lived on pay received in return for such labor should be recognized as workers, as set forth in the Trade Union and Labor Relations Adjustment Act.

22. Article 43 of the Convention stipulates:

1. Migrant workers shall enjoy equality of treatment with nationals of the State of employment in relation to:

   (a) Access to educational institutions and services subject to the admission requirements and other regulations of the institutions and services concerned;

   (b) Access to vocational guidance and placement services;

   (c) Access to vocational training and retraining facilities and institutions;

   (d) Access to housing, including social housing schemes, and protection against exploitation in respect of rents;

   (e) Access to social and health services, provided that the requirements for participation in the respective schemes are met;

   (f) Access to co-operatives and self-managed enterprises, which shall not imply a change of their migration status and shall be subject to the rules and regulations of the bodies concerned;

   (g) Access to and participation in cultural life.

2. States Parties shall promote conditions to ensure effective equality of treatment to enable migrant workers to enjoy the rights mentioned in paragraph 1 of the present article whenever the terms of their stay, as authorized by the State of

employment, meet the appropriate requirements.

    3. States of employment shall not prevent an employer of migrant workers from establishing housing or social or cultural facilities for them. Subject to article 70 of the present Convention, a State of employment may make the establishment of such facilities subject to the requirements generally applied in that State concerning their installation.

23. Article of 45 of the Convention stipulates:

    1. Members of the families of migrant workers shall, in the State of employment, enjoy equality of treatment with nationals of that State in relation to:

        (a) Access to educational institutions and services, subject to the admission requirements and other regulations of the stitutions and services concerned;

        (b) Access to vocational guidance and training institutions and services, provided that requirements for participation are met;

        (c) Access to social and health services, provided that requirements for participation in the respective schemes are met;

        (d) Access to and participation in cultural life.

    2. States of employment shall pursue a policy, where appropriate in collaboration with the States of origin, aimed at facilitating the integration of children of migrant workers in the local school system, particularly in respect of teaching them the local language.

    3. States of employment shall endeavour to facilitate for the children of migrant workers the teaching of their mother tongue and culture and, in this regard, States of origin shall collaborate whenever appropriate.

    4. States of employment may provide special schemes of education in the mother tongue of children of migrant workers, if necessary in collaboration with the States of origin.

24. Youngguk Kwon, "Presentation paper on the 3rd theme," Hearing documents for the ratification of the UN Migrant Workers Convention, National Human Rights Commission, Nov. 29, 2006, pp.62-63.

25. Article 2 of the Employment Security Act provides: No one shall be discriminated against in terms of vocational guidance and training service or work relations due to sex, age, religion, physical condition, social position or marital status.

26. Supreme Court ruling, Sept. 29, 1995. 95Do1331. The ruling states: " … no reason to exclude migrant workers due to lack of nationality as part of illustration … and the interpretation that migrant workers will be covered in application of the Act will not be considered ground for a breach of nulla poena sine lege, for this reason vocational guidance service toward migrant workers is to be covered by the article 19 of the Act."

27. Korea ratified ILO Convention No. 19, Convention on Equality of Treatment of National and Foreign Workers as regards Workmen's Compensation for Accident on March 29, 2001.

28. Supreme Court ruling, Sept. 15, 1995. 94Nu12067.

29. National Human Rights Commission Mar. 10, 2003. 02Jin-Cha30,31[nationality discrimination]. The Commission stated: "Migrant workers, being considered as workers under article 5 of Labor Standards Act irrespective of their sojourn status, are insured and compensated for industrial accident. The practice of excluding migrant workers from job rehabilitation training program operated in accordance with Industrial Accident Compensation Insurance Act is considered discriminatory due to nationality without any reasonable ground mentioned in article 30 para.2 of National Human Rights Commission Act. Therefore, it is necessary to improve retraining selection system so as not to exclude migrant workers."

30. Supreme Court ruling, Mar. 13, 2008. 2007Du26261.

31. Article 52 stipulates:

    1. Migrant workers in the State of employment shall have the right freely to choose their remunerated activity, subject to the following restrictions or conditions.
    2. For any migrant worker a State of employment may:
       (a) Restrict access to limited categories of employment, functions, services or activities where this is necessary in the interests of this State and provided for by national legislation;
       (b) Restrict free choice of remunerated activity in accordance with its legislation concerning recognition of occupational qualifications acquired outside its territory. However, States Parties concerned shall endeavour to provide for recognition of such qualifications.
    3. For migrant workers whose permission to work is limited in time, a State of employment may also:
       (a) Make the right freely to choose their remunerated activities subject to the condition that the migrant worker has resided lawfully in its territory for the purpose of remunerated activity for a period of time prescribed in its national legislation that should not exceed two years;
       (b) Limit access by a migrant worker to remunerated activities in pursuance of a policy of granting priority to its nationals or to persons who are assimilated to them for these purposes by virtue of legislation or bilateral or multilateral agreements. Any such limitation shall cease to apply to a migrant worker who has resided lawfully in its territory for the purpose of remunerated activity for a period of time prescribed in its national legislation that should not exceed five years.

4. States of employment shall prescribe the conditions under which a migrant worker who has been admitted to take up employment may be authorized to engage in work on his or her own account. Account shall be taken of the period during which the worker has already been lawfully in the State of employment.

32. Article 53 stipulates:

1. Members of a migrant worker's family who have themselves an authorization of residence or admission that is without limit of time or is automatically renewable shall be permitted freely to choose their remunerated activity under the same conditions as are applicable to the said migrant worker in accordance with article 52 of the present Convention.

2. With respect to members of a migrant worker's family who are not permitted freely to choose their remunerated activity, States Parties shall consider favourably granting them priority in obtaining permission to engage in a remunerated activity over other workers who seek admission to the State of employment, subject to applicable bilateral and multilateral agreements.

33. ILO Convention No. 143 on migrant workers (1975), article 14(a) states: "A Member may make the free choice of employment, … ,subject to the conditions that the migrant worker has resided … for a prescribed period not exceeding two years … ." This clause recognizes no national preferential treatment.

34. Ryszard Cholewinski, Migrant Workers in International Human Rights Law, Clarendon Press (Oxford) 1997, p.162.

35. Kwangsung Kim, *op. cit.* pp.208-209.

36. Committee on Economic, Social and Cultural Rights, Forty-Third Session Concluding Observation of the Committee on Economic, Social and Cultural Rights - Republic of Korea(E/C.12/KOR/CO/3), Dec. 17, 2009, para 21. Soojin Gong et al., "A study on Korean related laws for ratification of Migrant Workers Convention," Public Interest and Human Rights, Vol.9, 2011, p.16.

37. CEACR, Individual Observation concerning Discrimination (Employment and Occupation) Convention, 1958(No. 111) Republic of Korea (Doc No.(ilolex): 062009KOR111), 2009, para. 3.

38. Constitutional Court ruling, Sept. 29, 2011. 2007Hun-Ma1083, 2009Hun-Ma230.352.

39. Prof. Hongyup Choi shares the view on the necessity of amending the procedure of workplace transfer, but is of the view that the clause of the Act on the Employment of Foreign Workers not recognizing workplace transfer in principle would not contravene the Convention. Hongyup Choi, *op. cit.,* p.540.

40. Article 27 of the Convention provides:

1. With respect to social security, migrant workers and members of their families

shall enjoy in the State of employment the same treatment granted to nationals in so far as they fulfil the requirements provided for by the applicable legislation of that State and the applicable bilateral and multilateral treaties. The competent authorities of the State of origin and the State of employment can at any time establish the necessary arrangements to determine the modalities of application of this norm.

2. Where the applicable legislation does not allow migrant workers and members of their families a benefit, the States concerned shall examine the possibility of reimbursing interested persons the amount of contributions made by them with respect to that benefit on the basis of the treatment granted to nationals who are in similar circumstances.

41. Jinwan Park, *op. cit.,* p.164.

42. Article 28 of the Convention provides:
Migrant workers and members of their families shall have the right to receive any medical care that is urgently required for the preservation of their life or the avoidance of irreparable harm to their health on the basis of equality of treatment with nationals of the State concerned. Such emergency medical care shall not be refused them by reason of any irregularity with regard to stay or employment.

43. Article 30 of the Convention provides:
Each child of a migrant worker shall have the basic right of access to education on the basis of equality of treatment with nationals of the State concerned. Access to public pre-school educational institutions or schools shall not be refused or limited by reason of the irregular situation with respect to stay or employment of either parent or by reason of the irregularity of the child's stay in the State of employment.

44. Article 29 of the Convention provides:
Each child of a migrant worker shall have the right to a name, to registration of birth and to a nationality.

45. Several factors have been enumerated for low rate of ratification or accession: a lack of understanding or awareness of the Convention; conflict with national laws and legislation; contextual factors like adverse economic social climate. Martin Ruhs, "The human rights of migrant workers: why do so few countries care?," American Behavioral Scientist, Vol. 56, No. 9, 2012, pp.1282-1283.

46. Human Rights Committee, Report of the Working Group on the Universal Periodic Review: Republic of Korea, A/HRC/8/40, 29, May 2008. Yunho Seo, "Protection of the rights of migrant workers in migrant society," Ilkam Law Review, Vol. 26, 2013, pp.213-214.

References

Cholewinski, Ryszard, Migrant workers in International Human Rights Law, Clarendon Press (Oxford) 1997.

Bosniak, L.S., "Human rights, state sovereignty and the protection of undocumented migrants under the international migrant workers convention," International Migration Review, 1991.

Ruhs, Martin, "The human rights of migrant workers: why do so few countries care?," American Behavioral Scientist Vol. 56, No. 9, 2012.

Choi, Hongyup, "UN Migrant Workers Convention and Labor Law of Korea," Yeongnam Law Journal, Vol. 31, Oct. 2010.

Gong, Soojin et al., "A study on Korean related laws for ratification of Migrant Workers Convention," Public Interest and Human Rights, Vol. 9, 2011.

Kim, Kwangsung, "Remedial measures on related laws for protecting foreign worker's rights," The Journal of Labor Law 23, Dec. 2011.

Kwon, Youngguk, "Presentation paper on the 3rd theme," Hearing documents for the ratification of the UN Migrant Workers Convention, National Human Rights Commission, Nov. 29, 2006.

Park, Jinwan, "A Discourse on the constitutionality of rights in the Migrant Workers Convention," World Constitution Research, Vol. 16, No. 2, 2010.

Seo, Yunho, "Protection of the rights of migrant workers in migrant society," Ilkam Law Review, Vol. 26, 2013.

Constitutional Court ruling, Sept. 29, 2011.2007Hun-Ma1083, 2009Hun-Ma230.352.

Constitutional Court ruling, Aug. 30, 2007. 2004Hun-Ma670.

Constitutional Court ruling, Feb. 27, 1998. 94Hun-Ba13.26, 95Hun-Ba44 (Combined).

Supreme Court of Korea ruling, Sept. 15, 1995, 94Nu12067.

Supreme Court ruling, June 25, 2015, 2007Du4995.

Supreme Court ruling, Sept. 29, 1995, 95Do1331.

Supreme Court ruling, Sept. 15, 1995, 94Nu12067.

Supreme Court ruling, Mar. 13. 2008, 2007Du26261.

Seoul Administrative Court ruling, Feb. 7, 2006. 2005Gu-Hap18266.

Seoul High Court ruling, Feb. 1, 2007. 2006Nu6774.

National Human Rights Commission, Mar. 10, 2003. 02Jin-Cha30,31.

Committee on Economic, Social and Cultural Rights, Forty-Third Session Concluding Observation of the Committee on Economic, Social and Cultural Rights - Republic of Korea (E/C.12/KOR/CO/3), Dec. 17, 2009.

CEACR, Individual Observation concerning Discrimination (Employment and Occupation) Convention, 1958 (No. 111) Republic of Korea (Doc No.(ilolex):

062009KOR111), 2009.

Human Rights Committee, Report of the Working Group on the Universal Periodic Review: Republic of Korea, A/HRC/8/40, 2008. Convention, 1958 (No. 111) Republic of Korea (Doc No.(ilolex): 062009KOR111), 2009.

https://treaties.un.org/Pages/ViewDetails.aspx?src=IND&mtdsg_no=IV-13&chapter=4&lang=en.

International Legal Review on Japan's Claim to Dokdo and its Colonial Responsibility

DOH See-Hwan
Research Fellow
Northeast Asian History Foundation, Seoul, Korea

Abstract

Japan began claiming territorial sovereignty over Dokdo beginning in 1952 and has since strengthened its argument on three grounds: inherent territory from the 17th century, the doctrine of terra nullius and the San Francisco Peace Treaty. In other words, it argus that territorial sovereignty was established in the mid-17th century, reconfirmed with the Cabinet decision of 1905 to incorporate Dokdo, which was internationally recognized through the Peace Treaty.

In the course of Japan's changing focus in its assertion over Dokdo—from acquisition of the land in 1905, its statement made in 1952 claiming Dokdo being the inherent territory of Japan from 17th century, to recently the San Francisco Peace Treaty—it fundamentally reveals limitations in time series. By using the ground of occupancy, it changes and minimizes the issue into an international legal condition; its claim of Dokdo being the inherent territory of Japan distorts historical facts; it attempts to conceal its colonial aggression by arbitrarily interpreting conformity with the international legal principles. This series of assertions is a mere justification used to legitimize the assertions and illegal acts that have already been decided or executed based on the dynamics of international politics.

Thus, this paper will review the effect of international law revolving around historical substance of the three grounds Japan employed when claiming sovereignty over Dokdo. Then, changes in grounds for such argument based on international political dynamics will be reviewed in terms of intertemporal law and, in parallel, international legal issues found in recent studies of Japanese researchers on sovereignty over Dokdo and Japan's colonial responsibilities will be reviewed.

Conclusionally, Japan's claim to sovereignty over Dokdo asserted in line with Japanese colonialist history runs counter to the most basic undoing of colonial imperialism, that is, abandoning the land exploited by greed and violence. As such, Japan is left with responsibilities and obligations to fulfil under international law to build the Northeast Asian peace community in the 21ˢᵗ century.

Key Words

Sovereignty over Dokdo, Japanese colonial responsibility, *terra nullius*, inherent territory, San Francisco Treaty, Intertemporal law, Taft-Katsura Agreement, greed and violence, Northeast Asian peace community

1. INTRODUCTION

Concern has been raised that the Japanese government is set to bring up the issue of Dokdo in earnest under the premise that an agreement was reached on December 28, 2015 between the Korean and Japanese governments on the so-called "comfort women," the most critical one among all the issues the two nations have in hand to resolve.[1] Last February, Japan revised the guidelines for teaching and relevant manual that make it obligatory to specify Dokdo as the territory of Japan in the society textbooks used in elementary and junior high schools in Japan from next year. Not only that, Japan's claim to Dokdo is made plainly on the websites of the official residence of Prime Minister, Ministry of Foreign Affairs and the Office of Policy Planning and Coordination on Territory

Sovereignty under Chief Cabinet Secretary, provoking Korea regarding sovereignty over Dokdo.

Japan began claiming territorial sovereignty over Dokdo in 1952 and has since strengthened its argument on three grounds: inherent territory from the 17th century, the doctrine of *terra nullius* and the San Francisco Peace Treaty.[2] In other words, its argument can be summarized: territorial sovereignty was established in the mid-17th century, reconfirmed with the Cabinet decision of 1905 to incorporate Dokdo, which was internationally recognized with the Peace Treaty.

In the course of Japan's changing focus in its assertion over Dokdo—from acquisition of the land in 1905, its statement made in 1952 claiming Dokdo being the inherent territory of Japan from 17th century, to recently the San Francisco Peace Treaty—it fundamentally reveals limitations in time series. By using the ground of occupancy, it changes and minimizes the issue into an international legal condition; its claim of Dokdo being the inherent territory of Japan distorts historical facts; it attempts to conceal its colonial aggression by arbitrarily interpreting conformity with the international legal principles. This series of assertions is a mere justification used to legitimize the assertions and illegal acts that have already been decided or executed based on the dynamics of international politics.[3]

In essence, as its claim to sovereignty over Dokdo was integrated with its aggressive expansionist policies[4] to build an empire since the Meiji Restoration, it was intended to legitimize its claim under the doctrine of *terra nullius* amid wars of aggression in East Asia including the *Unyoho* Incident of 1875, the Sino-Japanese War of 1894 and the Russo-Japanese War of 1904. The unequal treaty signed as a result of the incident between modern *Joseon* and Japan on February 26, 1876, known as the Treaty of Ganghwa Island, did not state territorial demarcation. The order of *Dajokan*, the Grand Council of State, issued to complement the treaty on March 29, 1877 stated that Dokdo and the other island did not belong to Japan.[5] This significant decision of the Meiji government should be noted because the order cannot be found on the website of the Ministry of Foreign Affairs[6] and because the letter sent by Japan to Korea on July 13, 1962 made a contradictory argument that the early Meiji government recognized *Takeshima* as its territory.[7] Under the premise of contradictory limitations of arguments for acquisition of the land without sovereignty and that Dokdo was the Japanese territory from the Meiji government, the gist of the assertion Japan recently makes is the San francisco Peace Treaty[8] and Dean Rusk letter: the name of Dokdo was omitted in the process of establishing the treaty but the island remained the territory of Japan as evidenced by the Dean Rusk letter, which was written based on the information given by Japan. It should be noted again that the basis of such argument is in line with Japanese colonialism. As the nature of the San Francisco Treaty of 1951 changed from a punitive treaty to an anti-communist treaty based on the Cold War, Japan's claim to Dokdo is being legitimized based on colonialism as symbolized by the secret Taft-Katsura Agreement of 1905,[9] and this calls for a review on illegality[10] under international law.[11]

In other words, Japan strongly argues that its acts were legal under the law at that time[12] in an effort to be exonerated from its colonial responsibilities even when the Japan-Korea Annexation Treaty of 1910 holds no legal effects as the treaty was forcibly signed. In contrast, it claims sovereignty over Dokdo, deviating from the treaty between Korea and Japan, by changing the ground of argument from acquisition under *terra nullius*, being the inherent territory of Japan, to the San Francisco Treaty. Such arguments and their grounds are contradictory in applying the international intertemporal law.

Thus, this paper will review the effect of international law revolving around historical substance of the three grounds Japan employed when claiming sovereignty over Dokdo. Then, changes in grounds for such argument based on international political dynamics will be reviewed in terms of intertemporal law and, in parallel, international legal issues found in recent studies of Japanese researchers on sovereignty over Dokdo and

Japan's colonial responsibilities will be reviewed.

2. REVIEW ON THE GROUND OF "INHERENT TERRITORY OF JAPAN"

2-1. JAPAN's CLAIM

Japan's claim to Dokdo being its inherent territory is grounded on its awareness of the existence of the islet from the past which can be traced back with numerous documents and maps. It argued that in early 17th century, Japanese civilians used Dokdo as a navigational port and docking point for ships on the route to Ulleungdo, and as a fishing ground for sea lions and abalone with the official approval of the Tokugawa Shogunate. With this, it claims Japan established sovereignty over Dokdo in the mid 17th century.[13]

2-2. SUBSTANCE AND RECOGNITION

Inherent territory is a term used by Japan as the historical ground to claim sovereignty over Dokdo after it identified the limitation its doctrine of terra nullius entails, yet the term is considered "an invention of Japan" which, in its concept, denies the historical aspects of an area having territorial dispute. When its claim is premised on the inherent territory, Dokdo loses correlation with the Russo-Japanese war and annexation of Korea, and the Senkaku islands and Sino-Japanese war get denied of relevance because inherent territory holds an unalterable status in the course of or changes in history. Inherent territory means that the territory concerned originally belonged to Japan and is not a matter of dispute, but the term has recently been used in Korea and Japan to counteract Japan's position, which has intensified the disputes over Dokdo and Senkaku islands and calls for concern.[14]

2-2-1. APPROVAL

Kanae Taijudo, a Japanese international law scholar, stated regarding inherent territory: "the incorporation of territory made in the 38th year of the Meiji era by the Meiji government and subsequent national power was a sufficient replacement, in accordance with modern request, of the effective title Japan had in conformity of the 17th century international law."[15] Under the international law, however, a replacement with the title effective under modern international law is not required to maintain sovereignty over any inherent territory in history. Also, in that Japan never replaced the inherent historical title over numerous islands with occupation or any other title, Taijudo's statement for inherent territory entails a controversy under international legal principles.[16]

2-2-2. DISAPPROVAL

Haruki Wada, a Japanese history scholar, pointed out that the ground of inherent territory was unwarranted by explaining how it was created and used in Japan. This ground for claim was first used to request the handover of the Northern Territories, and the term was intended to mean it "never belonged to a foreign territory." Referring to the treaties involving the four Northern Territories signed between Russia and Japan, the claim that those islands "never belonged to Russia" can be valid, but such statement is limited to those four islands. Thus, such concept cannot be expanded to either Dokdo or Senkaku islands since those territories were controlled or owned by Korea and China, respectively, before being incorporated by Japan. Nevertheless, Japan began applying the term to Dokdo and Senkaku islands to justify its sovereignty, which sparked controversies over the term. This term is an "invention of Japan" which cannot be translated into other languages except for Japanese.[17] Also, if the term is literally applied, Okinawa and Hokkaido are not the territories of Japan, and only the four main islands belong to Japan.[18]

Norio Naka, a Japanese scholar of international social science, indicated that the inherent territory cannot be established. "Inherent territory" is not only a dangerous political term that may cause one to think and act for a war but also a meaningless term based on the wrong historical perception. Without defining from when and in what sense, the term lacks specificity and rings hollow. The use of inherent territory may well trigger questioning what is the inherent territory of Japan and calls for answering the questions like when was the beginning of the country as Japan and what is its scope. It seems no one can answer these questions.[19]

Narahiko Toyoshita, a Japanese political scientist, criticizes the inherent territory statement. Inherent territory is never a concept under international law. After all, it is a mere political concept invented by the Japanese government and the Ministry of Foreign Affairs who have as many as four disputed territories including the Senkaku islands, Takeshima and Northern Territories. Since the 1970s, Taiwan, China and Korea have quoted the concept, and now Southeast Asian countries are using the concept of inherent territory recklessly to legitimize their sovereignty.[20]

Kumiko Haba, a Japanese scholar of international politics, pointed out that inherent territory is a taboo word in the context of international politics in Europe. Inherent territory is used in relation to indigenous people in prehistoric times and ancient history. Any territory occupied by a country in the 19th or 20th century cannot be said as a native territory or land. In the 19th century, modernized countries "expanded" their territory against indigenous people or small countries, or if no humans reside, against mountains, rivers, territories and islands. If these are called inherent or native territories, that will trigger dispute and confrontation. In other words, Dokdo and Senkaku islands, incorporated by Japan in the 19th and 20th century, are not deemed inherent or native territories, and claiming as such would only induce a sense of victims and territorial nationalism, intensifying territorial disputes.[21]

2-2-3. CONCLUSION ON INHERENT TERRITORY

A negative view on inherent territory has been generally established in international politics and social science disciplines and has shown

signs of spreading to history studies. For instance, the second final report
of the Takeshima Issue Research Group published in March 2012 does
not mention inherent territory. Also, Satoshi Ikeuchi clearly expressed a
negative view on Japan's claim of inherent territory over Dokdo based on
historical research in his book *What is the Takeshima Issue?* published in
2012.[22]

2-3. LIMITATIONS OF INHERENT TERRITORY AND ITS BASIS

Japan's basis of claiming Dokdo using the concept of inherent territory,
which replaced the doctrine of *terra nullius* of 1905, should have been
established as a historical ground under international law since the dispute
over Ulleungdo began with the An Yong-bok incident of 1693 until
the incorporation of Dokdo in 1905. As Haruki Wada pointed out, it
is noteworthy to note that the border crossing prohibition on Tsushima
domain in 1696 and the order of *Dajokan* of the Meiji government in
1877 paradoxically run counter to the inherent territory argument. Under
this premise, the letter sent by Japan to Korea on July 13, 1962 stating that
the early Meiji government recognized Takeshima as its territory, combined
with the order of *Dajokan,* which was the prime state organization in the
Meiji era, being omitted in *10 Points to Understand the Takeshima Dispute*
published by the Japanese Ministry of Foreign Affairs make the meaning
of the issue be reconfirmed.

2-3-1. SEICHU NAITO'S ORDER BANNING PASSAGE TO TAKESHIMA IN EDO SHOGUNATE

Korea argues that Usan-do appearing in the 15th century literature
referred to Dokdo. In Japan, Japanese merchants were allowed by the
shogunate in the 17th century to go to Takeshima once a year to catch
abalone. In fact, Takeshima here refers to Ulleungdo. In 1692, many
people from Joseon came over to this island, making it hard for the
merchants to work, so they appealed to the shogunate to ban the Joseon

people from coming to the island. The shogunate ordered the Tsushima domain to negotiate with Joseon. Claiming Takeshima was its own island, a talk was proposed, but Roju Bungonokami Abe, the State Minister at that time, stated on the reason why the government allowed border crossing that "it was not intended for Japan to take the island of Joseon." "The island seemed Ulleungdo of Joseon," said Abe, clarifying that he would take action to prevent Japanese people from crossing the ocean. That action was taken in 1696.[23]

2-3-2. KAZUO HORI'S ORDER OF DAJOKAN IN THE MEIJI ERA

Following the successful Meiji Restoration, Japan proceeded with territory demarcation and establishment of relationship with neighboring countries. Japan pressed Joseon into signing the Japan–Korea Treaty of 1876 which did not specify the demarcation of border. To complement this, *Dajokan*, which governed the state affairs at that time, issued an order on March 29, 1877, which was pointed out in the 1987 paper of Professor Kazuo Hori of Kyoto University, *Japan's 1905 Incorporation of Takeshima*.[24]

In October 1876, an official of the Department of Geography, Ministry of Interior of Japan, asked about Takeshima (Ulleungdo) to Shimane Prefecture, and the prefecture studied and submitted "an inquiry about registration of the land of Takeshima and another island in the Sea of Japan" along with a map. The map titled Isotakeshima Ryakuzu (simplified map of Isotakeshima) had Isotakeshima (Ulleungdo) and smaller island Songdo drawn in the southeast direction from Isotakeshima to Oki. "Takeshima and the other island" referred to Ulleungdo and Dokdo (Takeshima), and the Ministry of Interior duly concluded following its own independent research and coinciding with the report of Shimane Prefecture, that "the two islands are the territories of Joseon, not Japan."[25]

The Ministry of Interior submitted the relevant inquiry to *Dajokan* on March 17, 1877. In an appendix, Takeshima is located 120-ri away northwest of Oki Island. Another island is called Songdo. The island is 80-ri away from Oki Island, and the other island is specified as Songdo (presently Dokdo). After deliberations, *Dajokan* concluded the opinion of the Ministry was correct, and *Dajokan* requested approval from Tomomi Iwakura on March 20. After reviewing the actions of the 17th century government in detail, *Dajokan* issued the oder on March 29, 1877, stating that Takeshima and the other island had nothing to do with our country (Japan). In the order, Ulleungdo and Dokdo were deemed as a group of islands and the two islands were declared non-Japanese territories based on a belief that they were the territories of Joseon. Thus, Japan demarcated the border with Joseon.

The finding of Kazuo Hori were supported by Naito Seitsu, professor at Shimane University, and Satoshi Ikeuchi, professor at Nagoya University while Masao Shimojo, professor at Takushoku University, denied the decision of *Dajokan* saying "it cannot be accurately concluded whether the other island in 'Takeshima and the other island' referred to Songdo (Dokdo)." The Ministry of Foreign Affairs has also ignored this decision of *Dajokan*.[26]

3. REVIEW ON THE GROUND OF TERRA NULLIUS

3-1. JAPAN's CLAIM

The doctrine of occupancy has been used by Japan to claim sovereignty over Dokdo following the Cabinet decision of 1905 which reconfirmed its intention to claim sovereignty over Dokdo. In the early 1900s, as residents of Oki Island, Shimane Prefecture, shored up their request for stabilizing sea lion fishing business, the Cabinet decision was made in January 1905 to incorporate Dokdo into the prefecture, which, Japan argues, reconfirmed its intention of possession, and the prefecture continued exercising sovereignty peacefully through administrative measures without any complaints from other country. Japan claims that its sovereignty over Dokdo, which by then had already been established, became clearer to other countries in terms of modern international law.[27]

3-2. PROCESS OF INCORPORATING DOKDO

A fisherman named Yozaburo Nakai who caught abalone near Oki Island went to Songdo to hunt sea lions in 1903, and in 1904, many people came to the shore who recklessly hunted sea lions, making hunting activities off the island more competitive. The fisherman submitted an application regarding the incorporation of Lyanko Island into Japan and lease of the island in September 1904. Amid the Russo-Japanese war, the Japanese government named the island Takeshima in its Cabinet decision on January 28, 1905 and incorporated it into Shimane Prefecture and Japanese main island.[28] The governor of Shimane Prefecture made a public announcement according to the government directive on February 22, 1905.[29]

Beginning with an invasion into the Korean Empire who announced its neutrality in war on January 21, 1904, the Russo-Japanese war broke out. The night before the breakout of the war in February 1904, the Japanese army took over Hansung, the capital of the Empire, further expanding the territory it conquered, and on February 23, 1904, Japan forced the Korean Empire into signing the Japan-Korea Treaty. The treaty was the first step in turning Joseon into the protectorate of Japan,[30] and specified that Japan may expropriate the areas needed for its military strategies for a certain period. On August 22, 1904, the Japan–Korea Protocol of 1904 was signed which coerced Joseon into engaging a diplomatic advisor sent by Japan.

An attack on Port Arthur began in August 1904, which was fought violently by General Nogi Maresuke who finally captured Port Arthur on January 1, 1905. The Japanese Navy had built observation posts on Ulleungdo to fight against the Baltic Fleet in East Sea, and began surveying the area after designating Dokdo as a candidate island for building another observation post, which was five days before Nakai submitted application.[31]

It was only natural that Nakai's application for incorporating Dokdo had a close relevance to the Russo-Japanese war. Enziro Yamaza, the Director of Political Affairs Bureau at the Ministry of Foreign Affairs, mentioned about the application that "Under the present circumstances, it is imperative that the island be incorporated. It is absolutely necessary to construct observation posts and install wireless or submarine cables for the surveillance of enemy ships. Particularly, diplomacy is free of such considerations." The incorporation of Dokdo was not about interests of the sea lion hunter, but it was intended to effectively fight against the Russian Navy taking advantage of the position and power obtained by occupying the Korean Peninsula.[32]

Following the victory of Japan, the rule of Korea by Japan was recognized by Russia with the Treaty of Portsmouth, and Japan forced the Japan-Korea Treaty signed on November 17, 1905 to make Korea the protectorate of Japan. The treaty deprived Korea of diplomatic sovereignty and sent Japanese Resident Generals. The decision on sovereignty over Dokdo made by the Japanese government was delivered to Korea on March 28, 1906.[33]

In 1910, five years after Japan's announcement of Dokdo being its own territory, the Korean peninsula was annexed into the Japanese territory. Incorporation of Dokdo in 1905 was a precursor to the annexation of the Korean peninsula and beginning of national tragedy.[34]

3-3. INTERNATIONAL LEGAL ISSUES OF THE DOCTRINE OF TERRA NULLIUS

The Cabinet decision of 1905 and notification No. 40 of Shimane Prefecture expressed territorial acquisition enacted in the modern legislative system, but they entail significant international legal issues.

First, the period between 1900 when the Imperial Decree No. 41[35] which specified Dokdo under the jurisdiction of Uldogun (county) was published in the official gazette as the Korean Empire's modern legislation, and 1905 when Japan made the Cabinet decision is within the "reasonable period" for effective control of a territory discovered by a state even though the Korean Empire's effective control was not sufficient. Thus, the Korean Empire held an incomplete title Dokdo which tentatively prevents other countries from occupying the territory when the Cabinet decision was made in 1905.

Second, the application for incorporating Lyanco Island and its lease made in 1904 stated "this island is located on the route that ships take going back and forth between the Japanese mainland, through Oki islands and Ulleungdo, and Joseon's Gangwon and Hamkyeong provinces." With Dokdo being the first foreign island located in the course from Japanese Oki Islands to Gangwon and Hamkyeong provinces, the mainland of Joseon, this statement demonstrated a close relationship Japan had with Joseon and showed that it had been believed Dokdo belonged to the territory of Joseon.

Third, the incorporation attempt to Dokdo by the Japanese government was made in the form of a Cabinet decision as it recognized the chances of failure if its attempt was officially found by the Korean Empire which had published Imperial Decree No. 41. Such was to avoid the burden of publishing it in the central government gazette while allowing administrative actions on Dokdo with the notification of Shimane Prefecture which provides a domestic legal ground.[36]

Fourth, any nullification of the agreements made between Korea and Japan before the incorporation of Dokdo requires prior notification. In that unilateral cancellation by a Cabinet decision does not have effect under international law, the incorporation of Dokdo of 1905 is neither legitimate nor legal.[37]

4. REVIEW ON THE GROUND FOR SOVEREIGNTY UNDER THE SAN FRANCISCO PEACE TREATY

4-1. JAPAN's CLAIM

Japan suggests that the San Francisco Treaty officially recognized Dokdo as the Japanese territory. It argued in the course of drafting the treaty when Korea requested to the U.S. to add Dokdo to the territories that Japan should abandon, however, the U.S. clearly rejected such request, saying "Dokdo was never treated as part of Korea, and the island is the Japanese territory."[38] Under such premise, Japan argued that the list of territories Japan had to renounce included "Korea including the islands of Quelpart (Jeju Island), Port Hamilton (Geomun Island) and Dagelet (Ulleng Island)" and intentionally excluded Dokdo.[39]

4-2. CHANGES IN THE POLICIES TOWARDS JAPAN

In 1945 when the Second World War ended, the US had the East Asian policies intended to weaken Japan while building a peaceful community with the Soviet Union and China. With those policies in mind, the Allied Forces established territorial policies towards Japan, which was solidified into the Potsdam Declaration. With Japan's acceptance of the declaration, an agreement was made between the Allied Forces and Japan on the joint territorial policy towards Japan.

In 1950, the nature and direction of the Treaty changed as the Cold War intensified and John Foster Dulles became the special representative. The biggest deviation was the conversion from a punitive treaty to an anti-communist treaty, which dropped Japan's responsibilities for war, cession of territory and reparations. Regarding territorial matters, those provisions related to the U.S. were specified in detail while the rest related to other neighboring countries were not. As a result, the wartime territorial policies towards Japan agreed by the Allied Forces as well as Japan were scrapped, but new territorial policy and principles were not discussed, agreed upon or decided under the San Francisco Treaty.

Under this assumption, the Japanese government has since 1952 repeatedly and continuously argued that the treaty was directly related to its sovereignty over Dokdo. Paradoxically, however, in 1949 after the change of U.S. policy towards Japan and the Peace Treaty being turned into an anti-communist treaty, Japan demanded to specify Dokdo as one of islands under the Japanese territory in the Peace Treaty, which was rejected, and Dokdo remained a non-Japanese territory.[40]

In addition, in April 1951 when Dulles made the second visit to Japan, the Japanese government reviewed the treaty drafted by the British government. At that time, the Japanese government, without the presence of Britain who drafted the treaty or Korea, a stakeholder in the treaty, and under a unilateral sponsorship of the U.S., had an intensive and exclusive review on the draft peace treaty created by the U.K. Foreign and Commonwealth Office (FMO). It should be noted that the Japanese acknowledged the FMO draft which stipulated Dokdo as the Korean territory, not Japanese territory. This was the official recognition of the Japanese government that Dokdo was the territory of Korea.[41]

In the meantime, a review on Article 2 of the Peace Treaty and international legal principles on the sovereignty of Dokdo from the perspective of a non-party to the treaty, it is noteworthy that at the second US-Britain summit to prepare the San Francisco Peace Treaty held in London from June 2 to 14, 1951, the U.S. and Great Britain did not recognize Korea as a party to the Treaty, but instead, agreed on the effect of treaties upon third states to grant Korea the rights to the benefits of Article 2 by adding Article 21.[42]

Also, a legal principle on the treaty which creates the objective regimes with the obligations valid *erga omnes* are not universally accepted. Even when this principle is recognized, the Peace Treaty can hardly be regarded as falling under this principle considering the attitudes that Korea, Soviet Union, China and Taiwan took at that time.[43]

4-3. ARTICLE 2(A) OF THE PEACE TREATY AND DEAN RUSK LETTER

Article 2(a) of the San Francisco Peace Treaty states that "Japan renounces all right, title and claim to Korea, including the islands of Quelpart (Jeju Island), Port Hamilton (Geomun Island) and Dagelet (Ulleng Island)." On this, Japan has countered that the provision was meant to leave Dokdo off from the list of islands Japan renounced. Japan claimed that Dokdo was not included in the territories Japan had to give up, thus since 1905 till now, Japan has maintained sovereignty over Dokdo.

Meanwhile, Yang Yoo-chan, the Korean ambassador to the US, requested to the US Secretary of State to revise the Treaty to add Dokdo to the islands Japan renounced, which were the islands of Quelpart, Port Hamilton and Dagelet. The U.S. did not accept the request, and as a result, Article 2(a) does not include Dokdo. The letter which Secretary of State Dean Rusk sent to the Korean embassy in the U.S. on August 10 explains the rason for such rejection. As regards the island of Dokdo, otherwise known as Takeshima or Liancourt Rocks, this normally uninhabited rock formation was according to our information never treated as part of Korea and, since about 1905, has been under the jurisdiction of the Okid Islands Office of Shimane Prefecture of Japan. The island does not appear ever before to have been claimed by Korea."[44]

It should be noted that the letter uses the premise of "according to our (U.S) information." Dokdo was excluded in the Peace Treaty based on the limited information the U.S. had.[45] Based on this premise, the letter emphasized that "since about 1905, Dokdo has been under the jurisdiction of the Okid Islands Office of Shimane Prefecture of Japan," which means the U.S. considered Japan's incorporation of Dokdo legitimate. Under the same premise, it stated "the island does not appear ever before to have been claimed by Korea." The limited information is, in other words, information after Japan's incorporation of Dokdo in 1905. Therefore, as discussed above, Japan's incorporation of Dokdo proved to have no effect under the legal principles, thus the Dean Rusk letter premised on Dokdo having been under the jurisdiction of the Oki Island Office of Shimane Prefecture since 1905 loses its meaning.[46]

5. A LEGAL REVIEW ON INTERTEMPORAL PRINCIPLES

5-1. THEORETICAL REVIEW ON INTERTEMPORAL LEGAL PRINCIPLES

5-1-1. CONCEPT

Intertemporal law governs which of the legal systems in successive periods is to be applied in a particular case. In the international relationship, new treaties and legislation reflect evolving legal norms. It is to determine whether the meaning of new legal norms and terms can replace that of the past legal norms and terms, and what status the legal effect maintains in time.[47]

5-1-2. DISTINCTION OF THE CREATION OF RIGHTS AND EXISTENCE OF RIGHTS

Intertemporal law is a method of interpreting law. The reason why political factors are said to be involved in intertemporal law is because it is necessary to have a dynamic understanding of the nature of legal norms, especially the rights.

First, when treaties are signed to create rights or impose obligations or events occur, subsequent legal effects are made based on the intention of the parties involved. The principle of international legal relations is dependent on the formation of agreement among the parties. This formation of agreement is premised on mutual benefit and impartiality. The principle that the meaning of rights should be defined under the law effective at the time of creation of such rights requires the continued existence of the rights under evolution of law. In other words, the existence of the rights can maintain their effect to the extent where justice and equality is fulfilled under the dynamic orders of international society. This nature of dynamic orders in international legal relationship can be found in cases where the legal principles of change of circumstances, prohibition of abuse of rights, prescription, desuetude or obsolescence, jus cogens are recognized.

Second, the principle of pacta sunt servanda and the principle of non-retroactivity of law, which protect the stability of legal relations established under international law, are the basic principles, but because of their static nature, they may make light of definitions or specific validity while giving weight only on legal stability. The principle of changes of circumstances is considered a representative legal principle which reflects the evolutionary nature of legal norms and rights. The circumstances which formed the basis on which the parties made an agreement changed rapidly and markedly as time goes by, would impose too much a burden on the parties and undermine impartiality if the original agreements are forced on the parties. If such circumstantial changes had been expected, the parties would not have signed the treaties in the first place or would have made different provisions, and in these cases, a discharge of such treaty can be argued based on the principle of changes of circumstances. What matters in continuing the relationship under the treaties is whether the identicalness and equality of the basis of agreement between the parties has been maintained.[48]

5-1-3. HARMONY OF STABILITY AND CHANGE

Then, when it comes to intertemporal law, should the legal relationship rapidly respond to and be interlinked with the changes of legal norms and events? The legal norms and facts evolve with the times and their meaning may change. In international society, changes in legal norms are slow and hard to make compared with changes of legal facts owing to a defect of the legislative institution. If the ground for rights has to be made anew to continue the legal relationship as legal facts at the time of creation or the meaning of events change, stability in international relationship may well be seriously undermined. Thus, in the case of Island of Palmas, Arbitrator Max Huber emphasized the first principle of intertemporal law, that is, the legal relationship should be determined by the law effective at the time of creation of rights under the legal facts. This should be interpreted that the second principle, that is, the continuation of the rights should be maintained anew according to an evolution of law, should not be expanded to the determination of the legal facts.[49] Occasionally, however, the boundary of the determination of legal facts or determination of the rights may be blurry because the facts and rights are all regulated by and subject to law.[50]

5-2. Precedent: Island of Palmas Arbitration (1928)[51]

Arbitrator Huber stated that in intertemporal legal principle, the creation of rights and the existence of rights are required. The U.S., which was ceded the territory after its victory in a war by Spain, who discovered and obtained the right to the Island of Palmas in the 16th century, had a territorial dispute with the Netherlands who claimed that it obtained its sovereignty over the island after the Dutch East India corporation signed an agreement with the native chief in the 17th century. In this dispute, the arbitrator ruled that the ground for title of the Netherlands was effective.

On the claim of the U.S. who acquired the title to the Island of Palmas from Spain which discovered the island in the 16th century, Arbitrator Huber stated that the discovery alone bestowed only immature title and that, in addition to discovery, the Netherlands had effective occupation based on the legal requirements for acquisition of title developed in the 19th century and early 20th century, thus has established the effective title for the island. Huber stipulated that for the existence of rights, the rights had to be exercised and maintained in accordance with legal requirements evolved until the dispute arose.[52]

5-3. Intertemporal Review on Claims of Sovereignty over Dokdo

Beginning with an invasion into the Korean Empire who announced its neutrality in war on January 21, 1904, Japan forced the Korean Empire into signing the Japan-Korea Treaty on February 23, 1904. The Japanese Army stationed in Korea constantly threatened the Korean Empire to sign the first to third Japan-Korea Treaties, which were mere formality under international law to cover up the essence of aggression.[53] Japan's claim to sovereignty over Dokdo was made between August 22, 1904 when the first Japan-Korea Treaty was signed, which denied Joseon of diplomatic rights, and November 17, 1905 when the second Japan-Korea Treaty was signed, which deprived Joseon of sovereignty. Such territorial provocation ran against Article 3 of the Treaty which guaranteed territorial integrity of the Korean Empire and was thus illegal under international law. Nevertheless, Japan unduly deemed that Emperor Gojong's defying the denial of diplomatic rights and sending secret envoys violated the treaty, and forced the treaties onto Joseon to deprive its sovereignty, force Emperor Gojong to abdicate the throne and dissolve the Korean army. As Alexis Dudden pointed out, this colonialization of Joseon by Japan was abusive of international law. In that Japan's incorporation attempt of Dokdo coincided with its colonialization of the Korean peninsula which began with the Russo-Japanese war, its claim over Dokdo does not satisfy the *terra nullius* requirements under international law and is an obviously illegal aggression on the territorial sovereignty of its neighboring country.

　　While Japan argued the basis which legitimizes its colonial rule was 'law effective at that time,' that is, the Japan-Korea Annexation Treaty in 1910, it kept changing focus in its assertion over Dokdo since 1952 from acquisition of the land in 1905 to statement claiming Dokdo being the inherent territory of Japan and the San Francisco Peace Treaty. Its claim to Dokdo is contradictory in terms of intertemporal law and calls for a review. In the same line, after violating Korea's sovereignty over Dokdo and colonizing Korea during the Russo-Japanese war, Japan seems to have applied such contradictory intertemporal law to the process where it started from the Japan-Korea Treaty of 1905 to the Japan-Korea Annexation Treaty of 1910, under the assumption that connivance and condoning of Colonial Powers as symbolized by the secret Taft-Katsura Agreement of 1905 was legal under international law.

To sum up, the essence of intertemporal law is the principle that rights are defined under the law effective at the time of creation of rights and that the rights should exist in link with an evolution of law which was the basis of the rights. The existence of rights should be seen as maintaining its effects only to the extent where it remains in compliance with the justice and equality of the dynamic orders of international society. Under the international legal system premised on these dynamic orders, Japan's claim to sovereignty over Dokdo runs counter to the principles of the prohibition of abuse of rights, prescription, desuetude or obsolescence, and jus cogens. Also, in the case of Island of Palmas of 1928 which proposed the principles of intertemporal law, the ground for the Peace Treaty between the U.S. and Spain was denied, and the principle of effective exercise defined as a continuous and peaceful display of territorial sovereignty was upheld, which has significant implications to Korea's sovereignty over Dokdo.[54]

6. JAPAN'S COLONIAL RESPONSIBILITIES AND THE STUDIES ON SOVEREIGNTY OVER DOKDO

Even though Korea regained its territorial sovereignty over Dokdo as a result of independence gained in 1945, the Japanese government has complained that Korea is illegally occupying the island, citing *terra nullius* occupation in 1905 or inherent territory. Regarding this, it is noticeable that researches have been carried out in Japan on a need to consider the Dokdo issue not as a territorial dispute but as international legal view of history along with Japanese colonial responsibilities.

6-1. Haruki Wada's Proposal to Give up Dokdo

Haruki Wada criticized Japan's claim to territorial sovereignty over Dokdo and its argument that Korea's occupancy on the island is illegal, which shows lack of morality on the side of Japan who regrets its colonial rule. There is no other option for Japan but to give up Dokdo which is effectively occupied by Korea. Japan's continuous assertion over Dokdo without prospects has only embarrassingly worsened the relationship with Korea and sentiment among Koreans and Japanese. In other words, his proposal for giving up Dokdo contains the meaning of apology and compensation for colonial rule.

Wada pointed out that: Dokdo was the Japanese territory for 40 years from January 1905 to August 15, 1945; after Japan was defeated in the war and Korea obtained independence, the Supreme Commander of the Allied Powers excluded Dokdo from the Japanese territory in January 1946; and several disputes occurred after Dokdo was included inside the Rhee Seung Man line in 1952, but Korea has sent the guards since 1954 and maintained an effective occupancy until today. Wada asserts that Korea has effectively occupied Dokdo for far longer than the period Japan occupied. Besides, the Japanese sovereignty over Dokdo obtained in January 1905 was the beginning of aggression into Joseon, a precursor to five-year forced annexation of Korea and the start of national tragedy.[55]

In contrary, however, he suggested for the interests of both Koreans and Japanese, fishing of Shimane Prefecture fishermen be allowed around Dokdo and the island not be used in drawing the baseline for the exclusive economic zone (EEZ).[56]

6-2. Gentaro Serita's Theory of Opening up Dokdo

After analyzing sovereignty over Dokdo under international law, Gentaro Serita concluded that no justified reasons to support Dokdo being the territory of Korea were found.[57] Afterwards, Serita pointed out that Korea has effectively occupied Dokdo, and Japan is fighting with its neighbor over a rock islet of about 100 pyeong, likening its size to a thumb, emphasizing Korea and Japan should conclude a new treaty to resolve the issue.

The details of the treaty Serita proposes are: first of all, Japan extends a sincere apology to Korea such as the Japan-DPRK Pyongyang Declaration of 2002 and the statement made by Prime Minister Tomiichi Murayama in 1995 as Japan did not apologize for its colonial rule in the Treaty on Basic Relations between Japan and the Republic of Korea made in 1965. For future generations, Serita claimed that Japan should give up or hand over Dokdo to Korea and recognize Korea's sovereignty over Dokdo.

At the same time, however, Serita requests to Korea that Korea promises to define the EEZ using Ulleungdo, not Dokdo, as the baseline and that Korea designates Dokdo as a natural conservation zone and sets a 12-nautical mile no fishing zone to open up the area for all nations for scientific research.[58] Serita's proposal is similar to that of Wada, with a difference of opening up Dokdo internationally. Serita and Wada's proposals have something in common such as apologies for its colonial rule and sharing of interests between Korea and Japan.[59]

6-3. YOSHIO HIROSE'S LEGAL PRINCIPLES ON DECOLONIZATION

Yoshio Hirose analyzes the Japanese annexation of Korea and sovereignty over Dokdo from a new angle of international historical view using the concept of colonization and decolonization, which were rarely used in international legal discussion. Hirose states that before World War I, it was an era of colonization era; after World War I, it is an era of decolonization. Decolonization means "a complete outlawing, after the establishment of legal orders under the League of Nations, of acts of colonizing other countries, forcibly making other country into a protectorate, or territorial incorporation by colonial nations like Japan who joined the ranks of colonialization in the later stage." Hirose argues that it is a must to impose a retroactive nullification on new colonization by colonial nations in the era of League of Nations and its results based on the decolonization principle established by jus cogens under the Charter of the United Nations after World War II and the self-determination principles (established through UN Charter Article 1 Paragraph 2, Articles 11, 12, 13 and the Declaration on the Granting of Independence to Colonial Countries and Peoples of 1960).

Yet, for colonial policies before WWI, Hirose argues, the legal effects of decolonization formed under the UN Charter are limited to the undoing of colonization based on the recognition of effects, rather than outright nullification. The international legal effects of a series of the Japan-Korea Treaties signed in the run-up to annexation belong to this criteria.[60] In other words, annexation of Korea by Japan is effective and subject to undoing and compensations. In the same line, Dokdo became the Japanese territory as a result of effective occupation of Japan who was executing colonial activities which were acknowledged by law throughout the 19th century until WWI, but after WWI, new decolonization principles apply to Dokdo.[61]

Hirose explains that Japan's returning Taiwan and Sakhalin, the territories Japan legally obtained after the Sino-Japanese and Russo-Japanese Wars, to the respective original owners were one type of decolonization after WWII. As such, he argues, Dokdo should be subject to decolonization, and Korea's sovereignty over the island should be recognized. Considering the friendly relationship between the two nations, the current provisional EEZ should be maintained and not define the EEZ from Dokdo, and Hirose argues, it is desirable that a joint natural resources jurisdiction surrounding the island should be set and agreed upon.

6-4. ASSESSMENT OF THE RESEARCHES ON JAPAN's COLONIAL RESPONSIBILITIES AND ITS CLAIM OF SOVEREIGNTY OVER DOKDO

Haruki Wada's proposal for Japan to give up Dokdo, Gentaro Serita's theory of opening up Dokdo and Yoshio Hirose's legal principles on decolonization recognize Korea's sovereignty over Dokdo based on Japanese colonial responsibilities. Nevertheless, it should be noticed that all three researchers pointed out the same. First, fishing of fishermen living in the Shimane Prefecture should be allowed in the sea surrounding Dokdo to harmonize the interests of Koreans and Japanese. Second, they uniformly suggest that it is not acceptable to use Dokdo, an islet, as the baseline in drawing the EEZ.

On the proposal commonly suggested by these Japanese researchers, an answer can be found from the question asked by Haruki Wada himself as a solution to the Dokdo issue. Korea and Japan should come to the table to demarcate the territory as an old colonial country. When such table is prepared, the Korean representatives would say "Japan invaded Joseon in 1904 and annexed and ruled the Korean peninsular in 1910. All the land has been returned to Joseon and the southern part of the peninsula has been recognized as the territory of the Republic of Korea. The territory includes Ulleungdo and Dokdo. Japan should recognize this. Also, Korea did claim sovereignty over Tsushima Island in 1948, but has since withdrawn it." What should the Japanese representatives respond to this?[62] It should be noted that "Korea did not add the remarks about sovereignty over Tsushima Island" as Wada said. One cannot but question the validity of a solution which is premised on the interests of Japan even when it started from recognition of Korean sovereignty over Dokdo as a colonial responsibility of Japan.

In addition, Yoshio Hirose's legal principles on decolonization based on international legal historic view started from the assumption that Japanese sovereignty over the island as a result of colonial activities of Japan was effective under international law until WWI. Yet, it should be noted that international law effective when Japan annexed Korea saw new changes surrounding universal legal norms in Europe and the U.S., which was a departure from the 19th century when legal positivism ruled in international law. At international peace conferences held in the Hague in 1899 and 1907, the Convention with respect to the Laws and Customs of War on Land was established. Russian Jurist Fyodor F. Martens[63] who wrote the draft convention stipulated that when for want of legal provisions due to the lack of laws and immaturity of international law, the people and belligerents should be laid under the protection and ruling of international legal principles in accordance with the customs established in civilized nations, the laws of humanity and the requirements of public conscience, not left under an arbitrary judgement of military commanders.[64]

7. CONCLUSION

Regarding the three grounds Japan uses to claim sovereignty over Dokdo based on international political dynamics, issues involving intertemporal legal principles have been identified in line with the historical facts and international legal justice, and in parallel, issues found in Japanese studies on Japanese colonial responsibilities under international law have been reviewed.

Above all, Japan's assertions to claim territorial sovereignty over Dokdo entail contradiction in time series. Amid Japan's expansionist war of aggression, it raised the doctrine of *terra nullius* in 1905 to justify its claim over Dokdo. Since then, in 1952, it came up with a contradictory theory that Dokdo had been its inherent territory from the 17th century, then it recently moved its focus onto the San Francisco Peace Treaty. In the course of changing its focus, with the ground of occupancy, Japan has constantly changed and minimized the issue into whether an international legal condition is met; its claim of Dokdo being the inherent territory of Japan distorts historical facts; it attempts to conceal its colonial aggression by arbitrarily interpreting the legal conformity of the provisions of the San Francisco Treaty. Based on this premise, criticism raised by the Japanese academia on Japan's claim to Dokdo becomes noteworthy. The border crossing prohibition on Tsushima domain of 1696 and the order of *Dajokan* of the Meiji government in 1877, which have been used as the ground to overturn the inherent territory argument, as well as the incorporation of Dokdo by Shimane Prefecture in 1905 lack legal effects under international law as they run counter to the Imperial Decree No. 41 of 1900 which was proclaimed and published in the official gazette. The Dean Rusk letter, the ground to support the San Francisco Treaty, also turned out not to be effective under legal principles as the letter was written based on limited information provided by Japan after its incorporation of Dokdo in 1905. These assertions made by Japan are a mere justification used to legitimize the assertions and illegal acts that have already been decided or executed based on the dynamics of international politics.

Next, as an international legal issue, Japan's claim to Dokdo calls for a review from the perspective of contradictory application of intertemporal law as Japan has stuck to 'the law effective at that time' on the premise of 'legality of colonial rule.' After violating Korea's sovereignty over Dokdo during the Russo-Japanese war, Japan seems to have till today applied such contradictory intertemporal law to the process where it started from the Japan-Korea Treaty of 1905 to the Japan-Korea Annexation Treaty of 1910, under the assumption that connivance and condoning of Colonial Powers as symbolized by the secret Taft-Katsura Agreement of 1905 was legal under international law. Essentially, the essence of intertemporal law is the principle that rights are defined under the law effective at the time of creation of rights and that the rights should exist in link with an evolution of law which was the basis of the rights. The existence of rights should be seen as maintaining its effects only to the extent where it remains in compliance with the justice and equality of the dynamic orders of international society. Under the international legal system premised on these dynamic orders, Japan's claim to sovereignty over Dokdo runs counter to the principles of the prohibition of abuse of rights, prescription, desuetude or obsolescence, and jus cogens. Also, in the case of Island of

Palmas of 1928 which proposed the principles of intertemporal law, the ground for the Peace Treaty between the U.S. and Spain was denied, and the principle of effective exercise defined as a continuous and peaceful display of territorial sovereignty was upheld, which has significant implications to Korea's sovereignty over Dokdo.

In closing, colonialism should be truly overcome and undone through studies on territorial sovereignty over Dokdo as part of Japanese colonial responsibilities. Haruki Wada's proposal for Japan to give up Dokdo, Gentaro Serita's theory of opening up Dokdo and Yoshio Hirose's legal principles on decolonization recognize Korea's sovereignty over Dokdo and Japanese colonial responsibilities while they uniformly suggest that it is not acceptable to use Dokdo, an islet, as the baseline in drawing the EEZ and that joint fishing around the islet be allowed. It is natural to question the legitimacy of such solutions which intend to assure national interests even when they commonly recognize Korea's sovereignty over Dokdo and Japanese colonial responsibilities. Under this premise, it is necessary for Japan to have the equal action as "Korea's withdrawal of sovereignty over Tsushima in 1948" which was proposed by Haruki Wada. Regarding the argument that colonial rule was legal before World War I, as Shinichi Arai pointed out, international law which was effective when Japan forcibly annexed Korea was undergoing a new change in the West surrounding the norms of international law, which saw a departure from the 19th century international law where legal positivism ruled.

Recognizing this change, Japan's claim to sovereignty over Dokdo asserted in line with Japanese colonialist history runs counter to the most basic undoing of colonial imperialism, that is, abandoning the land exploited by greed and violence. As such, Japan is left with responsibilities and obligations to fulfil under international law to build the Northeast Asian peace community in the 21st century.[65]

Notes

1. Byung-ryull Kim, "A Proposal for Studies on Korea's Territorial Title over Dokdo," Journal of Territorial and Maritime Studies, Vol. 11, 2016, p. 6.

2. The Ministry of Foreign Affairs of Japan, 10 Points to Understand the Takeshima Dispute, 2014, p. 3.

3. Young-ran Hur, "Tokdo and the Settlement of Japan's Territorial Line in the Meiji Period: A case comparison between the incorporation of Liancourt Rocks and that of the other islands," Seoul International Law Journal, Vol. 10, No. 1, June 2003, p. 28.

4. Norino Naka divided Japanese territorial changes (demarcation) in history into: the formation of a centralized state in 1867-1873; the border demarcation as a nation state in 1874-1881; expansionism (the establishment of the empire) in 1882-1945; and a reduction in territorial base (decline of the empire). Japan's claim to Dokdo falls onto the period of the establishment of the empire. Norio Naka, "From the territorial issue to "border demarcation problem": Senkaku, Takeshima, Northern four islands to consider from the perspective of conflict resolution theory," Akashi Shoten, 2013.

5. Kazuo Hori, "Japan's Incorporation of Takeshima Island in 1905," Bulletin of Society for Study in Korean History, Vol. 24, 1987, pp. 97-125.

6. Considering when the Japan-Korea Treaty of 1876 was concluded, Japan was aggressively expanding its influence on Korea, the order of Dajokan shows paradoxically that it is very much likely that if Japan had not had a clear view about Dokdo being the territory of Japan, Japan would have incorporated Dokdo as its own territory. Sung-hwan Lee, "Modern Japanese History and Territorial issues: Senkaku Islands, Dokdo and Gando Problems," Journal of Japanese History, Vol. 40, Dec. 2014, pp. 18-19.

7. Haruki Wada, How to Resolve Territorial Issues in Northeast Asia: from Confrontation to Reconciliation, Sakyejul, 2013, p. 41.

8. Yuji Hosaka, "Sovereignty over Dokdo Reviewed with the Japan-Korea Treaties and the Secret Letters of Emperor Gojong," Journal of Korean-Japanese Military and Culture, Vol. 8, 2009, p. 185.

9. Heon-ik Kwon, "Parallax on Dokdo-Takeshima Dispute," Journal of Dokdo, No. 6, 2009, pp. 125-126.

10. Alexis Dudden points out that Japan's colonization of Korea is a representative misuse of international law. Alexis Dudden, Japan's Colonization of Korea: Discourse and Power, Univ. of Hawaii, 2006.

11. See-hwan Doh, "International Legal Implications of the San Francisco Peace Treaty and Dokdo's Sovereignty," Korean Yearbook of International Law, Vol. 4, 2017, pp.

55-77.

12. See-hwan Doh, "Considerations of the Korea-Japan Annexation Treaty from the Viewpoint of Historical Truth and International Law," The Korean Society of International Law, The Korean Journal of International Law, Vol. 55, No. 4, Dec. 2010, p. 14; See-hwan Doh, "A New Perspective on 'Comfort Women' in International Human Rights Law," The Korean Journal of International Law, Vol. 53, No. 3. Refer to: IV. New perspective in international human rights law; e. Interpretation of international human rights law and intertemporal law.

13. The Ministry of Foreign Affairs of Japan, 10 Points to Understand the Takeshima Dispute, 2014, p. 8.

14. Sung-hwan Lee, "New Trend and Analysis of the Research on Dokdo in Japan: Focusing on Social Science Fields," Journal of Japanese Culture, No. 49, Jan. 2014, p. 309.

15. Kanae Taijudo, International Law on Acquisition of Territory, Tokyo: Toshindo, 1998, p. 143.

16. Pae-keun Park, "Some Observations on Japanese Argument of the Territorial Titles over Dokdo (Liancourt Rocks): Original Title and/or Occupation," The Korean Journal of International Law, Vol. 50, No. 3, 2005, p. 105.

17. In Korea, "Dokdo is an integral part of Korean territory" is used while Japan uses "Takeshima is a part of Japanese territory." Japan also used other terms like Japan proper and Japan's inherent territory. Haruki Wada, *ibid.*, pp. 41-42.

18. Haruki Wada, *ibid.*, pp. 31-45.

19. Norio Naka, *op. cit.*, p. 34.

20. Narahiko Toyoshita, What is the Senkaku problem?, Iwanami Shoten, 2012, p. 142.

21. Kumiko Haba, "The danger of state-owned territorial theory surrounding the Senkaku Takeshima - from international politics in Europe -," Sekai, Vol. 839, 2013, p. 43.

22. Satoshi Ikeuchi, "What is the Takeshima Issue?," Nagoya University Press, 2012. Yet, as having a strong intention of resolving a conflict or contradiction between the inherent territory and incorporation of Dokdo into the Shimane Prefecture in 1905 and emphasizing the doctrine of terra nullius, Ikeuchi's denial of inherent territory is different from the above denial of inherent territory. Sung-hwan Lee, *ibid.*, Jan. 2014, p. 312.

23. Seichu Naito · Byeong-ryull Kim, Historical verification of Takeshima Island, Iwanami Shoten, 2007, p. 43; Haruki Wada, *op. cit.*, p. 221.

24. Kazuo Hori, *op. cit.*, pp. 97-125; Haruki Wada, *op. cit.*, p. 222.

25. "Registration of Land of Takeshima and Another Island in the Sea of Japan," The Kobunroku(the official documents and records), Mar. 1877. National Archives of

Japan.

26. Haruki Wada, *op. cit.*, pp. 224~225.

27. Ministry of Foreign Affairs of Japan, 10 Points to Understand the Takeshima Dispute, 2014, pp. 11~12.

28. In a Cabinet meeting held on the territory of an uninhabited island requested by a secret letter of Minister of Home Affairs Akimasa Yoshikawa on January 10, 1905, Prime Minister Taro Katsura proclaimed Dokdo was the Japanese territory on January 28, 1905.

29. Haruki Wada, *op. cit.*, p. 228.

30. Article 3 of the Japan-Korea Treaty signed on February 23, 1904 stipulates that: "The Imperial Government of Japan definitively guarantee the independence and territorial integrity of the Korean Empire." The treaty guaranteed the independence and territorial integrity of Korea, and Japan violated the treaty by incorporating Dokdo into the Shimane Prefecture in Japan. Hosaka, Yuji, *ibid.*, p. 191.

31. Naito Seichu · Kim Byeong-ryull, *op. cit.*, pp. 169~175.; Haruki Wada, *op. cit.*, 2013, p. 228.

32. Haruki Wada, *op. cit.*, p. 229.

33. *Ibid.*, p. 229.

34. *Ibid.*, p. 230.

35. When Japanese people cut down lumbers in Ulleungdo without permission, the Korean Empire government requested the Japanese government bring back those Japanese while it decided to strengthen the regional administrative legal system of Ulleungdo. Accordingly, at the Uijeongbu (State Council of Joseon) meeting held on October 24, 1900, it was decided that "Ulleungdo shall be renamed Uldo and the administrator (dogam) shall be promoted to county magistrate (gunsu) (Article 1)" and it was specified that "all of the districts of Ulleungdo as well as Jukdo and Seokdo (Dokdo) shall be placed under the jurisdiction of Uldo-gun (Uldo County)." The decision explicitly included Dokdo into the jurisdiction of Uldo-gun, and it was approved by the Emperor on October 25 in 1900 and published in the official gazette as Imperial Decree No. 41 on October 27. The decree clearly stated the historical fact that Korea held sovereignty over Dokdo as part of Ulleungdo.

36. Cheol-young Choi, "An International Legal review on the Cabinet Decision of the Japanese Government in 1905," Conference on a Historical and International Legal Review on Documents and Maps of Dokdo in Modern Korea and Japan, Northeast Asian History Foundation, Oct., 20, 2017, p. 100.

37. Sung-hwan Lee, "A Review on Japan's Dajokan Directive and Incorporation of Dokdo from the Perspective of Legal History," The Korean Journal of International Law, Vol. 62, No. 3, Sep. 2017, pp. 99~100.

38. The original Dean Rusk letter can be found at: https://en.wikisource.org/wiki/Rusk_note_of_1951.

39. The Ministry of Foreign Affairs of Japan, 10 Points to Understand the Takeshima Dispute, 2014, pp. 13~14.

40. Byung-Joon Jung, "San Francisco Peace Treaty with Japan and 'Dokdo Issue'," The Journal of Dokdo, No. 18, June 2015, p. 156.

41. Byung-Joon Jung, *ibid.*, p. 158.

42. Byung-Joon Jung, Dokdo 1947, Seoul: Dolbegae, 2011, pp. 613~617.

43. See-hwan Doh, *supra* note 11.

44. *Supra* note 38.

45. Byung-Joon Jung, Dokdo 1947, 2011, pp. 775~786.

46. Sung-hwan Lee, "Joseon-Japan/Korea-Japan Territory Treaties and Dokdo," Conference on a Historical and International Legal Review on Documents and Maps of Dokdo in Modern Korea and Japan, Northeast Asian History Foundation, Oct. 20, 2017, pp. 83~85.

47. Oh, Byung-Sun, "A Theoretical Inquiry into the Inter-temporal Law Problem in International Law," The Korean Journal of International Law, Vol. 57, No.1, 2012, pp. 73~74.

48. *Ibid.*, pp. 74~75.

49. Peter Malanczuk, Akehurst's Modern Introduction to International Law, Seventh Revised Edition, Routledge, 1997, pp. 155~157 at 156; R. Jennings, The Acquisition of Territory in International Law, 1963, p. 30; Oh, Byung-Sun, *ibid.*, p. 75.

50. Oh, Byung-Sun, *ibid.*, p. 76.

51. Island of Palmas case (Netherlands vs. USA), April 4, 1928, UN Reports of International Arbitral Awards, Vol. Ⅱ, 2006, p. 831.

52. See-hwan Doh, "The Palmas Island Case (the Netherlands vs. the U.S.)," A Study on International Precedents on Territory and Oceans, Pakyoungsa, 2017, pp. 3~14.

53. In the course of depriving Korea of its sovereignty, Japan took the following five steps in an effort to secure legitimacy under international law: (1) Japan-Korea Protocol signed on February 23, 1904, which usurped the right to use territory, (2) the first Japan-Korea Treaty signed on August 22, 1904, which deprived the Korea Empire of diplomatic rights, (3) the second Japan-Korea Treaty signed on November 17, 1905, which denied the Korea Empire of sovereignty, (4) the third Japan-Korea Treaty on July 24, 1907, which took away the right to decide military and domestic affairs, and (5) the Japan-Korea Annexation Treaty on August 22, 1910, which forced the annexation of the Korean Empire. See-hwan Doh, "Revisiting the Protectorate Treaty of 1905 from the Perspective of International Law," The Korean Journal of International Law, Vol. 60, No. 4, 2015, pp. 126~143.

54. Island of Palmas case (Netherlands, USA), *op. cit.*, p. 867.

55. Haruki Wada, *op. cit.*, p. 264.

56. Haruki Wada, *ibid.*, p. 265.

57. Gentaro Serita, The Territory of Japan, Chuokoronsha, 2006, pp. 185~187; Sung-hwan Lee, *op. cit.*, Jan. 2014, p. 313.

58. Gentaro Serita, *ibid.*, p. 308.

59. Sung-hwan Lee, *op. cit.*, 2014, pp. 313~314.

60. Yoshio Hirose, "Legality of Japan's annexation of Korea and the territorial title of the island of Takeshima from the viewpoint of contemporary international law," Meiji Gakuin Law Journal, Vol. 81, 2007, p. 288.

61. *Ibid.*, p. 295.

62. Haruki Wada, *op. cit.*, p. 10.

63. Norigatsu sasagawa, "Grotius and Martens Accepted in Harvard Draft: about the Characteristics of Nullified Legal Effect of Treaty which has been procured by the Coercion of a Representative of a State," Japan's Annexation of Korea and Present Day, Thaehaksa, 2009, pp. 615~656.

64. After WWII, the Nuremberg trials, where war criminals of Nazi Germany were tried, defined a crime against peace in addition to the traditional war crimes against international law on humanity. The defendant raised opposition against a trial on a new crime category created under the ex post facto law, not 'international law at that time.' Yet, the court cited the Martens clause, saying "that is beyond a noble declaration." The court dismissed the defendant argument saying the clause is a general regulation creating the legal basis to be applied to cases where specific provisions of war law do not apply. Lord Wright of Durley who wrote the Law Report of Trial of War Criminals (1949) of the United Nations War Crimes Commission assessed the Martens clause as "in a few words stating the whole animating and motivating principle of the law of war, and indeed of all law," emphasizing the universality of meaning of the clause, which does not stop at the law of war. Theodor Meron, "The Martens Clause Principles of Humanity and Dictates of Public Conscience," American Journal of International Law, 94(1). It was not that 'international law at that time' did not have any aspect of legal norms as the Martens clause did. Following the two rounds of world wars, the aspect of norms of international law developed. The view of 'international law at that time' needs to be assessed with a weight placed on this progressive aspect, rather than a regressive aspect of a Japanese positivism. Shinich Arai, "Thinking about legitimacy and illegality in history," Sekai, Vol. 681, Nov., 2000, pp. 270~284.

65. See-hwan Doh, "The San Francisco Peace Treaty and Territorial Sovereignty," Korea Times, April 28, 2017, p. 9.

The Response to the Gross Violation of Human Rights Abuses in North Korea: Problematizing Accountability

Andrew Wolman
Lecturer
City, University of London, City Law School, London, U.K.

Abstract

In the past few years, one deceptively simple concept has come to dominate the international discourse on human rights in North Korea: accountability. On first glance, this seems entirely appropriate, given the severity of the crimes committed by Kim Jong Un and his associates. In this essay, however, I will take a step back, to problematize the concept of accountability. Specifically, I will address five questions that have to date been largely ignored. First: what does accountability mean? Second: why is it desirable? Third: does the emphasis on accountability have any potentially negative consequences? Fourth: when is the right time to focus on accountability? And fifth: who benefits from the turn to accountability? While I do not intend this essay to imply that accountability is undesirable in any way, I do aim to show that it is a more complex principle than is often assumed, and should be the subject of serious thought and discussion, rather than unthinkingly adopted as the core objective for North Korean human rights advocates.

Key Words

North Korea, Accountability, Transitional Justice, Human Rights

1. INTRODUCTION

The world has been aware of grave atrocities committed by the North Korean regime for at least two decades, and during that period the international community has advanced a series of strategies to address the issue, including engagement, monitoring, investigation, naming and shaming, outcasting, and (most recently) sanctioning.[1] The tenor of this response began to shift with the publication of the 2014 final report of the Commission of Inquiry on Human Rights in the Democratic People's Republic of Korea ('CoI'), a three-person investigative body established by the UN Human Rights Council.[2] This report found that grave human rights abuses and crimes against humanity had been committed by the North Korean leadership, and urged that the situation be referred to the International Criminal Court ('ICC').[3] In short, the CoI report shifted the discourse from an international human rights law framework to an individual accountability-based international criminal law framework.[4]

In the few years, since the CoI's report on North Korean human rights abuses (and as a result of the shift to an international criminal law framework), the deceptively simple concept of accountability has come to dominate the international response to atrocities in North Korea.[5] Recent UN Human Rights Council and General Assembly resolutions on North Korean human rights emphasized the concept, as did former UN High Commissioner for Human Rights Navi Pillay.[6] According to Tomas Ojea Quintana, the current UN Special Rapporteur on the Situation of Human Rights in the Democratic People's Republic of Korea, the international community "must be guided by the pursuit of justice and accountability as a core tenet of the United Nations."[7]

Most recently, the concept of accountability was the explicit focus of the Group of Independent Experts on Accountability, which was established by the Human Rights Council in 2016 and issued an advanced version of its final report in March 2017.[8] Outside of the UN halls, the principle of accountability has likewise becoming the focal point of governmental and non-governmental discourse. The focus on accountability is visible in the work of civil society groups,[9] and in the statements of government representatives and prominent experts in the field.[10] According to Michael Kirby, the former head of the CoI, "accountability is the name of the game in human rights...otherwise it's all rhetoric."[11] For Kirby, the principle of accountability for North Korean human rights violators is simply "non-negotiable."[12]

This focus appears set to continue: the 2017 U.N. Human Rights Council resolution on North Korean human rights mandated the initiation of a review of information by "experts in legal accountability" in order to develop "possible strategies to be used in any future accountability process," and decided to strengthen the OHCHR Seoul office to allow it to implement the recommendations of the Group of Independent Experts on Accountability.[13]

At first glance, this emphasis on accountability seems entirely appropriate. The CoI Report showed beyond any doubt that grave human rights abuses and crimes against humanity continue to be committed in North Korea. Who could oppose any move to hold the perpetrators of these crimes to account? We are, after all, living in what has been termed the "age of human rights accountability."[14] The International Criminal Court, regional human rights courts and the U.N. have all propagated a "global accountability norm," or at least have tried to do so.[15] In the words of former High Commissioner for Human Rights Navi Pillay, "[a] ccountability for international crimes and gross human rights violations constitutes a central plank of the contemporary human rights agenda. Today, the question is no longer whether to ensure accountability, but when and how this is best achieved."[16]

Accordingly, there has been little questioning this new emphasis on accountability, by either academics or the mainstream NGO community. Rather, the idea of accountability has, by and large, been accepted as an unquestioned objective, with scholars moving on to study the (undoubtedly important) follow-up questions of how North Korean human rights violators can be held accountable, and precisely who should be held accountable. In this essay, I will take a step back and problematize the concept of accountability. Specifically, I will question what the concept of 'accountability' actually means in the North Korean context, why it may be considered desirable or undesirable, what the implications are of focusing on accountability at this particular point in time, and conclude by discussing which groups benefits from this turn to accountability. In addressing these questions, this essay will draw from the abundant critical literature in transitional justice and international criminal justice that has emerged in recent years, and that have provoked a rethinking of the idea of accountability, as well as virtually every other aspect of the field.[17]

2. WHAT DOES 'ACCOUNTABILITY' MEAN?

In order to explore the implications of focusing on accountability when addressing North Korean human rights abuses, the first step should be to understand the term's meaning. This is not a simple task. There is a wealth of literature attempting to define and conceptualize 'accountability' in a variety of contexts.[18] Indeed, scholars have argued that there is widespread "fragmentation" in the discourse of accountability, such that different disciplines and interest groups employ the term in quite distinct manners, resulting in a "Byzantine confusion."[19]

When one looks more narrowly at the human rights and transitional justice field, a fundamental split is evident in scholarly views of what the term accountability signifies. Some analysts, especially those with a legal background, have traditionally viewed the term as referring solely to individual criminal prosecution (whether through a domestic, hybrid or international forum).[20] Thus, according to the Transitional Justice Working Group, "'[a]ccountability' in transitional justice is a concept often associated with legal remedies applied to situations where atrocities have taken place."[21] Other scholars use the term to refer to a much broader range of processes, potentially including lustration, truth commissions, and various restorative justice mechanisms,[22] and to refer to measures targeting states, corporations, and other institutions, as well as natural persons.[23] Among those who employ the term 'accountability' in this broader sense, there is sometimes a tendency to view different forms of accountability on a spectrum, with criminal prosecution as the 'highest' or 'ultimate' form of accountability.[24] There is also often an underlying sentiment that assigning accountability to institutional entities leads to an evasion of responsibility by the individuals who make and carry out atrocities in that entity's name.[25]

Of course, the meaning of difficult concepts such as 'accountability' will naturally tend to be disputed and context-dependent; the more important question is what accountability means to key actors in the context of the current discourse on addressing North Korean human rights abuses. Here too, however, there is some lack of consistency. In some cases, commentators have used the term 'accountability' to refer to elements of the North Korean state and institutions (as well as individuals) as subject.[26] One analyst has even defined accountability particularly broadly to encompass "helping the victims" and "improving the situation in the country."[27] Others have used the term to signify criminal prosecution. Thus, for example, former Special Rapporteur on the Situation of Human Rights in the Democratic People's Republic of Korea Marzuki Darusman interchangeably used the terms 'accountability,' 'judicial accountability' and 'criminal accountability' when discussing the formation of the Group of Independent Experts.[28] This also seems to be the stance of major NGOs, who petitioned the UN to draft the Panel of Experts' mandate to focus on criminal accountability.[29]

At the UN level, the Group of Independent Experts on Accountability has most explicitly conceptualized accountability, in its final report.[30] According to the Group of Independent Experts, in order to successfully attain 'accountability,' a number of different measures are necessary. As a starting point (and as a matter of international law), some form of criminal prosecutions is required.[31] However, that is not all; ensuring accountability also requires "measures towards the realization of the right to know the truth about violations and the right to adequate, effective and prompt reparation."[32] That being said, in practice, the Group of Independent Experts on Accountability devotes the large majority of the analysis of options in its final report to individual criminal accountability, specifically criminal prosecution in North Korea, other countries, or through international or internationalized courts.[33] It then discusses more briefly other approaches to accountability, including data-gathering by the South Korean National Human Rights Commissions, condemnation by the Japanese Federation of Bar Associations, UN mechanisms such as the Working Group on Arbitrary Detentions, and targeted sanctions.[34]

Is it important to have a single agreed-upon definition for the concept of accountability? Maybe not, if an elastic concept allows for more creative attempts to address the problem. But without an accepted definition, it will be hard to understand what different actors mean, how to measure whether particular policies in fact promote accountability or not, and how to apply research findings from other situations.[35] Without passing judgment as to whether a broad or narrow definition of accountability is more appropriate, the remainder of this paper will focus on questions of accountability narrowly conceptualized as criminal prosecution, given that this aspect has so far been the focus of the most powerful international actors in the North Korean human rights field.

3. WHY DO WE WANT TO PROMOTE ACCOUNTABILITY?

Accepting for the moment that the term accountability in the North Korean context refers primarily to individual criminal prosecution, whether at the domestic or international level (or a hybrid of the two), the logical next question is why accountability is desirable?[36] Scholars have provided a number of different possible answers. At the most basic level, accountability mechanisms have the potential to sanction the perpetrators of crimes for their actions, through imprisonment or other forms of punishment, which is a form of retributive justice. Retribution "conveys a society's condemnation of the criminal act in question and of the perpetrator found responsible."[37] It helps individualize guilt and focuses attention on the objective act committed by the perpetrator.

In the context of widespread and grave state crimes (whether in North Korea or elsewhere), however, relatively few people would consider retribution to be the sole legitimate objective.[38] Deterrence of human rights abuses is also important, as is incentivizing good human rights behavior, and alleviating the suffering of those whose rights have already been violated. Exposing human rights abuses (and improvements, where they occur) is desirable. Preventing war is undoubtedly a fundamental human rights goal. Many would also add unification and regime change to the list of objectives in the North Korean context, along with societal reconciliation. Even aside from its direct link to retribution, one might also plausibly want to focus on accountability as a way to instrumentally further these other goals. According to Jeff King, legal accountability is "a means for achieving ends, and not something to be addressed primarily in terms of its intrinsic value."[39]

This instrumental role of accountability has indeed been lauded by some commentators both in the North Korean context and more generally in the context of transitional justice situations. Certainly, if defined as criminal prosecution (domestic or international), accountability would be likely to involve the compilation of information and testimony on human rights abuses, thus furthering the search for truth (although perhaps not as effectively as other transitional justice mechanisms).[40] Criminal trials could be expected to provide at least some comfort for victims, whether in the form of reparations, apologies, or simply by fulfilling an expectation of justice.[41] Some researchers argues that the use of prosecutions as a tool of transitional justice also helps bring peace to conflict-prone societies,[42] because it improves respect for the rule of law (either domestically or internationally),[43] or because it leads to reparations or national reconciliation.[44] Still others have claimed that criminal trials can have a demonstration effect.[45] According to Jane Stromseth, "by removing perpetrators of atrocities from positions in which they can control and abuse others, criminal trials (and processes such as rigorous vetting) can have a cathartic impact by assuring the population that old patterns of impunity and exploitation are no longer tolerated."[46] In the North Korean context, NGOs have highlighted the benefits of accountability for bringing redress to victims of human rights abuses.[47]

Given the ongoing nature of North Korean abuses, one particularly important goal for many people would be deterrence, which has indeed been stressed by the Group of Independent Experts in its discussions of accountability.[48] Some observers have argued that the focus on accountability could also have (and indeed may already be having) a deterrence effect.[49] According to anecdotal reports, North Korean officials have already modified certain practices out of a fear of being held accountable, for example by ceasing forced abortions in detention centers and the use of torture in long term labor facilities, and by ending policies of imprisoning entire families to punish a single family member.[50] In addition to potential local effects, the international community may be incrementally acting to deter crimes by abusive regimes elsewhere in the world by strengthening a global accountability norm. This would make some sense under deterrence theory, which holds that a perceived increase in the likelihood of punishment leads to a decreased expected net value of engaging in criminal activities, and (assuming rational actors) less crime.[51]

On the other hand, another school of thought has downplayed the likelihood of accountability proceedings having a significant deterrent effect for future abuses.[52] Criminological research has long highlighted the importance of certainty of punishment to any deterrence effect, and at the current time there seems to be relatively little chance of North Korean leaders ever facing punishment (at least absent a change of power through war or rebellion that they would in any case be unlikely to survive unscathed).[53] Even if North Korea's leaders do perceive a likelihood of future prosecution, top figures such as Kim Jong Un have, one suspects, already committed severe enough crimes to receive harsh sentences regardless or future actions, thus diminishing the influence that any deterrence effect might have for them to change future behavior.[54]

4. ARE THERE ANY POTENTIAL DOWNSIDES TO FOCUSING ON ACCOUNTABILITY?

While accountability is oftentimes accepted as an unquestionably beneficial principle, it is also worth considering whether there are any downsides to the current emphasis on accountability in the North Korean context. Potentially, there could be two types of disadvantages. First, the emphasis on accountability could take the focus away from other potentially desirable objectives, and the techniques and strategies needed to attain them. As Sarkin and Davi have noted, while different transitional justice methods may be used at the same time, more frequently, a society "will have one dominant type of justice at the heart of its endeavours and this will be reflected in one dominant transitional justice mechanism."[55] If this is the case, and if the more important objective is 'peace,' 'security,' 'unification,' 'regime change' or any of a number of other plausible end goals, would it not make sense to think creatively about achieving those goals by all possible means, rather than just hoping that they will be furthered indirectly by promoting accountability? This was the approach of the UN Human Rights Council in its initial reports on Syria and Libya, which prioritized termination of abuses rather than accountability.[56] The counter-argument, however, is that engagement (along with other routes to attempt to influence North Korean behavior) has been attempted for years by the U.N., European countries, and others, with little if any result. To the extent that North Korea shows an interest in greater engagement in the future, then these other tracks can be re-invigorated.

Second, focusing on accountability could actually be counter-productive in terms of attaining the other desirable objectives discussed in the previous section, such as peace, deterrence, the rule of law, finding out the truth about the past, etc. Researchers have long argued that there are tensions and contradictions inherent in the transitional justice process, and pressing for accountability may not be the optimal strategy for achieving other worthwhile objectives.[57] For example, the use of accountability mechanisms has been seen in some cases as producing more violence in unstable countries, a situation that few would find desirable.[58] Advocates of restorative justice also argue that retributive justice measures are not good for bringing about healing for victims, and argue that such mechanisms "have a tendency to exacerbate tensions and pressures already heightened with a society."[59] Numerous scholars have challenged the reliability of histories revealed through criminal court proceedings, and outlined their limited scope for providing thorough explanations of past events.[60]

Most significant, of course, is the question of whether Kim Jong Un and his associates might (at some point) be discouraged from voluntarily stepping down or initiating peaceful unification due to a fear that they would immediately be held accountable – and thrown in jail – once they gave up power. Snyder and Vinjamuri, for example, argue that accountability mechanisms can encourage human rights abusers to disrupt democratization processes to avoid the prospect of prosecution.[61] This, of course, is a variant of the peace versus justice argument that has plagued transitional justice debates for the past two decades. While fear of accountability would certainly seem to add to the incentive to stay in power, as has arguably been the case with Assad in Syria and Bashir in Sudan, to name perhaps the only two current leaders to approach the Kim regime's brutality, it must be noted that Kim and his confederates have shown no apparent interest in stepping down or unification to date, so it seems unlikely that they would be tempted into doing so through, for example, the provision of a comfortable exile or amnesty.

Do these potential downsides outweigh the advantages of focusing on accountability? The answer to this question will depend on one's ethical framework, evaluation of the situation, and position in society. As will be discussed later, the effects of focusing on accountability are felt differently by different actors. The question, however, should not be ignored, or dismissed as illegitimate. It is not unreasonable to prioritize prevention and termination of human rights violations (or other objectives) as a greater priority than accountability, as indeed many observers have stated as much over the years.[62]

5. WHEN IS THE RIGHT TIME TO ADDRESS ACCOUNTABILITY?

Assuming one accepts the importance of accountability for North Korean human rights violations, it is still important to question whether now is the right time to focus on the issue. As a practical matter, there seems little chance of successfully trying and punishing North Korean leaders prior to a transition.[63] However, important decisions about future trials can be made at a pre-transition stage, and indeed the Special Rapporteur on the Situation of Human Rights in the DPRK has emphasized that "issues around accountability should be addressed at an early stage, and with long-term strategies in mind [and] should not be done [...] at the last minute of a change process."[64] Thus one, important issue is whether accountability should be demanded immediately, immediately after transition, or at some later time. The question is controversial, but there is widespread agreement that it is a meaningful one; to put it concisely, timing matters in transitional justice.[65] Some scholars argue that an early focus on reconciliation followed by later moves towards accountability leads to more stable transitions.[66] Others disagree, and argue that rapid justice is necessary to build confidence in democracy or deter extraconstitutional actions.[67] In any case, the optimal timing is likely to depend on important unknown factors, such as whether unification will quickly succeed the Kim regime's fall, whether the current regime leaves power voluntarily, and what role China will play in the process.[68] Given these uncertainties, hasty decision-making may be counter-productive.

One factor that mitigates against choosing to rely on accountability mechanisms at this time is that North Koreans themselves – the primary victims of the regime's abuses – are not yet in the position to influence decisions that are being made about their future, for the simple reason that outside observers have no way to survey public opinion in North Korea, and even if they did, North Koreans lack the freedom to speak their minds.[69] However, many scholars have emphasized the importance of ensuring that victims have input into transitional justice decisions in North Korea and elsewhere.[70] According to Robins, transitional justice "gains its moral legitimacy from the fact that victims are deserving and the claim and the practice of transitional justice has the aim of acknowledging victims and providing redress."[71] Indeed the UN itself advocates for the "centrality of victims" to the design and implementation of transitional justice programs.[72]

Of course, one can ask North Korean escapees who have made it to South Korea about their views on transitional justice, and this has been done: the majority of those surveyed supported prosecutions in court.[73] However, as is often the case with exile communities, the escapees are not representative (in terms of geographic origin, gender, or political views), they are not as invested in the future of North Korea as those that still live there, and they are influenced by the different groups and governments which have assisted them after their escape. Thus, their views should not be taken as proxies for those of the millions of other victims still in the country. Research in other transitional contexts has shown that prosecution is often not the foremost concern of victims (or at least not the only concern).[74]

If in practice the focus on accountability simply involves the documentation of abuses so that at some point in the future perpetrators can be held accountable, then the more difficult questions of whether, when, where and how to engage in prosecutions can be addressed later. However, recording North Korean human rights violations has been undertaken for well over a decade by governments, non-governmental organizations, and international organizations.[75] It appears clear that many in the international community consider 'accountability' to also involve a commitment to engage in an imminent start to prosecutions, if and when a venue becomes available.[76]

6. CONCLUSION: WHO BENEFITS FROM THE PUSH FOR ACCOUNTABILITY?

In light of the preceding discussion, this essay will conclude with a brief examination of which groups most benefit from the push for accountability. I would argue that for different reasons three discreet communities most noticeably benefit from pressing for accountability: the international justice community; the South Korean human rights establishment, and conservative anti-North Korean actors. Accordingly these three groups lie at the center of the international community's current move to emphasize accountability.

First, and most significantly, there is the international justice community, made up of (mainly) UN representatives, representatives of certain Western states, and activists at human rights NGOs or in academia.[77] For this community, accountability is a cardinal principle of 21st century international society. The quest for accountability is of particular importance because achieving accountability in North Korea would have (the theory goes) a general deterrence effect for dictatorial regimes all around the world.[78] It would show that criminal justice is not simply reserved for weak African rebels and deposed leaders, but rather is a serious threat for everyone in the world who commits atrocities, regardless of their current level of power, geographical location, or the presence of alliances with major countries such as China.[79] In short, the hope is that the non-impunity norm will become so well ingrained in international practice that potential human rights abusers will reasonably fear that they will, at some point, be held accountable for their crimes. This is a worthwhile (if, some would argue, quixotic) goal, but is not one likely to be held strongly by North Korean themselves, who would likely care more about the future stability of their country, promoting regime change, and specific deterrence (that is, deterrence within North Korea itself).[80]

The second group is made up of establishment human rights figures from South Korea, such as Ambassador Lee Jung-Hoon, Judge Sang Hyun Song, and groups such as the North Korean Database for Human Rights and the Citizens' Alliance for North Korean Human Rights.[81] For South Korean establishment figures, there is an underlying assumption that North-South reunification will occur with the fall of the Kim regime.[82] Thus, certain objectives that usually inform transitional justice processes – such as promoting democracy, stability, human rights, and the rule of law – are often overlooked, the belief being that a unified (and Seoul-dominated) Korea will automatically be democratic, stable, rights-respecting and follow the rule of law. There is, however, no guarantee that unification will come after the Kim regime falls. If not, then it might make sense to prioritize some of these other objectives.

The third group that benefits from the push for accountability can loosely be categorized as those conservative (or neo-conservative) elements in South Korea, the United States and Japan who are mainly interested in promoting regime change in North Korea, including through the use of force. For these actors, the push for accountability helps to delegitimize the North Korean regime and focus attention on the punishment of its major figures, which can only take place after they are overthrown. In this respect, the push for accountability in North Korea can be seen as mirroring the campaigns to hold Sadaam Hussein or Muammar Qadaffi responsible for their horrific crimes, each of which preceded (and helped justify, at least to a certain segment of liberal Western opinion) armed intervention in Iraq and Libya.

None of this is to say that accountability is undesirable. Any observer with a sense of justice would wish to see Kim and his henchmen in prison.

But accountability is not necessarily an uncomplicated objective, nor the sole appropriate focus for the international community. The timing of accountability matters, and the effects of accountability are felt differently by different actors. Thus, it is a concept that should be debated and justified, and not accepted uncritically. In doing so, the international community should recall that the needs and wishes of North Korean victims of the regime should come first, as they have suffered most directly from the Kim regime, and have the most to gain or lose from a successful or unsuccessful transitional justice experience.

Notes

1. *See generally*, Roberta Cohen, *Human Rights in North Korea – Addressing the Challenges, in* Transitional Justice in Unified Korea 75 (Baek Buhm-Suk & Ruti Teitel, eds., 2015); KINU Center for North Korean Human Rights Studies, Implementation Strategies for Policies on North Korean Human Rights (Korea Institute for National Unification, 2015).

2. U.N. Human Rights Council, Comm. of Inquiry on Human Rights in the DPRK, Report of the Detailed Findings of the Comm. of Inquiry on Human Rights in the DPRK, para. 432, A.HRC/25/CRP.1 (Feb. 7, 2014).

3. *Id.*, para. 1201(1).

4. Cohen, *Human Rights in North Korea, supra* note 1, at 80 ("the significance of the CoI report is that it established the legal foundation for holding the North Korean leadership to account").

5. KINU Center for North Korean Human Rights Studies, *supra* note 1, at 8 ("In 2014, North Korean human rights issue emerged as an important political agenda for the international community, going beyond from an issue to merely 'monitor' to one which calls for full 'accountability'"); Veronika Bílková, presentation at European Parliament Workshop, *Human Rights in North Korea: Accountability v. Engagement* (April 20, 2016), http://www.europarl.europa.eu/RegData/etudes/IDAN/2016/578004/EXPO_IDA(2016)578004_EN.pdf (last visited on July 17, 2017) ("Accountability issues vis-à-vis North Korea gained a prominent place on the international agenda especially since 2014 when the UN Commission of Inquiry published its report").

6. Open Letter from FIDH – International Federation for Human Rights et al to UN Human Rights Council, *Need for Enhanced Focus on Accountability in the DPRK* (Feb. 17, 2016), https://www.fidh.org/en/region/asia/north-korea/need-for-enhanced-focus-on-accountability-on-the-dprk (last visited on July 17, 2017) "In its own resolutions, the UN Human Rights Council has highlighted the need for accountability, a call that was echoed by the UN High Commissioner for Human Rights and many States during the plenary panel discussion at the 30th session of the Council"); G.A. Res. 69/188, U.N. Doc. A/RES/69/188 (Dec. 18, 2014) (calling on the UN Security Council to take "appropriate action to ensure accountability, including through consideration of referral of the situation in the Democratic People's Republic of Korea to the International Criminal Court").

7. John Power, *Bring a Regime to Justice? In Seoul, Rights Groups Play Long Game on N. Korea*, Christian Science Monitor (Mar. 13, 2017), https://www.csmonitor.com/

World/Asia-Pacific/2017/0313/Bring-a-regime-to-justice-In-Seoul-rights-groups-play-long-game-on-N.-Korea (last visited on July 17, 2017).

8. *See generally*, Group of Independent Experts on Accountability pursuant to Human Rights Council Resolution 31/18 on the situation of human rights in the Democratic People's Republic of Korea, at http://www.ohchr.org/EN/HRBodies/SP/CountriesMandates/KP/Pages/GroupofIndependentExpertsonAccountability.aspx (last visited on July 17, 2017).

9. *See, e.g.*, Open Letter from FIDH, *supra* note 6 (letter from major involved NGOs urging an "enhanced focus on accountability on the DPRK"; signatories include Human Rights Watch, FIDH, Amnesty International and the Citizens' Alliance for North Korean Human Rights). As its name suggests, the North Korea Accountability Project was recently founded by a group of civil society organizations to aid the UN in its efforts to bring accountability to North Korea. Presentation by Sylvia Caterini, Consultant for North Korea Accountability Project at European Parliament Workshop, *Human Rights in North Korea: Accountability v. Engagement* (April 20, 2016), http://www.europarl.europa.eu/RegData/etudes/IDAN/2016/578004/EXPO_IDA(2016)578004_EN.pdf (last visited on July 17, 2017).

10. For example, Jung-Hoon Lee, the South Korean Ambassador for Human Rights, recently called for a "global campaign on accountability" in North Korea, while Sang Hyun Song, former President of the International Criminal Court (ICC), who similarly stated that countries must work together to "strengthen the global system of accountability" as it applies to North Korea. *See* Lizzie Buehler, *The Future of Accountability in North Korea*, *Daily NK* (July 4, 2016), http://dailynk.com/english/m/read.php?num=13973&cataId=nk02501 (last visited on July 17, 2017).

11. Power, *supra* note 7.

12. Michael Kirby, *Overview*, *in* North Korean Human Rights: The Road Ahead 11 (Victor Cha & Marie DuMond, eds, 2015).

13. Hum. Rts. Counc. Res. 34/L.23, U.N. Doc. A/HRC/34/L.23 (Mar. 24, 2017) para. 12.

14. *See* Francesca Lessa & Leigh A. Payne, eds., Amnesty in the Age of Human Rights Accountability (2012).

15. Louise Mallinder, *Amnesties' Challenge to the Global Accountability Norm*, *in Amnesty in the Age of Human Rights Accountability* 69, 90 (Francesca Lessa & Leigh Payne, eds., 2012); Steven R. Ratner, *After Atrocity: Optimizing UN Action Toward Accountability for Human Rights Abuses*, 36 Mich. J. Int'l L. 541, 542 (2015); Ruti Teitel, *Transitional Justice and Judicial Activism – A Right to Accountability?*, 48 Cornell Int'l L.J. 385, 388 (2015).

16. Navanethem Pillay, Establishing Effective Accountability Mechanisms for Human Rights Violations, XLIX U.N. Chron. (Dec. 2012), https://unchronicle.un.org/article/establishing-effective-accountability-mechanisms-human-rights-violations (last visited on July 17, 2017).

17. *See, e.g.*, Christine Schwöbel, Critical Approaches to International Criminal Law: An Introduction (2014); Rosemary Nagy, *Transitional Justice as Global Project: Critical Reflections*, 29 Third World Q. 275 (2008); Jeremy Sarkin, Estelle Zinsstag & Stephan Parmentier, *Critical Issues in Transitional Justice: A Sysiphean Exercise*, 9 Hum. Rts. & Int'l L. Disc. 2 (2017); Jeremy Sarkin & Tetevi Davi, *Examining the Criticisms Levelled Against Transitional Justice: Towards an Understanding of the State of the Field*, 9 Hum. Rts. & Int'l L. Disc. 7, 7 (2017) ("almost every aspect and every component of every TJ mechanism in every place has been the subject of criticism to varying degrees").

18. *See, e.g.*, Robert Keohane, *The Concept of Accountability in World Politics and the Use of Force*, 24, MICH. J. INT'L L., 1121, 1123-24 (2003); Andreas Schedler, *Conceptualizing Accountability, in* The Self-Restraining State: Power and Accountability in New Democracies 13, 23 (Andreas Schedler et al., eds. 1999). Mark Bovens, Analysing and Assessing Accountability: A Conceptual Framework, 13 Eur. L.J., 447, 449 (2007).

19. Staffan Lindberg, *Accountability: the core concept and its subtypes*, Overseas Development Institute, Africa Power and Politics Programme Working Paper No. 1, 15 (2009). *See also,* Michael Dowdle, Public accountability: conceptual, historical and epistemic mappings, in Public accountability: designs, dilemmas and experiences (Michael Dowdle, ed., 2006) 1, 10. Jerry Mashaw, Accountability and Institutional Design: Some Thoughts on the Grammar of Governance, in Public accountability: designs, dilemmas and experiences 115, 117 (Michael Dowdle, ed., 2006).

20. Louise Mallinder & Kierna McEvoy, *Rethinking Amnesties: Atrocity, Accountability and Impunity in Post-Conflict Societies*, 6 Contemp. Soc. Sci. 107, 108 (2011) ("A key feature of the legalistic debates, which from our perspective tend to prevail in the area, is a narrow deployment of the term 'accountability' as synonymous with the prosecutions and punishment of individual perpetrators of serious human rights abuses"); Elin Skaar, Jemima García-Godos & Cath Collins, *The Accountability Challenge, in Transitional Justice, in* Latin America: The Uneven Road from Impunity Towards Accountability 1, 4 (Elin Skaar, Jemima García-Godos & Cath Collins, eds., 2016) ("In the TJ field, accountability is generally associated with criminal accountability"); Christine Bell, Transitional Justice 10 (2016) ("Trials are here seen as synonymous with accountability and the rule of law").

21. Transitional Justice Working Group, *Mapping Crimes Against Humanity in North Korea: Mass Graves, Killing Sites and Documentary Evidence* 50 (2017).

22. Carlos Fernandez Torne, *Truth Commissions and the Accountability Relationships they Generate: A New Framework to Evaluate their Impact*, 3 *Asian Journal of Peacebuilding* 233, 233 (2015) ("accountability refers to the process of holding public officials responsible for their actions, with the aim of restraining those who hold power. Truth commissions … are primarily mechanisms of accountability."); Colleen Murphy, *Transitional Justice, Retributive Justice and Accountability for Wrongdoing, in* Theorizing Transitional Justice 59 (Claudio Corradetti, Nir Eisikovits & Jack Rotondi, eds., 2015); Renée Jeffery, Amnesties, Accountability, and Human Rights 10 (2014) ("restorative justice is not opposed to accountability but, through its practices of truth-telling, apologies, compensation, repentance, and forgiveness, calls the perpetrators of wrongs to account for their actions").

23. *See* Jann Kleffner, *The Collective Accountability of Organized Armed Croups for System Crimes, in* System Criminality in International Law, (André Nollkaemper & Harmen van der Wilt, eds., 2009) 238; Ratner, *supra* note 15, at 556 ("I am not sure that individual accountability is more important than state accountability"); Carmen Valor, Corporate Social Responsibility and Corporate Citizenship: Towards Corporate Accountability, 110 Bus. & Soc. Rev. 191 (2005).

24. Skaar et al., *supra* note 20 at 4; Simon Robins, *Failing Victims: The Limits of Transitional Justice in Addressing the Needs of Victims of Violations*, 9 Hum. Rts. & Int'l L. Disc. 41, 51 (2017) ("despite the rhetoric of restoration that has permeated transitional justice, prosecution remains a mechanism that is privileged above all others"); Bell, *supra* note 20 (noting that the human rights movement "seemed to view criminal justice and punishment as the ultimate gold standard for former human rights abusers").

25. As famously stated by the judges at the Nuremberg Tribunal, "crimes against international law are committed by men, not by abstract entities, and only by punishing individuals who commit such crimes can the provisions of international law be enforced." Judicial Decisions: International Tribunal (Nuremberg), Judgment and Sentences, Oct. 1, 1946, 41 Am. J. Int'l. L. 172 (1947).

26. Buehler, *supra* note 10 (noting that Sung-ho Jhe called for "a combination of institutional responsibility and individual responsibility" for North Korea).

27. Bílková, *supra* note 5, at 7.

28. Marzuki Darusman, Video Presentation, North Korea – Violating its own People's Human Rights, at http://www.ohchr.org/EN/NewsEvents/Pages/NorthKoreaHumanRightsReport.aspx (last visited on July 17, 2017).

29. *See* Open Letter from FIDH, *supra* note 6.

30. Hum. Rts. Counc., *Report of the Group of Independent Experts on Accountability*, U.N. Doc. A/HRC/66/Add.1 (Feb. 24, 2017), paras. 11-17.

31. *Id.*, at para.12.

32. *Id.*, at para.14.

33. *Id.*, at paras.32-45; 50-61.

34. *Id.*, at paras.46-49; 62-67.

35. When there are multiple definitions for a concept being studied, then the extent to which any particular research findings are generally applicable often remains unclear. Chava Frankfort-Nachmias & David Nachmias Research Methods in the Social Sciences, 27 (5th edn. 1996); John Gerring & Paul Barresi, *Putting Ordinary Language to Work: A Min-Max Strategy of Concept Formation in the Social Sciences*, 15 J. Theor. Polit. 201, 202 (2003).

36. Jeff King, *The Instrumental Value of Legal Accountability*, *in* Accountability in the Contemporary Constitution 124, 124 (Nicholas Bamforth & Peter Leyland, eds., 2013) ("Any proposal to extend the domain of adjudication can reasonably be met with the following good faith question: why? What is valuable about doing that, and about legal accountability more generally?").

37. Brianne McGonicle Leyh, *Failing Victims: The Socialisation of Transitional Justice: Expanding Justice Theories Within the Field*, 9 Hum. Rts. & Int'l L. Disc. 83 (2017).

38. *See, e.g.*, Sarkin & Davi, *supra* note 17, at 6 ("long-term goals of transitional justice focus on the attainment of peace, stability and the rule of law in transitional societies"); UN Sec. Gen., The Rule of Law and Transitional Justice in Conflict and Post-Conflict Societies, U.N. Doc. S/2004/16 (Aug. 23, 2004) ("The challenges of post-conflict environments necessitate an approach that balances a variety of goals, including the pursuit of accountability, truth and reparation, the preservation of peace and the building of democracy and the rule of law").

39. King, *supra* note 36, at 124.

40. Jane Stromseth, *Pursuing Accountability for Atrocities after Conflict: What Impact on Building the Rule of Law?*, 38 Geo. J. Int'l. L. 251, 259 (2007) ("The selective, focused nature of criminal trials after massive atrocities also limits them as mechanisms for achieving a number of broad goals, such as a comprehensive account of a conflict and its causes").

41. *Id.* at 258 ("Holding individual perpetrators legally accountable can also provide some sense of justice and relief to victims and their families and potentially help to defuse grievances and curtail cycles of vengeance. by setting an example and making clear that wrong-doers will be held"). *But see*, Robins, *supra* note 24, at 47 ("It is almost universally presumed that prosecutions benefit victims and that impunity is in itself traumatic for survivors Despite these claims, there has been little empirical work on the issue of whether prosecutions of violators are of benefit to the victims of those tried").

42. Ratner, *supra* note 15, at 544.

43. Sarkin & Davi, *supra* note 17, at 12 ("Those in favour of retributive justice…argue that [without punishment] respect for the rule of law, which is often already weak where transitional justice is at issue, will continue to atrophy, leading to further abuses in future"); Stromseth, *supra* note 40, at 258 ("Prosecuting and punishing major offenders affirms and reinforces the core international legal rules prohibiting genocide, crimes against humanity, and war crimes").

44. Ratner, *supra* note 15, at 544 ("what is the point of individual accountability at all? We hear so many answers, from the UN High Commissioner for Human Rights, from victims, from NGOs: it's about meting out criminal justice to the perpetrators; it's about so-called closure for the victims; it's about reparations; it's about national reconciliation").

45. Stromseth, *supra* note 40, at 258 ("Bringing major perpetrators to justice demonstrating that their conduct is wrong and unacceptable-is an immediate and fundamental goal").

46. *Id.* at 262.

47. *See, e.g.,* Open Letter from FIDH, *supra* note 6 ("North Korea's countless victims deserve redress. Justice remains critical to end the pervasive impunity for the worst abuses in North Korea").

48. Lisa Schlein, *Experts: N. Korea Must be Held Accountable for Crimes Against Humanity*, VOA News (Mar. 13, 2017), https://www.voanews.com/a/experts-say-north-korea-must-be-held-accountable-for-crimes-against-humanity/3763130.html (last visited Sept. 12, 2017) (recommending the establishment of an ad hoc international tribunal, "which could act as a deterrent for future crimes").

49. Cohen, *Human Rights in North Korea, supra* note 1, at 83 ("the more the COI report is seen as the basis for holding North Koreans accountable at eventual trials, the more it might work as a deterrent"); Oknam Yi & David Sungjae Hong, *Start Thinking Now About Transitional Justice in a Post-Transition North Korea,* PacNet: 51 (July 11, 2013).

50. Roberta Cohen, *Human Rights and Humanitarian Planning for Crisis in North Korea*, XIX Intl. J. Kor. Stud. 1 (2015).

51. Daniel Nagin, *Deterrence, in* Correctional Theory: Context and Consequences 72 (Francis Culle & Cheryl Lero Jonson, eds., 2012).

52. Stromseth, *supra* note 40, at 258-59.

53. Kevin Kennedy, *A Critical Appraisal of Criminal Deterrence Theory*, 88 Dickinson L. Rev. 1, 4-5 (1984); Daniel Nagin, *Deterrence, in* Correctional Theory: Context and

Consequences 84 (Francis Culle & Cheryl Lero Jonson, eds., 2012).

54. Of course, accountability could be used as a negotiating tool, with threats of prosecution pulled off the table in exchange for better future behavior, and indeed North Korea has shown some willingness to negotiate on this point, but such a strategy would run counter to basic notions of justice and has not been embraced to date by other states. Cohen, *Human Rights in North Korea, supra* note 1, at 81-82.

55. Sarkin and Davi, *supra* note 17, at 13.

56. Ratner, *supra* note 15, at 553 ("in situations where atrocities are ongoing, termination is more important than accountability. Thus, the Human Rights Council's commission on Syria focused on cessation first, barely mentioning accountability. And the report of the commission on Libya is also very guarded in this respect").

57. Mirjan Damaska, *What is the Point of International Criminal Justice*, 83 Chi-Kent L. Rev. 329, 331 ("the professed goals do not constitute a harmonious whole; rather, they pull in different directions, diminishing each other's power and creating tensions").

58. Stromseth, *supra* note 40, at 252 ("In some situations, accountability mechanisms may actually trigger further violence")

59. Sarkin and Davi, *supra* note 17, at 13.

60. *See, e.g.*, Henry Rousso, The Haunting Past: History, Memory and Justice in Contemporary France (2002); Richard Evans, *History, Memory and the Law: The Historian as Expert Witness*, 41 His. & Theory 326 (2002); Ian Buruma, The Wages of Guilt: Memoires of War in Germany and Japan 142 (1995).

61. Jack Snyder & Leslie Vinjamuri, *Trials and Errors: Principle and Pragmatism in Strategies of International Justice*, 28 Int'l. Sec. 5, 5 (2003/2004).

62. Ratner, *supra* note 15, at 543 ("even as I've written about and participated in UN accountability processes, I have always been pulled toward seeing prevention and termination of human rights violations as a far greater priority").

63. *Id.* at 549-50 ("Where, at the other extreme, the government that committed the abuses is still in power—where, in a word, there is no transition—as with Sri Lanka since 2009, the obstacles to accountability are enormous, maybe even insurmountable for as long as that regime is in power").

64. U.N. Gen. Ass., Report of the Special Rapporteur on the Situation of Human Rights in the Democratic People's Republic of Korea, A/70/362 (Sep. 8, 2015) ¶ 50.

65. Paul Gready, The Era of Transitional Justice 18 (2011); Pierre Hazan, *Measuring the Impact of Punishment and Forgiveness: A Framework for Evaluating Transitional Justice*, 88 Int. Rev. Red Cross, 19, 27-8 (2006); Constantin Goschler, *German Reunification and the Challenge of Transitional Justice, in* Transitional Justice in

Unified Korea 132 (Baek Buhm-Suk & Ruti Teitel, eds., 2015) ("the feasibility of transitional justice in the case of North Korea will very much depend on the if and when of reunification").

66) Laurel Fletcher, Harvey Weinstein & Jamie Rowen, *Context, Timing and the Dynamics of Transitional Justice: A Historical Perspective*, 31 Hum. Rts. Q. 163, 165 (2009); Tricia Olsen, Leigh Payne & Andrew Reiter, Transitional Justice in Balance (2010).

67. Kathryn Sikkink & Carrie Booth Walling, *The Impact of Human Rights Trials in Latin America*, 44 J. Peace Res. 427 (2007); Hunjoon Kim & Kathryn Sikkink, *Explaining the Deterrence Effect of Human Rights Prosecutions for Transitional Countries*, 54 Int. Stud. Q. 939 (2010).

68. Baek Buhm-Suk, Lisa Collins & Kim Yuri, *Transitional Justice in Post-Unification Korea: Challenges and Prospects, in* Transitional Justice in Unified Korea 12 (Baek Buhm-Suk & Ruti Teitel, eds., 2015) ("the manner in which unification occurs will certainly determine if and how transitional justice will be implemented and what mechanisms will be employed").

69. *Id.* at 18 ("currently surveying North Koreans in North Korea about transitional justice and unification is impossible").

70. Laurel Fletcher, Harvey Weinstein & Jamie Rowen, *Context, Timing and the Dynamics of Transitional Justice: A Historical Perspective*, 31 Hum. Rts. Q. 163, 165 (2009); Robins, *supra* note 24, at 54 (it is "crucial that victims themselves have agency and voice in the process"); "Victim exclusion and marginalization can lead to processes that do not achieve their full potential"; Sarkin & Davi, *supra* note 17, at 15; Baek, Collins & Kim, *supra* note 68, at 12 (it is "necessary to ensure that North Koreans feel a sense of ownership of the transitional justice process so that they do not question its legitimacy"); Goschler, *supra* note 65, at 132 ("the sentiments of the North Korean population should be taken seriously to avoid a situation where transitional justice might be considered as a foreign imposition").

71. Robins, *supra* note 24, at 44.

72. U.N. Sec. Gen., Guidance Note: *United Nations Approach to Transitional Justice* 6 (Mar. 2010) ("Successful transitional justice programmes recognize the centrality of victims and their special status in the design and implementation of such processes").

73. Transitional Justice Working Group, *supra* note 21, at 51.

74. Stromseth, *supra* note 40, at 252 ("Although some victims demand trial and punishment of perpetrators, others place greater emphasis on public acknowledgement of their suffering and on reparations or some tangible form of assistance"); Robins, *supra* note 24, at 52 ("a desire for prosecution is often only one of many demands, and frequently not the first priority of victims of violations, at least in states where

other needs remain urgent."); Ratner, *supra* note 15, at 544.

75. *See, e.g.*, Database Center for North Korean Human Rights, 2016 White Paper on North Korean Human Rights (2016); U.N. General Assembly, Resolution on the Situation of Human Rights in the Democratic People's Republic of Korea, A/RES/69/188 (December 18, 2014); U.N. Human Rights Council, Report of the Commission of Inquiry on Human Rights in the Democratic People's Republic of Korea, A/HRC/25/63 (2014); Republic of Korea Ministry of Unification, 2015 White Paper on Human Rights in North Korea (2015).

76. This is most evident in the final report of the Group of Independent Experts on Accountability, which mentioned documentation but focused primarily on the current availability of trial venues. Hum. Rts. Counc., *Report of the Group of Independent Experts on Accountability, supra* note 30.

77. Some have noted the existence of a "transitional justice industry." Leyh, *supra* note 37, at 84.

78. *See*, Baek, Collins & Kim, *supra* note 68, at 19 (North Korea remains "an affront to the international accountability norm").

79. *See* Open Letter from FIDH, *supra* note 5 ("the [Human Rights] Council's own credibility demands a focus on accountability").

80. Stromseth, *supra* note 40, at 261 ("Domestic leaders often perceive international leaders and donors as more concerned about sending a general deterrent message regarding atrocities than about the specific, long-term needs of the particular post-conflict society directly involved").

81. *See*, Buehler, *supra* note 10.

82. *See, e.g.,* Baek Buhm-Suk & Ruti Teitel, eds., Transitional Justice in Unified Korea (2015). Of course, from a South Korean perspective it makes sense to plan for a potential unification, which is a constitutionally mandated national goal, in order to ensure that the process goes smoothly if this eventuality ever does come to pass.

Korea-U.S. Bilateral Trade Relations at Crossroads U.S. Trade Remedy Investigations and Ensuing WTO Litigation

LEE Jae Min
Professor
Seoul National University, School of Law, Seoul, Korea

Abstract

Since the conclusion of the Korea-U.S. FTA in 2012, United States' trade remedy investigations against Korean products have grown in numbers and intensified in scope. In particular, recent application of novel investigative practices, such as targeted dumping, adverse facts available and particular market situation, has made these topics the focal points of the bilateral discussions and consultation. In retrospect, some of the measures currently in place by the United States could have been dealt with by the Korea-U.S. FTA of 2012 and now an amended Korea-U.S. FTA in 2018. More elaborated provisions and detailed guidelines could have been inserted and reflected in the texts of the bilateral FTA. Recent bilateral discussions and disputes reflect the absence of such critical provisions and guidelines in the FTA. In future trade agreement negotiations, whether bilaterally or multilaterally, efforts should be made to develop and elaborate provisions regulating trade remedy investigations of contracting parties in a more meaningful way, and those provisions should be included in the texts of such agreements so as to reflect new trends of trade remedy investigation at the moment.

Key Words

Trade Remedy Investigations, Antidumping Investigations, Countervailing Duty Investigations, Adverse Facts Available, Particular Market Situation, Targeted Dumping

1. INTRODUCTION

The economic and trade relationship between the United States and Korea has been always pivotal for Korea. As a matter of fact, the United States is the second-largest trading partner of Korea, after China. Many Korean companies rely upon their exports to the U.S. market as a critical component of their business operation. Not surprisingly, Korea has been one of the most frequent targets of U.S. trade remedy measures – a term that collectively refers to antidumping investigation, countervailing duty investigation and safeguards investigation. While safeguards investigations are relatively rare because they are exceptional measures addressing 'fair trade,' antidumping measures and countervailing measures have been frequent and constant. As such, many Korean companies tend to remember these two measures first when they first hear WTO Agreements or free trade agreements.

Since 2008, with the advent of the global protectionism and ensuing measures in the United States, there is increasing concern on the part of the Korean government and industries regarding trade restrictive measures in the United States. In particular, the concern is directed at trade remedy investigations and measures of the United States Department of Commerce. Over the past several years, trade remedy investigations against Korean companies have grown in numbers and intensified in scope. In particular, recent application of novel investigative practices has been directed at Korean exports, most notably targeted dumping, adverse facts available ("AFA") and particular market situation ("PMS"). All these measures can be said to be the latest attempt of the United States to take advantage of the 'gray area' of 'gaps' of the WTO's *Agreement on Implementation of Article VI of the General Agreement on Tariffs and Trade 1994* (Antidumping Agreement) and *Agreement on Subsidies and Countervailing Measures* (SCM Agreement). Investigating authorities of the United States have been understood to focus on silence or a lack of specific provision in these agreements on specifics of trade remedy investigations, and to expand its discretionary authority as much as feasible.

As a result, exporters have been negatively affected by these new measures. Substantially high antidumping and/or countervailing duty margins have been imposed. The Korean government has undertaken a series of bilateral discussions with the U.S. counterpart, but the disputes have not been resolved. Korea has subsequently decided to challenge these measures at the WTO panels and the Appellate Body.

Trade remedy issues are just one aspect of the recent bilateral trade disputes between the two countries. In addition to the conventional trade remedy measures, there are new trade restrictive measures such as import restriction based on national security under Section 232 of the U.S. trade law.[1] While these new measures are now causing acute concerns in Korea, trade remedy measures still remain as one of the most important and chronic worries on the part of the exporters and the government. Korea has become one of the major targets of U.S. trade remedy investigations.

2. EXAMPLE OF CHANGING TRENDS IN TRADE REMEDY INVESTIGATIONS

In 2015, the United States amended its rule on the determination of subsidy rates and anti-dumping margin through the American Trade Enforcement Effectiveness Act of 2015, which constitutes Title V of Trade Preference Extension Act ("TPEA"). TPEA made changes to US Tariff Act to give a broad discretion to the law enforcement agencies such as the Department of Commerce and the International Trade Commission.

Under the new legislation, the U.S. Department of Commerce is given a discretion to apply subsidy rates or anti-dumping margin calculated in any prior proceeding under the same AD or CVD order, including "the highest such rate of margin." In addition, the U.S. Department of Commerce need not "corroborate" the accuracy of any subsidy rate or dumping margin obtained from a prior proceeding under the same order, and it need not estimate what the subsidy rate or dumping margin would have been if the non-cooperative foreign respondent had cooperated nor demonstrate that the selected rate or margin "reflects an alleged commercial reality." Since this amendment, it is very evident that the U.S. Department of Commerce has increasingly applied subsidy rates or dumping margins calculated using AFA on the reasons of a foreign respondent's alleged failure to cooperate.

One of prime example of such trend is the recent imposition of antidumping and countervailing duties on two Korean steel producers, POSCO and Hyundai Steel Company ("Hyundai") in a case called as *Countervailing Duty Investigation of Certain Hot-Rolled Steel Flat Products from the Republic of Korea.* The U.S. Department of Commerce investigated POSCO and Hyundai Steel for both antidumping and countervailing duties. AD and CVD Preliminary determination showed that both POSCO and Hyundai received *de minimis* subsidy rates. However, during the verification process, the U.S. Department applied AFA to POSCO for the failure to report certain cross-owned input suppliers, and facilities located in a foreign economic zone (FEZ), as well as for certain loans presented to Daewoo International Corporation ("DWI"),[2] an affiliated trading company of POSCO.[3] The U.S. Department of Commerce applied AFA to Hyundai for its failure to report its location in an FEZ. As a result of application of adverse facts available, the U.S. Department of Commerce imposed 57.04 percent of countervailing duty on POSCO, 3.89 percent on Hyundai Steel Company. Most notable in this case is the striking discrepancy between the subsidy rate imposed on POSCO in the preliminary and final determination, and the subsidy rate as imposed on POSCO and Hyundai. Since both POSCO and Hyundai had failed to report its location in an FEZ, it can be safely assumed that the discrepancy between subsidy rates of POSCO and Hyundai might be due to the application of AFA based upon the failure by POSCO to report certain loans presented to its affiliated trading company DWI and the debt restructuring program of DWI.

This is not an isolated case. Rather, similar AFA has been applied to foreign respondents from Brazil, Turkey, Italia, Japan, India, Australia, Canada and Indonesia. In *Imports of Certain Uncoated Paper from China and Indonesia (CVD)*, the U.S. Department of Commerce applied AFA to four out of seven respondents, with highest subsidy rate being 176.75 percent.[4]

The U.S. Department of Commerce states that its determination of CVD rates are conducted in accordance with the new provision on applying facts available. However, many foreign respondents and their home governments question the legality of the amendment giving broad discretion relating to AFA and its application by the U.S. Department of Commerce. Canada filed a request for consultations, dated 30 March 2016, to the WTO Dispute Settlement Proceeding[5] after one of its respondents in countervailing duty investigation in *Supercalendered Paper from Canada* was subject to adverse facts available. Furthermore, Government of Canada, had made an attempt to make a motion to submit *amici curiae* to the U.S. Court of International Trade (U.S. CIT) in *Changzhou Trina Solar Energy v. United States* (161 F.Supp.3d 1343).[6] While the motion was declined by U.S. CIT, it indicates that the respondent at issue, Resolute, has at least some intention of bringing the case to U.S. CIT.

3. TRADE REMEDY ISSUES IN KOREA-U.S. FTA

While the Korea-U.S. FTA has been regarded as one of the important achievements of the Korean government in the trade sector, it has left a bitter-sweet memory to Korea in terms of trade remedy investigation of the United States. Knowing that Korean goods had been frequent targets of AD and CVD investigations in the United States, addressing this issue was one of the top priorities of the Korean government during the negotiation of the Korea-U.S. FTA (2005-2007). And yet, the United States strongly opposed to any substantive change in its trade remedy investigation mechanism, underscoring that it did not receive a mandate to amend it from the U.S. Congress – which was true to some extent as the U.S. Congress viewed trade remedy measures as the last line of defense of U.S. industries in a new landscape of free trade. As a result, only minor procedural issues were able to be included in the agreement such as notification and consultation requirement upon initiation of a new investigation. Few changes, if any, took place in the real practice of the trade remedy investigations of the United States.

In the wake of the Korea-U.S. FTA, frustration has been going up, because many exporters assumed, albeit erroneously, that the FTA may remedy the trade remedy investigation system. In fact, the trade remedy investigations continued to stay in the same course, and from 2015 with the introduction of TPEA, investigation practices turned its course for the worse.

Not surprisingly, when the two countries initiated their discussion to amend the Korea-U.S. FTA starting from last September, this issue again became one of the top priorities on the Korean part. The two countries have agreed, in principle, on the contents of the amendments and modifications in late March 2018. While specific contents of the amendments and modifications have not been disclosed to the public yet, it is being reported that yet again only minor changes have been made in the trade remedy sector. Thus, it seems that the concerns over and problems in the trade remedy sector will continue to haunt the Korean exporters for the time being.

4. CURRENT SITUATIONS AND DISPUTES

Recent trade remedy investigation practices and methodologies have become one of the major challenges of Korean manufacturers and exporters to the U.S. market. While specific disputes have arisen relating to particular industries, these issues have not been just confined to some selective industries, but rather have been representative of the general reaction of the exporters at large.

● Targeted dumping determination and continued application of zeroing[7]

In 2013, the U.S. Department of Commerce found targeted dumping in its investigation of large residential washers from Korea. As a result of the finding, it applied zeroing, resulting in inflation of the dumping margin. Korea initiated a WTO dispute settlement proceeding. After the panel and the Appellate Body proceeding, Korea prevailed in 2015. The United States refused to implement the rulings and recommendation of the WTO's Dispute Settlement Body. Korea was authorized to retaliate in January 2018.

● "Adverse facts available" finding and application[8]

In 2017, it its countervailing duty investigation against Korean steel products, the U.S. Department of Commerce found less-than-optimal cooperation from the respondent (POSCO). The claimed lack of cooperation on the part of the respondent was directly related to the changed investigating practice on the part of the U.S. investigating authority in a way that expands the scope of investigation and broaden the contents of requested information in a shortened deadlines. As a result, it decided to apply AFA which increased the CVD margin substantially. Korea brought a WTO challenge in February 2018, and the case is still pending.

This new phenomenon is the outcome of the legislative changes made in 2015. At that time, the U.S. Congress at the request of the Obama

Administration amended the rule on the determination of subsidy and antidumping rates through the American Trade Enforcement Effectiveness Act of 2015, which constitutes Title V of Trade Preference Extension Act (TPEA). More specifically, the TPEA's Section 502 amended Section 776 of the Tariff Act of 1930 as amended with respect to the finding and application of "adverse facts available." This legislative change basically provides a wide range of latitude to the United States Department of Commerce. Under the new legislation, the U.S. agency is now given a discretion to apply subsidy or antidumping rates from a variety of different options when certain conditions are met. These proxy rates include those calculated from any prior proceeding under the same AD or CVD order. Effectively, the new measure means that the United States Department of Commerce is enabled to use "the highest calculated rate for a single transaction as the adverse facts available margin."[9]

● **Particular market situation finding and application**[10]

In 2017, in its antidumping investigation against Korean steel products (OCTG), the U.S. Department of Commerce determined that the Korean manufacturers utilized raw materials from a non-market economy country (that is, China) and thus the Korean domestic market constitutes a particular market situation. As a result of the finding, the U.S. Department of Commerce applied a different methodology in calculating normal value (NV), which then led to the increase of the AD margin. Korea initiated its challenge at the WTO in May 2018, and the case is now pending at the WTO.

It should be noted that these critical new practice of trade remedy investigation "on the field" has been actually engineered in previous administrations.[11] Legislative changes had then been made even before the current Trump Administration came in in January 2017.[12] The current situation wherein Korean exporters are facing a wide range of obstacles in the course of defending themselves in trade remedy investigations is not just a passing incident. Instead, this is the reflection of a gradual changes in law and practice of the United States when it comes to trade remedy investigations against foreign product imports. The focus of such changes is placed on how to enhance the authority and expand discretion of the investigating authority (that is, the United States Department of Commerce) in conducting these investigations.[13] While the WTO's Antidumping Agreement does underscore the importance of procedural fairness and the foreign exporters' right to defend themselves,[14] it also recognizes a rather wide latitude of decision making process for an investigating authority of WTO Member states.[15]

So, the agreement itself reflects the competing objectives between one line of thought (favoring the views of exporters) and another line of thought (favoring the views of the importing states). The competing views even hampered the adoption of the preamble of the agreement. The situation is not that different with respect to the WTO Agreement on Subsidies and Countervailing Measures (SCM Agreement) which regulated the companion countervailing duty investigations. The SCM Agreement is also another WTO covered agreement which does not include a preamble. Under these circumstances, it would be quite difficult, if not entirely impossible, for one group of Members to tell definitively that a particular way of exercising the discretion of an investigating authority of a WTO Member in a specific manner is by nature in violation of the agreement. Finding of violation in fact requires more in-depth analyses for a long time, and any outcome of such analyses are arguably vulnerable to criticism of the Members who happen to disagree.

As such, it is indeed quite challenging for other countries to take issue with the expansion of discretion of the investigation authority of a Member *per se*. It can be said that the covered agreements do not provide sufficient details and elaboration in this respect, which apparently now opens the door for some Members to explore the possibility of expanding the discretion of the investigating authority, allegedly within the confinement of the provisions of the agreements. It seems that the efforts of the United States for the past several years in particular are reflective of this trend in the global community and this reality of the texts of the agreements.

5. A CRITICAL CHALLENGE: UNCLEAR SCOPE OF THE DISCRETION OF THE INVESTIGATING AUTHORITY

While specific legal issues are all different and based on the texts of the Antidumping Agreement and the SCM Agreement, arguably there is one commonality, based on Korea's own experience, in the recent trend of new trade remedy investigation of the United States. That is expansion of the discretion of the investigating authority to the fullest, and arguably beyond the limit authorized by the Antidumping Agreement and SCM Agreement. Instead of relying on investigative practices that have been and can be challenged relatively easily based on the explicit text of these agreements, the U.S. Department of Commerce apparently seems to be looking to the 'unwritten' part of the agreements. One of such examples is the inherent discretion of an investigating authority.[16] All these measures that Korea has raised bilaterally and multilaterally are related to the scope of discretion on the part of the investigating authority.

The problem is, the text is unclear as to the specific aspects of the exercise of discretion of investigating authorities in actual investigations. Other than pronouncement of basic principles in abstract, application of the principle in specific contexts and investigations does not always a clear-cut conclusion.

By way of example, there is jurisprudence that procedural due process should be kept in trade remedy investigations. Likewise, there is jurisprudence that an investigating authority should make best efforts to conduct fair and reasonable investigations. That said, there is few jurisprudence or regulation as to what type of information an investigating authority can request, how much an investigating authority should consider logistical difficulties of responding companies, how long or short deadlines can be. Most importantly, assessing specific factual situations or information is regarded to fall under the jurisdiction of an investigating authority.[17]

The recent trend of the introduction of new investigating practices and methodologies arguably indicate that the United States has found the utility of relying upon this aspect of the Antidumping Agreement and SCM Agreement. It may have learned, from its experience in the WTO panel and Appellate Body proceedings, that exercising discretion to the fullest or sometimes over the limit is easier to apply and defend, as opposed to going down the path where specific textual hook can be identified. Presumably, the panels and the Appellate Body have been more open and flexible, or even deferential, when it comes to a specific instance of exercise of discretion in a specific investigation. As a matter of fact, a deferential standard of review of a WTO panel is also codified in Article 17.6 of the Antidumping Agreement.[18] Furthermore, even if the measures at issue are found to be WTO-inconsistent, these types of discretion-related measures are relatively easier to remedy once an adverse ruling is issued. The investigating authority can only re-open the investigation and re-do the finding, by requesting more focused and detailed information. On top of that, these discretion related issues are not necessarily codified in laws and regulations, which make them difficult to be challenged "as such." Thus, any burden from an adverse ruling from the WTO is arguably less than it would be the case otherwise.

Such being the case, it can be said that the fate of the Korea's recent challenges at the WTO is not entirely clear. In particular, the AFA and PMS disputes pose novel issues with few precedents, if any. At the same time, they are substantially fact-specific and case-specific in nature. So, it would be indeed interesting to see how panels and the Appellate Body react to these issues and disputes. Likewise, it would be also interesting how the United States would react to any adverse ruling from the WTO.

6. CONCLUDING THOUGHT: MISSED OPPORTUNITIES AND FUTURE LESSONS

In retrospect, Korea should have been more mindful of the changing direction of the U.S. government in terms of exploring various import restrictive measures and elaborating trade remedy investigation practices and methodologies. Korea should have been more assertive in reflecting its concern in the bilateral FTA with the United States. More detailed provisions could have been contemplated and inserted into the FTA's trade remedy chapter, so that investigating authorities' wide discretion could be regulated properly. Due to the strong opposition of the United States, the trade remedy chapter of the FTA fail to address some of the core concerns of Korean exporters at that time and guard against ever-expanding scope of the discretion of the investigating authority. As a result, during the past three years since 2015 when major Korean exporters have been struggling with the new trade remedy investigation practices and methodologies, the provisions of the FTA have remained largely irrelevant. This phenomenon has spread the perception among businesses and industries in Korea about the tangible benefit of the FTA.

Some of the measures currently in place by the United States could have been dealt with by the FTA. At least, provisions could have been introduced into the text of the FTA regarding trade remedy investigations, such that Korea's voice can be reflected and concerns registered in formulating new changes in trade remedy investigations.

It is hoped that in future instances of FTA negotiations, whether bilaterally or multilaterally, states might want to be apprised of the importance of properly addressing these issues in the prospective trade agreements. Simply referring to the WTO Agreements may not be able to ensure that antidumping investigations and countervailing duty investigations are conducted in fair and reasonable manner in all respects. This is so because, unfortunately, there are loopholes and gaps in the texts of the WTO Agreements themselves, and the efforts to update and amend the agreements have been still elusive due to the moribund situation of the DDA negotiations.

To the extent that only few rules are contained in the texts and that a wide latitude of discretion is provided to an investigating authority, it seems possible that such discretion can be applied in a way that puts foreign respondents in a more difficult situation. Under the current texts of the WTO Agreements, these types of measures certainly harbor a protectionist intent, but their incompatibility with WTO Agreements are more complicated than they seem: some of them arguably stand on a borderline between compatibility and incompatibility while others apparently constitute violation of the agreements.

In the absence of the amendment of the Antidumping Agreement and SCM Agreement, only FTAs will be able to fill the gap and elaborate the text, so that trade remedy investigations are reasonable and fair both in form and in substance.

Notes

1. Section 232 is codifies the "national security clause", where it enables the U.S. President to impose restrictions on imports that the United States Department of Commerce determines threaten the national security of the United States. Rachel F. Fefer & Vivian C. Jones, Cong. Research Serv., IF10667, Section 232 of the Trade Expansion Act of 1962 (2018), https://fas.org/sgp/crs/misc/IF10667.pdf. For steel products *see The Effect of Imports of Steel on the National Security*, U.S. Dep't Com. Bureau Indus. & Sec. Office Tech. Evaluation 55 (Jan. 11, 2018), https://www.awpa.org/wp-content/uploads/2018/02/Section-232-Investigation-of-Steel-Imports-DOCs-Report-and-Recommenda....pdf; *The Effect of Imports of Aluminum on the National Security*, U.S. Dep't Com. Bureau Indus. & Sec. Office Tech. Evaluation 104 (Jan. 17, 2018), https://www.bis.doc.gov/index.php/forms-documents/aluminum/2223-the-effect-of-imports-of-aluminum-on-the-national-security-with-redactions-2 0180117/file.

2. Issues and decision memorandum for this investigation also shows that POSCO had failed to report on supplies from its affiliates located in Korea, and US Department of Commerce also applied AFA on that information as well.

3. A memorandum regarding the CVD investigation states that "the Government of Korea did not provide the requested information about DWI's Creditor's Council," which was formed during restructuring of DWI during the 2000s.

4. The memorandum for this investigation shows that the respondent did not respond to questionnaire within deadline, and the CVD rate was entirely based on adverse facts available.

5. *United States - Countervailing Measures on Supercalendered Paper from Canada* (DS505)

6. Not to be confused with *Changzhou Trina Solar Energy v. United States* (100 F.Supp.3d 1314) in which the issue of adverse facts available was not addressed.

7. *United States - Anti-Dumping and Countervailing Measures on Large Residential Washers from Korea*, WT/DS464 (Authorization to retaliate requested (including 22.6 arbitration) on 22 January 2018).

8. *United States - Anti-Dumping and Countervailing Duties on Certain Products and the Use of Facts Available*, WT/DS539 (Consultation filed on 20 February 2018).

9. See Alexander V. Sverdlov, "Change is Coming: What to Expect from the Recent Amendments to the Trade Remedy Laws," 47 *Georgetown Journal of International Law* 161 (2015), available at https://www.law.georgetown.edu/academics/law-journals/gjil/recent/upload/Sverdlov.pdf(last visited on November 28, 2018).

10. *Issues and Decision Memorandum for the Final Results of the 2015-2016 Administrative Review of the Antidumping Duty Order on Certain Oil Country Tubular Goods from the Republic of Korea* (Apr. 17, 2018) at 17 ("Commerce continues to determine that the circumstances present during the instant review remained largely unchanged from those in the prior review which led to the finding of a particular market situation in Korea in OCTG from Korea POR 1. Therefore, Commerce continues to find that, based on the collective impact of Korean HRC subsidies, Korean imports of HRC from China, strategic alliances, and government involvement in the Korean electricity market, a particular market situation exists in Korea which distorts the OCTG costs of production").

11. *Refer to* The Economist, "Obama a Dangerous Protectionist?" (dated on February 26, 2008), retrieved from https://www.economist.com/blogs/freeexchange/2008/02/obama_a_dangerous_protectionis (last visited on July 30, 2017); Jeffrey J. Schott, "Trade Policy and the Obama Administration," 44(3) *Business Economics* 150 (2009); Ryan McMaken, "It's Not Just Trump: Obama's Protectionists Are Attacking Chinese Steel", Mises Institute (dated on June 7, 2016), retrieved from https://mises.org/blog/its-not-just-trump-obamas-protectionists-are-attacking-chinese-steel (last visited on July 30, 2017).

12. For instance, in 2015, the United States of America (U.S.) amended its rule on the determination of subsidy rates and anti-dumping margins through the American Trade Enforcement Effectiveness Act of 2015, which constitutes Title V of Trade Preference Extension Act (TPEA). The TPEA' Section 502 amended Section 776 of the Tariff Act of 1930 relating to facts available. The TPEA made changes to US Tariff Act to give a broad discretion to the law enforcement agencies such as the Department of Commerce (US DOC) and the International Trade Commission (ITC). Under the new legislation, the US DOC is given a discretion to apply subsidy rates or anti-dumping margins calculated in any prior proceeding under the same AD or CVD order, including "the highest such rate of margin." According to one observation, USDOC now has discretion to apply a rate calculated from a small set of transactions, for a small set of companies, to the point where it is possible for US DOC to use "the highest calculated rate for a single transaction as the adverse facts available margin." Alexander V. Sverdlov, "Change is Coming: What to Expect from the Recent Amendments to the Trade Remedy Laws," 47 *Georgetown Journal of International Law* 161 (2015), available at https://www.law.georgetown.edu/academics/law-journals/gjil/recent/upload/Sverdlov.pdf (last visited on July 30, 2017).

13. *See ibid.*

14. *See* Antidumping Agreement, Article 6.

15. *See ibid.*, at Article 17.6.

16. With respect to AFA, Article 6.8 of Antidumping Agreement states that:

> "In cases in which any interested party refuses access to, or otherwise does not provide, necessary information within a reasonable period or significantly impedes the investigation, preliminary and final determinations, affirmative or negative, may be made on the basis of the facts available. The provisions of Annex II shall be observed in the application of this paragraph."

Annex II of Antidumping Agreement, under the title of "Best Information Available" further clarifies procedures of applying facts available. Paragraph 1 to paragraph 4 are provisions that set forth how the request for information should be made, and paragraph 5 states that "[e]ven though the information provided may not be ideal in all respects, this should not justify the authorities from disregarding it, provided the interested party has acted to the best of its ability." Paragraph 6 provides that when the investigating authority decides not to accept the information provided by the respondent, the investigating party should inform respondent of such decision with reasons, and should give the respondent an opportunity to provide further explanations within a reasonable period.

The investigating agency has discretion over decision on which fact among the "facts available" to apply, within boundaries of both Article 6.8 and Annex II of Antidumping Agreement. In practice, it is expected that the investigating agency would choose the most adverse information among the facts available towards the foreign respondent within the boundaries of WTO Agreements.

17. The WTO Panel recognizes that the facts available mechanism would ensure that the work of an investigating authority should not be frustrated or hampered by non-cooperation on the part of interest parties. For instance, the Panel in *E.C.-Countervailing Measures on DRAM Chips* (DS299) noted that the Article 12.7 of SCM Agreement "identifies the circumstances in which investigating authorities may overcome a lack of information, in the response of the interested parties, by using 'facts' which are otherwise 'available' to the investigating authority."

WTO Panel also confirms that the investigating authority has wide discretion when it chooses and weighs information available in applying facts available to non-cooperating respondents. The same Panel in the DS299 stated that "[t]here is no rule in the SCM Agreement that stops the investigating authority from taking into account information from all sources."

However, one critical requirement set by the WTO Panel is that any facts available must be *facts,* not just assumption or assertion. Therefore, any application of facts available must have a "factual foundation," as noted by the Panel in *China-GOES* (DS414), and the investigating authority is expected to employ "the best information available," as noted by the Appellate Body in *Mexico - Anti-Dumping Measure.*

18. This article is interpreted as not permitting a WTO panel to conduct *de novo* review of determination by investigating authorities. The Appellate Body precedents have also made it clear that a panel "may not conduct a *de novo* review of the evidence" nor it can "substitute its judgment for that of the investigating authority," and noted that the role of a panel is a "reviewer of agency action," not "initial trier of fact."

SPECIAL REPORTS

Tasks for Adopting 'the Civil Society Charter' towards Peace and Human Rights in East Asia: Overcoming the San Francisco Peace Treaty System[1]

LEE Jang-Hie
Professor Emeritus
Hankuk University of Foreign Studies, Law School, Seoul, Korea

Key Words

Colonialism, Long Division of the Korean peninsula, THAAD, Navi Pillay, Durban Declaration, Peaceful East Asian Community, CSCE, Civil Society Charter, NGOs.

1. PRESENT SITUATION IN EAST ASIA

East Asia is at a critical turning point after 17 years has passed in the 21st century. East Asian countries, including Korea-China-Japan, have become the center of the world in terms of economic development. Even in terms of education, East Asian countries are increasingly ranking above the international standards. These shifting trends look very familiar as we observe that China became a member of the G20 along with the United States and the Republic Korea (hereafter ROK) hosted the G20 summit in Seoul in 2010.

However, Korea-China-Japan have failed to obtain an international political leadership and capability equal to their growing economic dominance. One of the main reasons is the absence of a common voice in the world stage due to the lack of regional collaboration. In fact, the level of regional integration among East Asian countries is significantly lower than that of the European Union (EU) in Europe, the Organization of American States (OAS) in the Americas, and the African Union (AU) in Africa.[2] Of course, there has been some progress such as 'ASEAN + 3,' which evolved from the Association of Southeast Asian Nations (ASEAN) by including three Northeast Asian countries and promoting regional collaboration between the Southeast and Northeast Asian countries. The main focus of these attempts, however, has been on the mediation of economic interests; as a result, they have failed to create a more inclusive regional community by incorporating issues such as historical reconciliation, peace and culture. Historical reconciliation from colonialism has been discussed in three East Asian countries, i.e. Korea-China-Japan. East Asia is still suffering from historical conflicts stemming from colonialism in the 19th century and lacks an alliance of cultural and historical identities. There are two main reasons for this situation: surviving colonialism and the 70-year-long division of South and North Korea.

First of all, surviving colonialism has made the regional collaboration between countries very difficult. East Asia has been unable to eliminate all of the scars of colonialism and imperialism made by the 19th century European powers. The deep wounds caused by colonialism and imperialism are still causing ethnic conflict in each country in addition to historical conflicts, territorial disputes and ideological tensions. Between ROK and Japan, there are unresolved historical conflicts rooted in colonialism, such as the comfort women issue and compensation for victims of the atomic bomb and forced labor under the Japanese colonial rule. Furthermore, Japan started to justify the history of territorial and colonial invasions on March 30, 2011, by adopting a misinterpreted historical textbook for future generations. Since 2003, China has utilized carefully employed plans in order to degrade Korean history through national projects including Xia Shang Zhou Chronology Project, Northeast Project, Ancient Chinese Culture Exploration Project, and Liao He Civilization Theory.

Secondly, the long division of ROK and North Korea created a new Cold War structure in East Asia, hindering regional collaboration. The world shifted away from the Cold War and ideological conflicts after the dissolution of the USSR in 1986, the unification of Germany in 1990, and the collapse of Eastern Europe. Furthermore, the Warsaw Treaty Organization, a mutual defense treaty subscribed by eight communist states in Eastern Europe, disappeared, and Eastern European countries including Rumania and Poland joined the North Atlantic Treaty Organization (NATO), a collective defense system led by the United States, Canada and countries in Western Europe. Nonetheless, however, there are still many obstacles against the regional collaboration of East Asia, such as the possible formation of a new Cold War structure between Korean-US-Japan and North Korea-China-Russia due to North Korea's nuclear test issue and nuclear armed intercontinental ballistic missiles (ICBMs), Japanese comfort women & Dokdo territorial issues between ROK and Japan.

Furthermore, Japanese prime minister Abe Shinzo, came back to political power again in 2013. His extreme right wing inclination & support for colonialism and militarism has caused many regional conflicts with neighbor countries in North East Asia. For instance, the Japanese education ministry, in its guideline on a history book released in 2014, said Dokdo was "Japan's sovereign territory," and was under "illegal occupation by ROK that the Japanese government is protesting against it."[3]

On December 28, 2015, Japan and ROK declared in Seoul the adoption of the Korea-Japan verbal agreement regarding the issues on the sexual victims of Japanese military during the Korea-Japan Ministerial Talks. The 12.28 Agreement does not specify the admittance of legal responsibility. Specifically, state responsibility for a state crime under international law regarding "organized violation of women's human rights during war" was not specified in the Agreement. The Agreement merely contains emotional expressions such as "admit responsibility as the Prime Minister of Japan." No specific statements regarding legal responsibility were made in the Agreement. Japanese Foreign Minister Gishida publicly states that legal responsibility was not admitted in front of the Japanese press. Abe said that his cabinet was not considering issuing a letter of apology to Korean "comfort women."[4] Navi Pillay (Former UN High Commissioner for Human Rights) criticized the Japanese government regarding the above agreement in a media interview.

On February 7, 2016, the Ministry of Defense said that ROK and the US had started THAAD (Terminal High Altitude Area Defense) talks.[5] Seoul' adoption of the U.S.-made anti-missile system means putting itself at the center of the hegemonic contest between the world's two superpowers. Behind the US policy to contain China in the region, the US seeks to enhance the trilateral alliance with Japan and Korea. Unlike Japan's strong backing the U.S. policy, ROK has managed to juggle its ties with the United states and China. Peking has made its objections to THAAD very clear, being concerned that the related radar system is very wide in scope and intrusive in nature. In the mean time, China committed retaliatory actions against ROK for its planned deployment of THAAD battery in ROK.

The Korean armistice ending the Korean War temporarily is still valid and still in force, despite North Korea's claim that it has been nullified, according to the top UN spokesman.[6]

Now, the Korean Peninsula and North East Asia was militarily under fire. Speculation was growing over the high possibility of a seventh nuclear test by North Korea following its successful test-launch of an intercontinental ballistic missile (ICBM), on late November in 2017. Pyongyang is purportedly capable of mounting a nuclear warhead on the ICBM, which is believed to be able to reach Alaska.[7] Now North Korea intensified provocations, conducting its six nuclear tests on September 3rd in 2016 and launching missiles, including ICBMs.

The fundamental background of regional conflicts in East Asia traces back to Cold war oder from the long division of the Korean peninsula and unresolved issues from Japanese colonialism.

2. PROBLEMS TO BE RESOLVED IN EAST ASIA

2-1. HISTORICAL BACKGROUND

On August 15th in 1945, colonialism came to an end due to Japanese Empire's acceptance of Potsdam Declaration and Japan's unconditional surrender. Two years earlier, the Cairo Declaration of 1943 had proclaimed the necessity to "establish the nation of freedom and independence" in consideration of "the slavish conditions of Chosun people." Potsdam Declaration was a reaffirmation of the Cairo Declaration.

As a result, the Korean Peninsula regained independence from Japanese Empire. However, Japan did not express any apology for plundering her natural resources, food supplies as well as her cultural assets nor for persecuting people involved in independence movement nor its ethic extermination. Moreover, Japan intervened in Korean citizens' struggle to establish a new country, and concreting the division of Korea into North and South by supporting American army during the Korean War. Japan did not liquidate her colonial legacy; what's more, its manifest legacy lives on to testify in the very form of Korea's north-south division. This colonial issue traces back to the International Military Tribunal for the Far East lead by the United States and England who, while never denying the rule of colonialism, nevertheless overlooked Japan's responsibility even while the afore-said of Japan to incorporating her into the cold war system. Accordingly, North and South Koreas were excluded from the agenda of San Francisco Peace Treaty and Japan's compensation issues were deferred.

2-2. SURVIVING COLONIALISM AND THE LONG DIVISION OF THE KOREAN PENINSULA

Colonialism and long division are a serious threat to building a peaceful East Asia community through regional collaboration and historical reconciliation. Furthermore, unsettled problems of colonialism and the continued division of Korea slowed down the development of democracy in East Asian countries and caused serious internal conflicts in terms of establishing of ethnic spirit.

2-3. New Liberalism

At the same time Korea-China-Japan indiscriminately accepted new liberalism, which is different from Asia's universal cultural norms and values, while also promoting competition and English as the absolute good; this caused the polarization of life qualities, worsening the impoverished conditions of the poor. From now on, the three nations should try to make contributions to Asia and the international society by resolving historical conflicts caused by colonialism and reestablishing the universal norms of East Asia from an ethnical perspective. In addition, the three countries should respect human dignity and rights and define the universal norms and values of East Asia that will enhance the international social responsibilities of private companies.

3. TOTAL ELIMINATION OF COLONIALISM IN COMPLIANCE WITH THE UN DURBAN DECLARATION IN 2001 AND INTERNATIONAL PRACTICES

Our demand to get rid of colonialism is not out-of-date. Indeed, this demand complies with the demands of the UN and the international society. On August 23 2010, at an international academic conference hosted by the Northeast Asian History Foundation, Mushakoji Kinhide, director of the Asia Pacific Research Center of Osaka University of Economics and Law) suggested that colonial crimes should be viewed from the perspective of *lex ferenda*, meaning "future law" used in the sense of "what the law should be."[8]

First, the Durban Declaration--adopted in South Africa in 2001 at the "World Conference against Racism" held by the United Nations--clearly stated that getting rid of colonialism is a historical task. During the months of August and September, 2001, the United Nations organized the "World Conference against Racism, Racial Discrimination, Xenophobia and Related Intolerance." The Durban Declaration adopted at this conference claims for the first time that slavery and the slave-trading system is a crime against humanity. Also, it was confirmed that colonialism should be criticized and that a recurrence of this crime should be prevented. Furthermore, the United Nations declared that it is a historical task to eliminate the slavery and colonial control that has haunted the people in Africa and Asia for the last centuries and announced specific plans to take action. This revolutionary announcement applies not only to countries in Europe and America but also to all past colonial countries including Japan.

Second, there was a case in which France asked for additional compensation for forced draftees even if there had been a complete settlement of all the claims during the composite dialogue between Germany and France in 1960. In response, Germany created Donation Agreement for Better Mutual Understanding between Germany & French[9] in March, 1981, and promised to make a contribution in the amount of 250 million German Mark (DM). The partial change was made to the original settlement, but an equivalent political agreement was made.

Third, Libya which had suffered from Italian colonial rule between 1911 and 1943 received an official apology from the Italian government, a promise to return national treasures looted during the colonial period, and reparation in the amount of 5 billion US dollars in investment money on August 30, 2009; the two countries finally signed a friendship treaty, ending their agonizing colonial history.[10]

4. MEASURES TO BUILD A PEACEFUL EAST ASIAN COMMUNITY

At present, the Japanese government tries to justify its history of colonial occupation and the Chinese government tries to distort ancient history. What actions should be taken to resolve this situation? First of all, who should lead the way to end colonialism and the division of the Korean Peninsula?[11] The early settlement of colonial issues is a critical matter for East Asian countries; once they pass this step, they can recover and establish rightful cultural and historical identities so that they can build a peaceful East Asian community in the 21st century. However, we should never leave this matter in the hands of East Asian sovereign states seeking national interests. Non-governmental organizations (NGO) that love peace and justice beyond selfish national interests must take the initiative in this matter. Therefore, the role of NGOs such as Asian NGO Peace–Network (hereafter 'ANPN') as a "Non-State Actor" with initiative and drive is necessary to bring about historical reconciliation and regional peace.

Second, in what way should this problem be handled? It should be pointed out that East Asian countries have numerous cultural and historical heritages. Therefore, the first step to build a peaceful East Asia is to establish "universal norms and values" based on the culture and history of East Asia. Instead of taking various nationalistic views, we should take an East Asian point of view based on universal culture and history. By establishing universal norms and values, East Asia should play a central role in making an East Asian peace community. Non-state actors should initiate the measures and encourage member countries to accept them through persuasion and pressure.

Third, what are the difficulties? Who will take on the role of leadership? Who takes the initiative is a critical matter in establishing the universal rules and values of East Asia community. As is well known, East Asia has a heterogeneous nature in terms of culture, economic status and geography. Korea-China-Japan, however, are close to each other geographically, culturally and economically; the three countries should start with regional collaborations and gradually expand to the ten ASEAN countries. Among the three countries, Korea has never been a threat to the other two. Therefore, Korea is the most suitable candidate to be a mediator. East Asia has not been able to recover its unique historical and cultural identities both spiritually and culturally. Now we should take a leap forward in establishing historical and cultural identities and set up the universal rules and values of East Asia rather than simply seek economic prosperity.

Fourth, we must study and learn from the experiences of many European countries on how to overcome historical and ethnic conflicts.[12] There was a very strong movement among European countries to institutionalize hope for the peace and prosperity of Europe through historical reconciliations among themselves. The first attempt was made in May 1949 by creating the Council of Europe with ten member states.[13] Now, the member states have grown to 47. European countries founded the Council of Europe (May 5, 1949) and established the European Court of Human and Rights as a separate entity from the council based on the European Convention on Human Rights (November 1950)[14] and the Commissioner for Human Rights that makes suggestions on the human rights report. The Council of Europe's most famous achievement is the European Convention on Human Rights, which was adopted in 1950 following a report by the Council of Europe's Parliamentary Assembly, and followed on from the United Nations 'Universal Declaration of Human Rights' (UDHR). The Convention created the European Court of Human Rights in Strasbourg.

Also, European countries intentionally adopted the European Social Charters in 1961 at the Council of Europe in order to protect economic, social and cultural rights that were not included in the European Convention on Human Rights. The European Committee of Social Rights was also established to monitor the implementation of the European Social Charter.

Also, the Helsinki final act[15] of the Conference on Security and Cooperation in Europe (CSCE), established in 1975, has made a contribution to regional collaboration and regional integration both directly and indirectly, especially CSCE played a crtical role in German unification process.[16] It is noteworthy that non-state actors actively stirred up the public opinion for regional collaboration and took on a role in founding the Council of Europe and CSCE.

5. TASKS FOR ADOPTING 'THE CIVIL SOCIETY CHARTER' TOWARDS PEACE AND HUMAN RIGHTS IN EAST ASIA FOR OVERCOMING THE SAN FRANCISCO PEACE TREATY SYSTEM

What are the details of universal norms and values[17] for adopting the Asian Social Charter at the NGOs level? What should be the foundations of the East Asian peace community and what should be included in specific action plans? The pursuing values of East Asia such as peace, prosperity, and human rights should go beyond the nationalistic perspective and acquire a new identity from an East Asian perspective.

The Asian Social Charter at the NGOs level should be based on the universal norms and value in East Asia as follows:
1) Universal norms must include Common peace, prosperity and human rights in East Asia based on the international law
2) Universal values must embrace cultural identity of East Asia and civil value of East Asia
3) Principles of action should include complete elimination of colonialism, resolution of historical conflicts, international social responsibilities of the private sector (observance of ISO 26,000)[18]
4) 'The Civil Society Charter' based on the aforementioned three principles should be adopted at "East Asia NGOs Conference on Peace and Human Right."

5) Specific task are suggested as follows:
   (a) Publication of a common East Asian history textbook
   (b) Publication of a survey on the historical conflicts in East Asia
   (c) Exchange and cooperation project to enhance cultural understanding
   (d) Establishment of the East Asia Peace Education Center
   (e) Establishment of East Asia University
   (f) Development of East Asian history reconciliation index and peace index

6) Initiative Organization: Asian NGO Peace Network as a "Non-State Actors"(ANPN).
   (a) Members: NGOs from "ASEAN+ 3"
   (b) Utilization of the human resource network of those who participate in the "International NGOs Conference on History and Peace"[19]
   (c) Cooperation with the UNESCO Asia Pacific members

7) Road Map : Three steps for creating the Council of Asia
   (a) First step: ANPN (NGOs: Universal Norms & Values/Steering Committee)
   (b) Second step: Adopting the Civil Society Charter at "East Asia NGOs Conference on Peace, Prosperity and Human Right."
   (c) Third step: Development for Council of Asia at the GO level. The Council of Asia member states maintain their full sovereignty but commit themselves through the Asian Social Charter and cooperate on the basis of common values and common political decisions.

8) Final Objective can be summarized as follow:
   (a) Institutionalization of universal rules and values of East Asia and principles of action by adopting the Asian Social Charter in "East Asia NGOs Conference on Peace, Prosperity and Human Right."
   (b) Declaration of East Asian version of Durban Declaration
   (c) Establishment of a permanent acting organization and campaign for establishing the Council of Asia at the NGOs level.

6. CLOSING REMARKS

East Asia, which was once devastated by colonialism and imperialism, has now become economically prosperous. The rich East Asian countries must develop the correct historical and philosophical perspective based on East Asian values in order to make continuous contributions to peace, prosperity and human rights in both Asia and the broader international society. If East Asian countries show uncritical obeisance to the new liberalism chasing after competitiveness, English, and material prosperity, economic prosperity will act as a big hindrance in the development of East Asia. To build a long-standing, peaceful East Asia, we must start by establishing universal norms and values based on Asian cultural identity. This task will never be realized if we rely solely on the selfishness of our own national interests. In this time of global society where the cultural heritage of a nation is being protected and preserved as the world's cultural heritage, people need to change their self-centered view of history. We must learn lessons from European experience.[20]

In this regard, The "Asian NGO Peace-Network(ANPN)," as a non-state actor aspiring towards peace, prosperity, and human rights beyond national boundaries, should come forward with an action program and a road map. The Asian NGO Peace-Network must put pressure on governments and organize regional collaboration campaigns in order to establish and institutionalize our hope for the peace, prosperity and human rights of East Asians. As a result, the Council of Asia, the Asian Court of Human Rights at the Go level and the Asian Social Charter on the NGOs level will gradually be institutionalized. We must make an Asian version of the Durban Declaration among the ASEAN+3 countries, and the Asian NGO Peace-Network must take an initiative in this process. Another option is to organize the Regional Operation Committee by networking with all of the professional participants of the many gatherings of the International NGOs Conference on History and Peace. ANPN should devise a multilateral peace mechanism within the Conference on Peace and Human Right in East Asia which could coincide with individual peace interests of the participating states.

Notes

1. This article is a modified version of my paper on "Tasks for Establishing Universal Norms & Value towards Peaceful Community Building in East Asia,"presented at 2017 International NGOs Conference on History and Peace, Specialists Round Table 1, July 12-15, 2017, Korea University, Seoul, Materials Book, pp. 178-185.

2. Jose E. Alvarez, International Organization as Law-makers, Oxford University Press (2006), pp. 116-117.

3. "Japanese exam asks about 'unlawful occupation' of Dokdo," The Korea Times, June 20, 2016.

4. "Abe reject apology letter for comfort women victims," The Korea Times, October 16, 2016.

5. "THAAD talks will begin this week," The Korea Times, February 21, 2016.

6. "U.N. : Korean War armistice still in force," The Korea Times, March 25, 2016.

7. "N. Korea's next step is to conduct 6th nuclear Test," The Korea Times, July 8, 2017.

8. Kinhide Mushakoji, "The Illegality and the Historial Lesson of the Japanese 'Annexion' of Korea," International Conference on Reexamining the Legal Validity of Japan's Annexation of Korea from the Prospective of International Law organized by Northeast Asian History Foundation (June 22, 2009), Materials Book, pp. 35-36.

9. This explanation may be inconsistent with the original version.

10. Jang-Hie Lee, "A Review of the Italy-Lybia Colonial Reparation in the Perspective of International Law," International Conference on Reexamination of the System of the Korea-Japan Treaty in 1965 and the Responsibility of Colonial Rule, North East History Foundation (June 22, 2012), Materials Book, pp. 61-98.

11. The proper way to overcome the division of Korea is to let Koreans be main agents of the process with support from neighboring countries.

12. Dennis Sammut, "European expression in attaining human rights, civic values, and universal norms," 2011 International NGOs Conference on History and Peace, Specialists Round Table 1(August 18-22, 2011, Younsei Univ. Seoul), Materials Book, pp. 161-162.

13. The Treaty of London or the Statute of the Council of Europe was signed in London on that day by ten states: Belgium, Denmark, France, Ireland, Italy, Luxembourg, the Netherlands, Norway, Sweden and the United Kingdom. Many other states followed, especially after the democratic transitions in central and eastern Europe during the early 1990s, and the Council of Europe now includes all European states except Belarus, Vatican City and European territories with limited recognition such as Artsakh, Abkhazia, South Ossetia, Northern Cyprus, Transnistria, and Kosovo.

14. The Court supervises compliance with the European Convention on Human Rights

and thus functions as the highest European court. It is to this court that Europeans can bring cases if they believe that a member country has violated their fundamental rights and freedoms.

15. CSCE has been changed to OSCE (Organization for Security and Cooperation in Europe). Please refer to OSCE Handbook, third edition, June 2000.

16. Theodor Schweisfurth, "Einfuehring," KSZE, Dokumente der KSZE, Beck-Texte im dtv, pp. XI-LXIV.

17. Ki-Joon Hong, "Two Track Approaches to Common Norm Building in North east Asia," 2013 International NGOs Conference on History and Peace, Specialists & NGOs workshop (July 22th-25nd, 2011, Kyung Hee Univ. Seoul), Materials Book, pp. 294-298.

18. Martin Neureiter, "ISO 26000-the future global Standard on Social Responsibility," International Conference, Convergence of Corporate Governance & Social Responsibility (January 28, 2011), hosted by Institute for Legal Studies, Sogang University Law School, Material Book, pp. 12-22.

19. Example: The 2016 International NGO Conference on History Education for Peace in East Asia and Europe (6-10 July 2016, The Hague, Leiden, Utrecht, Amsterdam, The Netherlands) co-organized by History NGO Forum for Peace in East Asia and European Association of History Education.

20. Inga Niehaus, "Overcoming Exclusive Nationalism and Historic Understanding beyond National Borders through Textbook Revision," 2010 Coordinating Committee Meeting for the International NGOs Conference on History and Peace, The Role of Global Civil Society towards Historical Reconciliation in East Asia, International Symposium, October 3, 2010, North York Civic Centre, Proceedings, pp. 75-76.

The Approaches of the Highest Courts in the Republic of Korea and Japan towards the Meaning of the Framework of the San Francisco Peace Treaty with Japan of 1951

KANG Pyoung-Keun
Professor
Korea University, School of Law, Seoul, Korea

Key Words

Peace treaty, League of Nations, War of Aggression, Sex-slavery Victims, War Reparations

1. INTRODUCTION

A war is important under international law. Territories and governments were changed, and many new states were created after the war. After the World War I, the concept of war and practices relating thereto has been changed. There are many instances where a war is terminated without any peace treaties. A peace treaty is an international instrument to terminate hostilities between belligerents and to declare a permanent peace between them, and also to construct international society politically and legally.

Under the Covenant of the League of Nations, member states did not have right to resort to war. A peaceful solution was sought after while war activities were suspended for 9 months under the Covenant. States were committed to renouncing war as their national policies under the Paris

Pact of 1928. Under international law developed after the World War II, war is illegal. State can only use military force for self-defense or through the UN authorized resolutions. Individuals planning and prosecuting war were punished as international criminals after the World War II.

For a long time, belligerent states were treated as equals with victorious states even when they were defeated in war. The terms and conditions of a peace treaty were negotiated between them. When a belligerent state surrendered unconditionally, all or part of her territories were taken by a victorious state which was able to dictate the terms of a peace treaty to that effect. After the World War I, however, conquering activities were disdained. In 1931, U.S. State Secretary Stimson criticized the Japanese conquest of Manchuria as invalidating international law.

After the World War II, Axis states were criminalized for their wars of aggression. They were treated differently from belligerents in other wars. They were forced to surrender without condition as aggressors and their leaders were punished as committing crimes against war and peace under the customary laws of war and the Paris Pact.

Peace treaties with Axis states were not made on the basis of negotiations between the belligerent powers, but the Allied and Associated Powers declared unilaterally the termination of war with them. No peace treaty was made with Germany. As for Japan, the situation was different. Even though Japan surrendered unconditionally, Japan was able to negotiate terms and conditions with the U.S. and the Great Britain representing 48 Allied Powers declaring war against Japan.

2. THE BACKGROUND OF THE SAN FRANCISCO PEACE TREATY

At the Cairo Conference in November, 1943, the leaders of the U.S., U.K., and China made it clear that the reason for them to fight war was to restrain and punish the aggression of Japan. They were determined to strip

Japan of all the islands in the Pacific occupied by Japan since 1914 and all the territories stolen by Japan from the Chinese including Manchuria, Formosa, and the Pescadores should be restored to the Republic of China. Japan was to be expelled from all other territories taken by violence and greed. The three Allied Powers determined that Korean people being enslaved should be free and independent in due course.

At the Potsdam Conference in July, 1945, the three leaders called upon Japan to surrender unconditionally and declared that Japanese sovereignty should be limited to the 4 main islands and such minor islands to be determined later. The San Francisco Peace Treaty with Japan was signed on 8 September 1951 in San Francisco between Japan and 48 Allied Powers. Neither the Republic of China (ROC) nor the People's Republic of China (PRC) was invited to the San Francisco Peace Conference, and neither were parties to the Peace Treaty with Japan. The Republic of Korea (ROK) was not invited to the Conference and she did not sign the Peace Treaty with Japan, either. Japan and ROC made a peace treaty between them on 28 April 1952 when the Peace Treaty with Japan took into effect.

3. JUDGEMENTS BY THE SUPREME COURT OF JAPAN

In 2007, the Supreme Court of Japan delivered its judgment in light of damage claims made by workers and sex-slavery victims with the nationality of PRC to the effect that PRC, even though not a signatory, was subjected to the San Francisco Peace Treaty with Japan.[1] The Court proclaimed on the basis of the so-called "Framework of the San Francisco Peace Treaty" that individuals were not able to raise claims arising out of war activities before the Courts in Japan. According to the Framework, Japan was obligated to provide restitutions with Allied Powers under the condition that all the claims in light of activities during the war were mutually renounced; that Allied Powers were empowered to dispose all the properties of Japan and her subjects in their own territories; and that war restitutions including service reparations should be made through special arrangements between Japan and each Allied Powers.

Due to the importance of the San Francisco Peace Treaty between Japan and 48 Allied Powers with regard to the post-war reparations, the Treaty was determined to be applicable to the states who did not participate in the San Francisco Peace Conference. The Court decided that, without the Framework, diverse claims arising out of war activities would be raised in forms of civil actions before the Courts in various levels, and that it would be impossible to achieve the purposes of the San Francisco Peace Treaty to terminate war situations between Japan and the 48 Allied Powers and to make friendship for the future.

Under the Framework, the waiver of the contracting parties to the Treaty meant to avoid the situations where individuals made claims in civil cases before the Courts. It was determined that individual claims were not extinguished but devoid of being dealt with in civil court actions. Therefore, although the claims were not able to be disputed in civil actions before the Courts, the obligors were able to perform voluntarily to satisfy the claims alleged by the victims in accordance to the forms and conditions of each individual and particular claims. The Court opined that each state was able to dispose individual claims of their own subjects by concluding peace treaties to terminate wars. Japan agreed to waive the right to raise claims including individual claims mutually by making bilateral agreements on war reparations or for waiver of claims. Peace agreements or reparation agreements on bilateral terms between Japan and other states or other regions who did not participate into making the San Francisco Peace Treaty also had the effect of making claims including individual claims being renounced mutually.[2]

The Supreme Court of Japan noted that even though Article 2 of the Agreement of 1967 between Japan and Malaysia provided in abstract way for 'complete and ultimate settlement,'[3] the Contracting Parties waived effectively all the claims arising out of war activities including individual claims in accordance with the Framework. The Court based itself upon the concept of the Framework of the post-war settlement which was applicable to the states whether or not parties to the San Francisco Peace Treaty. The Court opined that the San Francisco Peace Treaty had provisions for the third parties, and that, by exercising their own personal jurisdiction over their nationals in concluding a peace treaty to terminate war situations, the Parties to the San Francisco Peace Treaty were able to waive the right to initiate claims based on claims of individual nationals before national courts. The Court deemed that all the damage claims made by the victims of forced labor and sexual slavery were arising either out of war situations and prosecution of war. The Court decided that since any peace treaties should terminate war situations, they entail provisions for the waiver of the right to initiate claims before national courts. It was decided that any agreement would have the same effect of having such right waived even though it did not incorporate provisions from the San Francisco Peace Treaty.

Under the Framework, Japan was obliged to make a special arrangement with the States who had alleged to be victimized because of war with Japan. Due to such arrangement made under the Framework, individuals were not able to initiate civil actions based on their alleged claims before the national courts of the States to the arrangement. Due to the framework under which the Japan-Malaysia Agreement of 1967 was concluded, individual nationals lost their rights to initiate claims before the courts of each contracting parties to the Agreement although it was not clear about the meanings of the 'complete and ultimate settlement' in Article 2 of the Japan-Malaysia Agreement of 1967.

According to the thrust of the judgments by the Supreme Court of Japan, the Framework of the San Francisco Peace Treaty is applicable to the nationals of the PRC or ROC, and to the nationals of the Two Koreas. The judgments of 2007 by the Japanese Court closed firmly the door to the victims of forced labor and sexual slavery during the war activities by Japan to seek judicial remedies from the Japanese courts.

4. JUDGMENTS BY THE COURTS IN KOREA

In a case challenging against the act of omission by the Korean Government involving Article 3 of Agreement on the Settlement of Problem concerning Property and Claims and the Economic Cooperation between the Republic of Korea and Japan on 22 June 1965 (hereinafter "the Agreement of 1965"), the Constitutional Court of Korea quoted the decision of 26 August 2005 by the Joint Government- Private Committee co-chaired by the then Prime Minister and to which the respondent is a member representing the government as saying that the Agreement of 1965 was signed with the purpose of resolving the financial, civil debtor/creditor relationship between Korea and Japan based on Article 4 of the San Francisco Peace Treaty and that the Japanese government has legal liability for 'illegal acts against humanity' involving state power such as the problem of 'comfort women,' who were forced into sexual slavery by the Japanese military during World War II, which are not considered to have been resolved under the Agreement of 1965.

The Constitutional Court decided that the provisions of the Agreement of 1965 are spelt out in general and abstract terms, and that it is not clear whether or not Japan's compensation for comfort women victims falls under the claims mentioned in the Agreement of 1965. It was confirmed that the difference in positions between the two countries has led to a 'dispute' over interpretation and implementation of the Agreement of 1965 on the legal relationship of the complaining comfort women victims.

In the same vein, the Supreme Court of Korea decided in a case involving forced laborers against Japanese companies that the Agreement of 1965 was not negotiated for Japanese compensation for colonial control but for 'the purpose of resolving the financial, civil debtor/creditor relationship between Korea and Japan based on Article 4 of the San Francisco Peace Treaty.'

As to the very similar facts involving forced laborers and sexual slaves, the Courts of Japan and Korea took very different approaches from each other. The Supreme Court of Japan decided with confidence that all the questions were settled completely and ultimately, even under the abstract terms of Article 2 of the Japan-Malaysia Agreement of 1967. The settlement of all the claims meant that those claims were unable to be raised in civil actions before the courts in Japan.

To the contrary, the Supreme Court of Korea decided that even though States may have the claims of their nationals settled by concluding treaties, the Agreement of 1965 cannot be interpreted to have the effect of extinguishing claims concerned in addition to the waiver of the right to protect their nationals unless there were clear terms to that effect. While the Supreme Court of Japan decided that it was not necessary to legislate for another domestic measures to implement the loss of the right to initiate civil actions for judicial remedies, the Supreme Court of Korea decided that it was necessary to make legislations of having the effect of extinguishing claims as Japan had enacted an act to dispose properties of Koreans in Japan.

The Supreme Court of Japan misinterpreted the provisions of Article 21 of the San Francisco Peace Treaty under which Article 14(a)2 does not apply to Korea but to China. Therefore, the Framework of mutual waiver between Contracting Parties based on Article 14(a)2 may not be applicable to Korea since Korea was not able to dispose overseas properties of Japan or the nationals of Japan. As for those properties situated below 38th Parallel of the Korean Peninsula, it was the U.S. Military Government who disposed them, and it was Japan who recognized the validity of dispositions of property of Japan and Japanese nationals by the U.S. Military Government in Korea.

5. CONCLUSION

The Courts in Korea and Japan dealt with the cases involving victims of forced labor and sexual slavery which are very similar in factual terms.

Nevertheless, the logical results reached by them were far away from each other. The Supreme Court of Japan interpreted very broadly the relevant provisions of the San Francisco Peace Treaty by inventing the terms of art of 'The Framework of the San Francisco Peace Treaty.' The Framework was heavily relied upon by the Supreme Court of Japan to deter victims of forced labor and sexual slavery from initiating damage claims before the courts in Japan. It applies to the nationals of the third parties to the San Francisco Peace Treaty including China and Korea with the effect of precluding any claims being initiated based upon the prosecution of war by Japan.

The Constitutional Court and the Supreme Court of Korea made it clear that individual claims may not be extinguished unless the relevant treaties have provided for such effects clearly and concretely. Contrary to the Supreme Court of Japan, the counterparts of Korea decided that the loss of the right to initiate claims before the courts should be based on domestic legislation. The Supreme Court of Japan used the concept of the Framework to achieve general effects of having individual rights to claim damages being lost before the Courts in Japan. Its attitudes are quite different from those of the Government of Japan, because the latter tenaciously oppose the idea of the existence of any war situations between Korea and Japan. It is one of the many occasions where Japan looks Janus-faced in particular with regard to the matter of post-bellum justice.

Notes

1. Nishimatsu Construction Co. v. Song Jixiao et.al., 2004(Ju) 1658, Minshu Vol. 61, No. 3, Supreme Court of Japan (2nd Petty Bench), 27 April 2007. Available at http://www.courts.go.jp/app/hanrei_en/detail?id=893, (last visited on 30 March 2018) (English translation); Ko Hanako et.al., v. Japan, Supreme Court of Japan (1st Petty Bench), 27 April 2007. Available at http://www.courts.go.jp/app/files/hanrei_jp/591/034591_hanrei.pdf, last visited on 30 March 2018 (in Japanese).

2. Among the various peace treaties involving Japan, the Treaty of Peace between the Governments of India and Japan provides as follows : "Article VI (a) India waives all reparations claims against Japan. (b) Except as otherwise provided in this Treaty, India waives all claims of India and Indian nationals arising out of action taken by Japan and its nationals in the course of the prosecution of the war as also claims of India arising from the fact that it participated in the occupation of Japan."

3. The Article 2 of the Japan-Malaysia Agreement provides that "The government of Malaysia agrees that all problems arising from the unfortunate incidents that occurred during World War II, which might affect a good relationship between Japan and Malaysia, have been hereby settled completely and ultimately."

Assessment of Korea's 3-Year Pilot Refugee Resettlement Program (2015~2017)

LEE Seryon
Professor
Chonbuk National University, School of Law, Jeonju, Korea

Key Words

UNHCR, Resettlement, Refugee, Korea's Refugee Act, Sharing Responsibility

1. INTRODUCTION*

The 1951 Convention relating to the Status of Refugees (hereinafter, "Refugee Convention"), supplemented by its 1967 Protocol, is indisputably the cornerstone of the international system on refugee protection.[1] Although the Refugee Convention has contributed to a theoretical framework for the protection of refugees at the international level,[2] it does not fit easily with some of the current refugee crisis particularly involving persons in armed conflicts.[3] It was commonly understood among international lawyers that war-related refugees would not have a right to protection within the frame of Refugee Convention as civilians in areas of war and civil war were generally subject to inhumane treatment, rather than maltreatment.[4]

However, UNHCR broadens the definition of a refugee in the Refugee Convention[5] based on UNHCR's Statute by extending the protection to individuals who are outside their country of origin and unable or unwilling to return there owing to serious threats to life, physical integrity or freedom resulting from generalized violence or event seriously disturbing public order. The annual report released by UNHCR estimated that a total of 68.5 million people were forcibly displaced worldwide by persecution, conflict, violence or human rights violation at the end of 2017.[6] Out of 25.4 million refugees that are under the mandate of UNHCR and UNRWA, more than 4.2 million people are of concern to the Asia-Pacific Region.[7] The refugee population in Asia-Pacific region increased by 21% from 2016 largely due to the arrival of refugees from Myanmar in Bangladesh.[8] Resettlement under UNHCR auspices involves the selection and transfer of refugees from a State in which they have sought protection to a third state, which agrees to admit them as refugees and grant a permanent residence status.[9] In 2017, UNHCR projected that some 1.2 million refugees are in need of resettlement as a durable solution, which represents a substantial increase in number compared to five years ago (859,300), due mainly to the Syria crisis as well as protracted refugee situations in Africa. A total of 35 countries[10] accepted UNHCR's resettlement submissions in 2017. Yet, the total number of refugees who benefit from the resettlement program amounted to less than 1% of the total refugee population. With the increasing number of displaced populations worldwide, UNHCR has been calling on States to initiate or expand resettlement program.

2. KOREA'S RESPONSE : A 3-YEAR PILOT RESETTLEMENT PROGRAM

2-1. OVERVIEW OF THE PROGRAM

In response to the UNHCR's call for responsibility-sharing, the Republic of Korea (hereinafter, "Korea") launched a three-year pilot resettlement program (2015 - 2017) and resettled 86 Myanmar refugees from camps in Thailand. Korea is the only country in the Asian region that has an independent refugee law, covering a comprehensive range areas concerning protection of those persons.[11] In October 2014, the Korean government made a field visit to Thailand and assessed the feasibility of initiating such a program in the country. The Ministry of Justice organized the first consultation meeting of Working Group on Resettlement in January 2015, also participated in the Annual Tripartite Consultations on Resettlement organized by UNHCR in June 2015, an annual gathering of resettlement countries, NGOs, and other affiliated groups.

On July 1, 2015, a Memorandum of Understanding was concluded between the Ministry of Justice of Korea and the Office of the UNHCR for the resettlement of refugees to the Republic of Korea. The agreement between the two parties set the institutional framework for cooperation and collaboration including, but not limited to, modalities of the selection process, departure arrangements, integration, protection of personal data.

Table 1. The accepted refugees through Korea's Resettlement Program

Year	2015	2016	2017	Total
No. of Families	4	7	5	16
No. of Adults	9	17	11	37
No. of Children	13	17	19	49
Total No. of Persons	22	34	30	86
Ethnicity	Karen	Karen	Karen/ Rohingya	

Of the many factors that triggered the Korean government's decision to initiate a refugee resettlement program, the following two factors were pointed out by UNHCR:[12] the first possible reason was Korea's increased engagement in humanitarian affairs over the recent years as Korea's annual financial contribution towards UNHCR was quadrupled from 2012 to 2016. In 2017, the Korean government's contribution alone reached more than 21 million USD and Korea became a member of so called '20 million club' of major donors to UNHCR.

Table 2. Contribution to UNHCR in 2017[13]

	Donor	Contributions (USD)
1	United States of America	1,450,360,238
2	Germany	476,918,668
3	EU	436,036,986
4	Japan	152,359,773
5	United Kingdom	136,219,370
6	Sweden	111,958,945
7	Norway	98,941,956
8	Canada	81,879,293
9	Private donors in Spain	80,749,997
10	Netherlands	75,711,468
11	Denmark	58,370,565
12	Italy	51,417,322
13	France	39,733,899
14	Australia	39,715,089
15	Private Donors in U.S	39,463,883
16	Private Donors in the Republic of Korea	35,818,585
25	Republic of Korea	21,845,151

Second, Korea's resettlement program had a solid legal basis from its Refugee Act. Article 24 of the Refugee Act explicitly stipulates that the resettled refugees will be given refugee status upon arrival and will enjoy the various rights in accordance with Chapter IV of the Refuge Act, which includes same treatment for social security and other provisions as Korean nationals (Art.31), an entitlement to basic livelihood security (Art.31) and guarantee of education (Art.33), and Korean language education (Art.34). The details as to specific requirement and procedure for granting resettlement are set forth in the Enforcement Decree of the Refugee Act, which further provides that a recognized refugee's entitlement to education for social integration (Art.14) and vocational training (Art.15).[14]

2-2. SELECTION PROCESS

It takes approximately four months from the initial request by Ministry of Justice of Korea to UNHCR to official admittance and arrival of resettled refugees in Korea. The Ministry of Justice conducts document review and interviews in refugee camps in Thailand, followed by medical examination by International Organization for Migration. Once the final decision is notified to UNHCR, a pre-departure orientation is prepared for the selected refugees. Although UNHCR's selection criteria for resettlement formed the basis for Korea's selecting candidates for resettled refugees, Korean government paid particular attention to other elements such as integration possibilities in Korean society and showed its preference for admitting families. Drawing attention to Korea's selection criteria based on likeliness of adaptation, UNHCR recommended that Korean government give priorities in selecting resettled refugees to legal or physical protection needs and specific vulnerabilities related to age, gender and medical or physical conditions such as survivors of violence and/or torture, women and girls at risk and children.[15]

2-3. SUPPORT FOR SETTLEMENT AND EVALUATION OF THE PROGRAM

Upon arrival in Korea, the resettled refugees stayed at the Immigration Reception Center (IRC), which was established in 2014 to accommodate asylum-seekers and resettled refugees. In principle, resettled refuges are required to spend for six months to gain a basic grounding to adjust to their new environment. As a part of social integration program at the IRC, the resettled refugees underwent an intensive Korean language program along with various courses to adapt to a daily life in Korea. The language lessons are particularly important for the recognized refugees as the language proficiency is one of the requirements for naturalization in Korea. The support by the Korean government during their stay at the IRC included music or food therapy, which could be useful in the treatment of traumatized refugees as well as financial allowance on a monthly basis to each household. After the resettled refugees left the IRC, the Incheon Immigration Office (IIC) took over the responsibilities to oversee the social integration process. The IIC facilitated the network of local groups to employment possibilities and developed a pool of mentors to help the refugees to build a life in Korea. The mandate by mentors included an assistance with the challenges the refugees might encounter in day-to-day life.

Although there is still room for much improvement, Korea's 3-year trial of resettlement program seems to be a successful endeavor. The Korean government efficiently utilized the existing social integration programs and networks with a number of civil societies for multicultural communities. Given the relatively low levels of public awareness on Korea's refugee resettlement project nationwide, the Korean government needs to create a positive environment by explaining the benefits for both resettled refugees and the receiving society in general as well as Korea's commitment in international community.

3. LOOKING FORWARD

UNHCR identified key principles in conducting resettlement as responsibility of States and the principle of non-refoulment. As the New York Declaration for Refugees and Migrants expressed the political will of world leaders to protect rights and share responsibility on a global scale, the protection of refugees in on the verge of becoming a collective responsibility the international community. While the Refugee Convention itself does guarantee the rights of qualified refugees, it is not quite clear on the substances of the rights of 'unconventional' refugees who might still be in need of protection due to humanitarian reasons. The common concern with refugee issues would be how to efficiently incorporate both the drive for protection and the value of deterrence for security reasons.

Korea has rather recently embarked on this so-called responsibility-sharing journey by taking a number of active steps such as enacting Refugee Law and launching a resettlement program with the collaboration of UNHCR. Moreover, the Korean government has recently decided to extend its resettlement project for the next two years to admit 120 individuals at the maximum. With these initiatives, Korea could be an epitome of refugee protection in Asia by shedding some light on the path towards realizing responsibility-sharing in times of humanitarian crisis.

Notes

* Some part of this paper was presented at the Academic Workshop held on April 22, 2018 at Islamic University of Indonesia (UII), Yogyakarta, Indonesia.

1. The Convention Relating to the Status of Refugee, July 28, 1951, 189 U.N.T.S 137 (entered into force on April 22, 1954); Protocol Relating to the Status of Refugees, Jan. 31, 1967, 19 U.N.T.S 267, entered into forced Oct. 4, 1967. However, James C. Hathaway asserts that the two foundational treaties of the international human rights system--the ICCPR and ICESCR—also applies to the refugee entitlements, *The Rights of Refugees Under International Law* (Cambridge University Press, 2005), p. 8.

2. Guy S. Goodwin-Gill and Jane McAdam, *The Refugee in International Law* (Oxford University 2007), p. 9. However, the authors further note that whether the influence of the Convention is actually or potentially positive for refugees deserves further inquiry.

3. In fact, the Refugee Convention was negotiated in the aftermath of World War II initially to deal with the European problem of 1.25 million refugees arising out of the post-war chaos. *Refugees, Asylum Seekers and the Rule of Law*, Edited by Susan Kneebone (Cambridge University Press, 2009), p. 5. James C. Simeon, *Critical Issues in International Refugee Law : Strategies towards interpretative harmony* (Cambridge University, 2010), p. 184. The original refugee regime itself also emerged only after the Peace of Westphalia as a way to deal with religious minorities. However, this agreement is foreshadowed in the Peace of Augsburg, in 1955. The latter treaty concluded a settlement under which the formula cuius regio, eius religio (whose the region, his the religion) allowed the rulers in Germany to determine whether their states would be wither Lutheran or Catholic. The Peace of Westphalia built upon this foundation by arguing for the right as jus emigrandi (the right to emigrate with one's personal property) as a universal right. It is in this very context that the term refugee emerged.

4. Paul Tiedemann, "The Ambivalence of Current Refugee Law Between Solidarity with "Friends" and Solidarity with "Human Beings"," *Journal of Human Rights Social Work*, Vol. 1, 2016, p. 179.

5. UNHCR Refugee Resettlement Handbook, p. 20. However, extended definitions are also contained in regional instruments in Africa and Latin America: The definition in Article 1 of the 1951 Convention is supplemented by regional instruments in Africa and Latin America: In Africa, Article I (2) of the 1969 OAU Convention governing specific aspects of refugee problems in Africa extends the refugee definition to: *"every person who, owing to external aggression, occupation, foreign domination or events seriously disturbing public order in either part or the whole of his country of*

origin or nationality, is compelled to leave his place of habitual residence in order to seek refuge in another place outside his country of origin or nationality"; In Latin America, Conclusion III of the 1984 Cartagena Declaration extends the refugee definition to: "*persons who have fled their country because their lives, safety or freedom have been threatened by generalised violence, foreign aggression, internal conflicts, massive violation of human rights or other circumstances which have seriously disturbed public order,*" available at https://emergency.unhcr.org/entry/114761/refugee-definition.

6. UNHCR Global Trends: Forced Displacement in 2016, p. 2. This number includes 22.5 million refugees including those under UNHCR mandate as well as those registered under UNRWA, 40.3 million internally displaced people and 2.8 million asylum-seekers. See also UNHCR Statistical Yearbook available at http://www.unhcr.org/figures-at-a-glance.html.

7. *Supra* note 6, p. 14. Table 1: Refugee population by UNHCR regions at the end of 2016.

8. *Ibid.* p. 13.

9. UNHCR Resettlement Handbook, Revised Version, 2001, p. 3.

10. As of December, 2017, the following countries currently offer resettlement / humanitarian admission: Argentina, Australia, Austria, Belgium, Brazil, Bulgaria, Canada, Chile, Croatia, Czech Republic, Denmark, Estonia, Finland, France, Germany, Hungary, Iceland, Italy, Ireland, Japan, Rep. of Korea, Latvia, Liechtenstein, Lithuania, Luxembourg, Monaco, Netherlands, New Zealand, Norway, Portugal, Romania, Slovenia, Spain, Sweden, Switzerland, United Kingdom, Uruguay, and the United States of America. http://www.unhcr.org/56fa35b16, p. 7.

11. Only the following five countries have signed or acceded to the 1951 Refugee Convention in Asia : Cambodia, China, Japan, Philippines, and the Republic of Korea. For a legislative history of Korea's Refugee Act, *See* Seryon Lee, *Korea's Refugee Act: Towards Fuller Implementation of the Refugee Convention,* Korean Yearbook of International Law, Vol. 2, 2015.

12. Review of the Pilot Resettlement Programme in the Republic of Korea, UNHCR, December 2017, p. 8

13. http://www.unhcr.org/5954c4257.pdf.

14. Article 24 (Acceptance of Refugees Seeking Resettlement) reads that: (1) The Minister of Justice may permit resettlement in the Republic of Korea of refugees seeking resettlement, after the Foreigners Policy Committee reviews the size of the group seeking resettlement, their regions of origin in accordance with Article 8 of the Basic Act on Treatment of Foreigners Residing in Korea. Permission for resettlement shall be deemed recognition of refugee status pursuant to Article 18(1).

15. *Supra* note 12, p. 18.

Cooperation between Courts in Cross-Border Insolvency Matters: Korean Practice

KIM Young-Seok
Judge
Seoul Bankruptcy Court, Seoul, Korea

Key Words

Cross-border Insolvency, Cooperation, JIN Guidelines, Judicial Network Insolvency, Seoul Bankruptcy Court

1. COOPERATION IN CROSS-BORDER INSOLVENCY MATTERS

1.1. INTRODUCTION

The number of Cross-Border insolvency cases has been growing very rapidly with a variety of issues, such as whether to repatriate proceeds of debtor's estate, how to treat foreign tax claims in terms of priority, and how to solve the conflicts between maritime lien and automatic stay. These issues might seem to be solved by enacting provisions of Private International Law on Insolvency like Article 7 through 18[1] of Regulation (EU) No. 2015/848 of the European Parliament and of the Council of 20th May, 2015 in Insolvency Proceeding (hereinafter the "the recast EIR"). In addition to that, for the group of companies cases, procedural consolidation, substantial consolidation and separate proceedings[2] have been discussing as effective or efficient alternatives to the current method.

However, these ways of enacting, combining of proceedings or establishing new procedures may have some limits because different principles of applicable laws[3] established by each country's unique precedents and diverse legal bases are not likely to resolve the problems perfectly, but rather to cause unhealthy forum shopping.

1.2. COOPERATION AS A USEFUL TOOL

Following this global trend, the Seoul Bankruptcy Court (hereinafter 'SBCourt')[4] drafted "Procedural Guideline No. 504 (Cooperation between Courts in Cross-Border Insolvency Matters)"(hereinafter "Guideline No. 504") based on Article 641 of the Debtor Rehabilitation and Bankruptcy Act (hereinafter "DRBA"), which is a Korean National Insolvency Law.[5] Actually, the SBCourt has already cooperated twice with the Federal Court of Australia and the U.S. Bankruptcy Court for the Eastern District of Virginia by using the Guideline No. 504 successfully.

2. LEGAL BASIS OF COOPERATION IN KOREA

2.1. ARTICLE 641 OF THE DRBA

The one and only rule stipulating about cooperation between courts in Cross-Border insolvency matters is the Article 641, in which we can find when we are allowed to cooperate with foreign court or foreign representative, on what specific issues we can discuss about, and how concrete means we can use to solve the hardships caused by Cross-Border issues.

The text of the Article 641 is as follows:

Debtor Rehabilitation and Bankruptcy Act

Article 641 (Cooperation)

(1) The court shall cooperate with any foreign court and foreign representative with respect to the matters falling under each of the following subparagraphs in order to ensure the smooth and fair execution of domestic insolvency procedures, foreign insolvency procedures or between multiple foreign insolvency procedures that are proceeding over the same debtor and other debtors related with the former:

1. The exchange of opinions;
2. The management and supervision of the debtor's business and properties;
3. The coordination of the progression of multiple procedures;
4. Other necessary matters.

(2) The court may exchange information and opinions directly with any foreign court or foreign representative in order for the cooperation referred to in the provisions of paragraph (1).

(3) Any administrator and any trustee in insolvency who are in charge of domestic insolvency procedures may exchange information and opinions with any foreign court or foreign representative under the court's supervision.

(4) Any administrator and any trustee in insolvency in charge of domestic insolvency procedures may reach an agreement with any foreign court or foreign representative on the coordination of insolvency procedures after obtaining permission therefor from the court.

2.2. PROCEDURAL GUIDELINE NO. 504 OF THE SBCOURT

Based on Article 641(1) of the DRBA, the SBCourt stipulated more specific regulations on how to cooperate and communicate with foreign court and foreign representative through establishing the Guideline No. 504 named "Cooperation between courts in Cross-Border matters." According to the Guideline No. 504, the SBCourt can cooperate by (ⅰ) sending or transmitting copies of formal orders, judgments, etc., (ⅱ) two-way communication using telephone, video conference call, or other electronic means, (ⅲ) other methods as may be agreed by the two courts.

The text of the Guideline No. 504 is as follows:

Cooperation between courts in Cross-Border matters

Article 1 (Purpose)

The procedural guideline No 504. provides the specific methods and procedures for cooperating with foreign court or foreign representative based on the Article 641 of the DRBA, aiming not only to protect the interests of creditors and other interested entities, including the debtors (hereinafter "interested entities") in the parallel proceedings, but also to manage the Cross-Border insolvency proceedings efficiently and effectively.

Article 2 (Cooperation with Foreign courts)

① The SBCourt can exchange its opinions (hereinafter "communication") with foreign court or foreign representative (hereinafter "foreign courts") for fair and smooth process in the parallel proceedings by using communication means.

② The SBCourt shall respond promptly when receiving requests for communication from foreign courts.

③ Communication can be carried out through the following method:

    1. Sending or transmitting copies of judgments, decisions, orders, other official documents, etc. to the foreign courts;

    2. Two-way communications with the foreign courts using telephone, video conference call, or other electronic means;

3. Other methods as may be agreed by the SBCourt and the foreign courts.

Article 3 (Two-way communication)

① Judges who are in charge of domestic insolvency proceedings related to debtors may participate in the two-way communication, and interested entities may also participate in the two-way communication if the SBCourt considers it necessary.

② The SBCourt may decide the time and place of the two-way communication in consultation with foreign courts, and allow personnel other than judges to contact the person in charge of the foreign courts.

③ The SBCourt may record two-way communication with foreign courts, and handle documents of recording the two-way communication (hereinafter "transcripts of recording") as official documents if the foreign courts agree.

④ The SBCourt may order to maintain of the confidentiality in terms of the two-way communication related records, or transcripts of recording if the court considers it appropriate.

Article 4 (Cooperation of administrators)

① The administrator or trustee of domestic insolvency proceedings (hereinafter "administrators") can communicate with foreign courts after getting an approval of the SBCourt.

② If the administrators are given any requests of communication from foreign courts, the administrators shall report it to the SBCourt without delay and apply for approval for the communication with the foreign courts.

③ The SBCourt may help the administrators to communicate with foreign courts smoothly when receiving requests from the administrators for the help.

④ The administrators shall report the contents of the communication to the SBCourt after finishing communication with foreign courts.

Article 5 (Concluding of procedural agreements)

① The administrators can conclude procedural agreements (hereinafter "protocol") on the adjustment of insolvency proceedings with foreign courts after getting an approval of the SBCourt.

② The protocol provides only procedural matters in principle, but substantive matters may be prescribed to the extent specifically permitted by applicable law.

③ Concluding a protocol does not imply or allow the following matters:

    1. Waiver by the SBCourt or administrators of any powers concerning domestic insolvency proceedings, or confer of any authority to the foreign courts;

    2. Exclusion of rules that must be followed by the administrators according to the applicable law applied to domestic insolvency proceedings;

    3. Prevention the SBCourt from refusing to take an action in domestic insolvency proceedings that would be manifestly contrary to the public policy of the Korea or which not sufficiently protect the interests of interested entities;

    4. Altering substantive rights of interested entities in domestic insolvency proceedings.

> **Article 6(Participation)**
>
> ① The SBCourt may authorize interested entities to appear before and be heard by a foreign court, subject to approval of the foreign court to such appearance.
>
> ② If permitted by its law and otherwise appropriate, the SBCourt may authorize interested entities of a foreign proceeding to appear before and be heard on a specific matter by the SBCourt, without thereby becoming subject to the SBCourt's jurisdiction for any purpose other than the specific matter on which the entities are appearing.

3. COOPERATION PRACTICE IN THE SBCOURT

3.1. PROCESS

The SBCourt nominated a Cross-Border Cooperation and Coordination Judge (hereinafter "CBCC Judge") considering the importance of cooperation with foreign court and foreign representative.[6] The CBCC Judge takes a role of arranging proceedings, not only requests from domestic insolvency practitioners but also requests from foreign court or foreign representative.

Cooperation and Coordination process can apply equally to situations where foreign courts recognize domestic insolvency proceedings as foreign proceedings and grant reliefs relating to the domestic proceedings (so called the "Outbound case") and vice versa (so called the "Inbound case").[7]

Procedures in terms of the two kinds of cooperation are as follows:

3.1.1. Request From Domestic Insolvency Practitioner

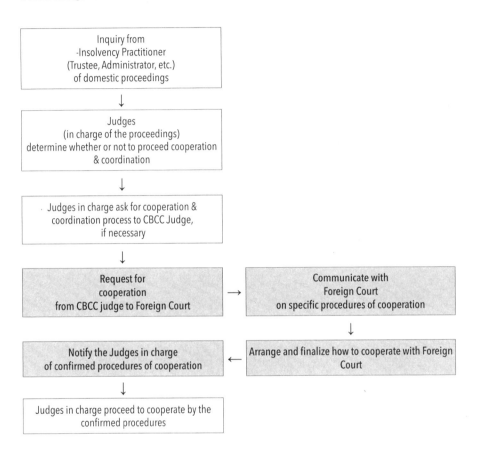

3.1.2. Request From Foreign Court of Foreign Representative

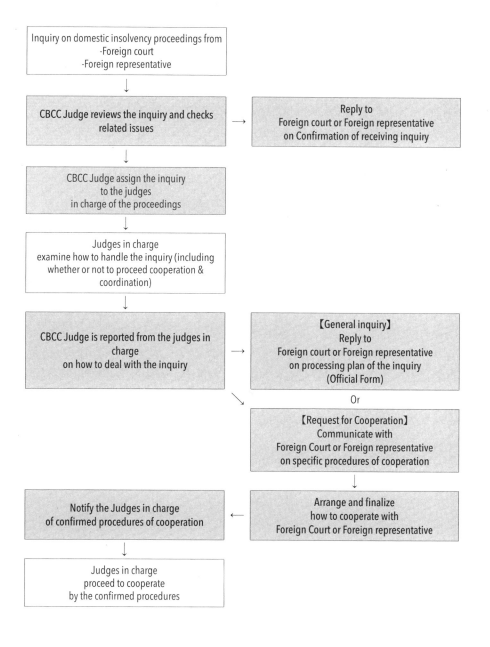

3.2. Cases

The SBCourt has undertaken two cooperation cases in terms of Cross-Border insolvency matters with foreign courts. The first one is with Federal Court of Australia (hereinafter "FCA"), and the second one is with U.S. Bankruptcy Court for the Eastern District of Virginia (hereinafter "EDVA").

3.2.1. FCA Case

The SBCourt received documents regarding the Hanjin Shipping Company (hereinafter "Hanjin") from the FCA on May 22th, 2017. It was a notification of contravention of the administrator of the Korean rehabilitation proceedings in terms of Hanjin based on "Cross-Border Insolvency Act 2008", Australian National Insolvency Law (hereinafter "Australian Law").

According to the Article 18 of Schedule 1, part 4 of the Australian Law,[8] which is same as the Article 18 of the UNCITRAL Model Law on Cross-Border Insolvency (hereinafter "Model Law"), the administrator should have informed the FCA promptly of the conversion of the Hanjin proceeding from a rehabilitation process into a bankruptcy process, which was caused by the comparison between going concern value and liquidation value.

As the CBCC judge, the author checked the documents, reviewed relating issues, and forwarded those documents to 21th Division of the SBCourt, the panel in charge, with some opinions on the occasion. The panel above decided to order the Trustee[9] of the bankruptcy proceeding of Hanjin to report the current situation and how to cope with the issues.

After being received the plan of submitting documents including Affidavit to the FCA directly by the Trustee on May 29th, 2017, the author sent the FCA an official letter of explaining the specific process which was undertaken in the SBCourt and the plan of the Trustee on June 1st, 2017.

3.2.2. EDVA Case

This case is the first cooperation case in terms of Inbound proceedings and also the first case that was initiated by the SBCourt's request, which has been recognized as a very meaningful cooperation case in Korea.

3.2.2.1. Case Brief

Raymond A. Yancey, a foreign representative of the foreign proceedings that was commenced in the EDVA with respect to the debtors who were once lived in Korea, applied for recognition of the foreign proceedings in the SBCourt on Mar. 7th, 2014. After reviewing the application, the SBCourt granted recognition of the Chapter 11 proceedings of the U.S. Bankruptcy Code, Case No. 10-18839-RGM as foreign proceedings based on Article 632 of the DRBA in the Case SBCourt 2014-KukSeung-1 on May 8th, 2014.

Meanwhile, Raymond A. Yancey, also applied for appointment of a "Cross-Border Insolvency Administrator"[10] who has the authority to perform the debtors' business and dispose of the debtors' estates located in Korea, in the SBCourt on Apr. 9th, 2014. After reviewing the application, the SBCourt granted a relief of appointing the Raymond A. Yancey as the Cross-Border Insolvency Administrator relating to a SBCourt 2014-KukSeung-1 based on Article 636(1) of the DRBA in the Case SBCourt 2014-KukJi-1 on May 26th, 2014.

During the pendency of the Chapter 11 proceedings in the EDVA, the Cross-Border Insolvency Administrator requested permission on repatriating the proceeds of the debtors' real estate in the Case SBCourt 2014-KukJi-1 on Oct. 26th, 2017, which is the issue of this cooperation with the EDVA.

3.2.2.2. Cooperation Process

The SBCourt requested cooperation to the EDVA based on the Article 641(1) of the DRBA and the Guideline No. 504 on Oct. 26th, 2017 explaining those national regulations and necessity to protect the interests of local creditors through cooperation. The EDVA accepted the SBCourt's request based on U.S. Bankruptcy Code 105(a)[11] with the "Order establishing protocol for communication with the Seoul Bankruptcy Court (South Korea)" on Oct. 30th, 2017.

After being given the order of protocol from the EDVA on Oct. 31st, 2017, the SBCourt asked a few questions[12] in terms of the Chapter 11 proceedings to confirm how well the Korean creditors have been protected and offered the same opportunity to participate in the U.S. proceedings, and exchanged a few issues with the EDVA from Nov. 8th, 2017 to Jan. 11th, 2018.

3.2.2.3. Conclusion

The SBCourt could find that the Korean creditors were given enough chance to participate in the proceedings in the EDVA and treated fairly during the pendency of the proceedings, and could not find any evidence that the repatriation of proceeds of real estate that was once owned by the debtors would be manifestly contrary to the public policy of the Korea through this cooperation.

Accordingly, the SBCourt decided to grant a relief of repatriating the proceeds of the real estate at issue to the Raymond A. Yancey, the Chapter 11 Trustee of the EDVA No. 10-18839-RGM, who is under the supervision of the EDVA on Jan. 18th, 2018.

Meanwhile, it was reported that the proceeds were transferred into the U.S. account of the Raymond A. Yancey as the Chapter 11 Trustee of the EDVA successfully from the Korean account of the Raymond A. Yancey as the Cross-Border Insolvency Administrator of the Korean proceeding on Feb. 13th, 2018.

4. DISCUSSION OF ADOPTING THE JIN GUIDELINES IN KOREA

4.1. THE JIN GUIDELINES

Regarding the cooperation process between courts, the Judicial Insolvency Network (hereinafter "JIN"), a network of insolvency judges from around the world, is now getting much attention from many countries or courts. This is because of the Guidelines for Communication and Cooperation between Courts in Cross-Border Insolvency Matters (hereinafter "JIN Guidelines") that the JIN established for the cooperation between courts. The JIN Guidelines consist of 14 guidelines as well as 6 introductions and 1 Annex (Joint Hearing) stipulating specific procedures and method of cooperation and fundamental principles.[13]

4.2. THE CURRENT STATUS OF THE JIN

The SBCourt established the Guideline No. 504 based on the JIN Guidelines, which is becoming a standard of cooperation among distinguished insolvency courts, including U.S. Bankruptcy Court (S.D.N.Y., Delaware and F.L.S.D.), Ontario Superior Court (CAN), England & Wales (U.K.) and New South Wales Supreme Court (AUS).

Due to the increasing interest on cooperation between courts, the SBCourt decided to participate in the JIN very recently, and the author representing the SBCourt has been invited as an observer to the JIN since Feb. 7th, 2018,[14] and is supposed to attend the meeting which will be held on a regular basis.

The current status of the JIN is as follows (as of Apr. 7th, 2018):

#	Court	Judges in charge	
		Name	Note
1	FCA (AUS)	Brigitte Markovic	
2	NSW Supreme Court (AUS)	Ashley Black	
3	Supreme Court of Bermuda (BER)	Ian Kawaley	
4	Eastern Caribbean Court (BVI)	Barry Leon	
5	Ontario Superior Court (CAN)	Geoffrey Morawetz	
6	Cayman Islands Judicial Administration (CAY)	Nick Segal	
7	Court of Appeal of England & Wales (U.K.)	Elizabeth Gloster	Member
8	Supreme Court of Singapore (SGP)	Kannen Ramesh / Aedit Abdullah	
9	Delaware Bankruptcy Court (U.S.)	Christopher Sontchi	
10	S.D.N.Y Bankruptcy Court (U.S.)	Robert Drain	
11	National Commercial Court (ARG)	Maria Cristina O'Reilly	
12	First Bankruptcy Court of Sao Paulo (BRA)	Daniel Costa	
13	F.L.S.D. Bankruptcy Court (U.S.)	-checking	
14	High Court of First Instance (HKG)	Jonathan Harris	
15	Tokyo District Court (JPN)	Daisaku Ueharai / Naoyuki Iwai	Observer
16	Seoul Bankruptcy Court (KOR)	Young Seok KIM	

4.3. DISCUSSION IN THE SBCOURT

The SBCourt is now considering adopting the JIN Guidelines as a very useful tool to cooperate with foreign court and foreign representative, which would provide effective mechanism for dealing with Cross-Border insolvency cases.[15] Revising the Guideline No. 504, such as adding Article 7 of incorporating the JIN Guidelines into the Guideline No. 504 with addendum could be a streamlined way of adopting the JIN Guidelines.

Sharing the common procedure of cooperation can give each court very reliable instruction of how to proceed and solve the difficulties caused by different legal systems and misunderstanding on the other proceeding.

This kind of cooperation is not just confined to the parallel proceedings, of course. The more practically active cooperation cases becomes, the better protection and maximization of the value of the debtor's assets we will accomplish in many Cross-Border insolvency cases.

Notes

1. The recast EIR provides specific principles of deciding applicable laws regarding Third parties' rights in rem (Article 8), Set-off (Article 9), Reservation of title (Article 10), Contracts relating to immoveable property (Article 11), Payment systems and financial markets (Article 12), Contracts of employment (Article 13), Effects on rights subject to registration (Article 14), European patents with unitary effect and Community trade marks (Article 15), Detrimental acts (Article 16), Protection of third-party purchasers (Article 17), Effects of insolvency proceedings on pending lawsuits or arbitral proceedings (Article 18) as well as the general rule (Article 7). For the details, please refer to Young Seok KIM, *Review on Regulation (EU) No 2015/848 of the European Parliament and of the Council of 20 May 2015 on Insolvency Proceedings (recast)*, Korea Private International Law Study, Vol. 21, December, 2015.

2. The recast EIR expresses this kind of proceedings as "group coordination proceeding," whereas the UNCITRAL uses "planning proceedings" to explain the similar concept in draft legislative provisions. For the recent discussion in UNCITRAL, please refer to UNCITRAL Working Group V 53th Session A/CN.9/WG/V/WP.158.

3. 『Act on Private International Law(hereinafter "APIL")』, Korean national law dealing with applicable laws, is now under revision but the draft has not included provisions in terms of Cross-border Insolvency matters so far. For the details, please refer to Official Gazette (No. 2018-17) of the Ministry of Justice in the Republic of Korea.

4. The SBCourt was transformed from the former bankruptcy division of the Seoul Central District Court. For the details, please refer to Young Seok KIM, *Cross-Border Insolvency in the Republic of Korea: Focus on Selected Maritime Issues*, Korean Yearbook of International Law (KYIL) Vol. 4, 2016, 104, 116.

5. As the current Cooperation and Coordination Judge in the Seoul Bankruptcy Court, the author drafted the procedural guideline No. 504, and has considered if there is anything to revise or add.

6. The author has been the CBCC Judge in the SBCourt so far since the cooperation system was first established in the court.

7. The SBCourt has the exclusive jurisdiction for the Inbound case which consists of recognition and relief. In other words, cases concerning recognition of and relief to foreign proceedings shall be placed under the exclusive jurisdiction of the SBCourt. Accordingly, the cooperation and coordination activities with respect to Inbound case are also within the scope of the SBCourt's task.

8. The text is as follows:

Article 18 (Subsequent information)

From the time of filing the application for recognition of the foreign proceeding, the foreign representative shall inform the court promptly of:

(a) Any substantial change in the status of the recognized foreign proceeding or the status of the foreign representative's appointment;

(b) Any other foreign proceeding regarding the same debtor that becomes known to the foreign representative.

9. An attorney was nominated as the Trustee in the Hanjin bankruptcy proceeding which was converted from the rehabilitation proceeding of the company, making the former administrator in the Hanjin rehabilitation proceeding lose his authority of administering Hanjin's insolvency proceeding.

10. Unlike the Model Law, the DRBA provides "Cross-Border Insolvency Administrator" in addition to the "foreign representative." The Article of the DRBA relating to the is as follows:

Article 637 (International Bankruptcy Custodians)

(1) Where any Cross-Border Insolvency Administrator is appointed, the authority to perform the debtor's business and manage and dispose of the debtor's properties shall be vested exclusively in such Cross-Border Insolvency Administrator.

(2) Where Cross-Border Insolvency Administrator intends to dispose of the debtor's properties, or remove the debtor's properties from the Republic of Korea, realize the debtor's properties, distribute dividends and perform any act that is prescribed by the court, such Cross-Border Insolvency Administrator shall obtain permission therefor from the court.

(3) The provisions of Section 1 of Chapter II of Part II and Section 1 of Chapter II of Part III shall apply mutatis mutandis to every Cross-Border Insolvency Administrator.

11. The EDVA seems to have no choice but to rely on this rule because the EDVA have not adopted the Judicial Insolvency Network Guidelines unlike other U.S. Bankruptcy Court for the District (S.D.N.Y., Delaware and F.L.S.D.). The text of the U.S. Bankruptcy Code 105(a) is as follows:

Article 105 (Power of court)

(a) The court may issue any order, process, or judgment that is necessary or appropriate to carry out the provisions of this title. No provision of this title providing for the raising of an issue by a party in interest shall be construed to preclude the court from, sua sponte, taking any action or making any determination necessary or appropriate to enforce or implement court orders or rules, or to prevent an abuse of process.

12. The author inquired of the EDVA about ① Information of Creditors who are

known to have nationality of the Korea (Korean Creditors) (such as name, address, allowed claims, etc.), ② How the Korean Creditors are classified and treated in the Liquidation Plan (such as repayment ratio, repayment period, etc.), ③ How the Korean Creditors are served, notified and given any chance to participate in the voting of the Liquidation Plan by due process (If not, please explain the reason why the Korean Creditors were not treated equally like other domestic creditors), ④ In case of requests from Korean Creditors who belatedly get to know the existence of the proceeding, can the Korean Creditors participate in the proceeding by subsequent filing of their claims even after the confirmation of the Liquidation Plan? (If not, are there any ways to protect Korean Creditors in good faith?)

13. For the details of JIN Guidelines, please refer to Supreme Court of Singapore, *Paving the Way for Improved Coordination of Cross-Border Insolvency Proceedings,* 12th Joint Multinational Judicial Colloquium (UNCITRAL/INSOL/World Bank), 2017. 3.

14. Supreme Court of Singapore publicized the join of the author and Japanese Judges (Daisaku UEHARAI, Naoyuki Iwai) from Tokyo District Court to the JIN through media releases of Feb. 7th, 2018 on their webpage. For the details, please refer to Supreme Court of Singapore, *Japan and South Korea Joins the Judicial Insolvency Network as Observers,* Media Releases (Feb. 7th, 2018), available at https://www.supremecourt.gov.sg/news/media-releases/japan-and-south-korea-joins-the-judicial-insolvency-network-as-observers.

15. This is also the purpose of the Model Law.

RECENT DEVELOPMENTS

Revised Bill of Korea's Act on Private International Law

LEE Gyooho
Professor of Law
Chung-Ang University, School of Law, Seoul, Korea

1. INTRODUCTION

The Committee for Revision of the Korean private international law, which consisted of 10 experts, was launched on June 2014 and run until December 2015. Its general meetings was held for 19 times and its subcommitteeg was held twice.

It discussed the following matters: (i) the reform of general provisions such as general jurisdiction, jurisdiction in related cases, jurisdiction in counterclaim, prorogation of jurisdiction based on choice of court or appearance of defendant, exclusive jurisdiction; and (ii) the improvement of special provisions related to jurisdiction such as claim, real property, domestic relation, inheritance, bills of exchange, promissory notes, checks, and maritime cases as well. It has wound up sharing consensus among the Committee members about the reform of international jurisdiction and finalizing it. However, it has failed to come up with choice of law issues on intellectual property rights.[1]

Afterwards, the International Legal Affairs Division of the Ministry of Justice in Korea consulted 4 legal experts of private international law to draft the governmental bill of private international law from January to December 2017.[2] The Ministry of Justice announced the revised bill for public notification from January 19 to February 28, 2018. After that, the public hearing on the revised bill was held on February 27, 2018 and the final draft of the revised bill was completed on March 2018. The final draft of the revised bill was sent to the Ministry of Legislation for its official review on March 2018. As of July 20, 2018, it is expected to be submitted to the National Assembly in 2018.

2. AN OVERVIEW OF THE REVISED BILL OF KOREA'S ACT ON PRIVATE INTERNATIONAL LAW

2-1. Structure

The current Korea's Act on Private International Law consists of as follows:

(i) Chapter I (General Provisions) comprising Article 1 (Purpose), Article 2 (International Jurisdiction), Article 3 (Law of Nationality), Article 4 (Law of Habitual Residence), Article 5 (Application of Foreign Law), Article 6 (Scope of Applicable Law), Article 7 (Mandatory Application of Acts of Republic of Korea), Article 8 (Exception to Designation of Applicable Law), Article 9 (Renvoi in Case of Designation of Applicable Law), and Article 10 (Provisions of Foreign Law Contrary to Social Order);

(ii) Chapter II (Person) comprising Article 11 (Legal Capacity), Article 12 (Judicial Declaration of Disappearance), Article 13 (Capacity), Article 14 (Adjudication on Commencement of Limited Guardianship or Adult Guardianship, etc.), Article 15 (Protection of Business Transaction), and Article 16 (Corporations and Other Organizations);

(iii) Chapter III (Juristic Act) comprising Article 17 (Method of Juristic Act) and Article 18 (Agency in Fact);

(iv) Real Property Rights (Chapter IV) comprising Article 19 (Applicable Law of Real Property Rights), Article 20 (Means of Transportation), Article 21 (Bearer Securities), Article 22 (Things in Transit), Article 23 (Stipulated Security Interests on Bonds, etc.), and Article 24 (Protection of Intellectual

Property Rights);

(v) Chapter V (Claims) comprising Article 25 (Party's Autonomy), Article 26 (Objective Connection at Time of Decision of Applicable Law), Article 27 (Consumer Contract), Article 28 (Employment Contract), Article 29 (Formation and Validity of Contract), Article 30 (Management of Affairs), Article 31 (Unjust Enrichment), Article 32 (Torts), Article 33 (Ex Post Facto Agreement on Applicable Law), Article 34 (Assignment of Claim and Acceptance of Obligation), and Article 35 (Transfer of Claim by Act);

(vi) Chapter VI (Family) comprising Article 36 (Establishment of Marriage), Article 37 (General Validity of Marriage), Article 38 (Marital Property System), Article 39 (Divorce), Article 40 (Children in Wedlock), Article 41 (Children out of Wedlock), Article 42 (Legitimation of Children Born out of Wedlock), Article 43 (Adoption and Its Dissolution), Article 44 (Consent), Article 45 (Legal Relations between Parents and Children), Article 46 (Duty to Support), and Article 47 (Other Kinship), Article 48 (Guardianship);

(vii) Chapter VII (Inheritance) comprising Article 49 (Inheritance) and Article 50 (Will);

(viii) Chapter VIII (Note and Check) comprising Article 51 (Capacity), Article 52 (Qualification for Drawee of Check), Article 53 (Method), Article 54 (Validity), Article 55 (Acquisition of Underlying Claim), Article 56 (Partial Acceptance and Partial Payment), Article 57 (Method of Action for Exercise and Preservation of Rights), Article 58 (Loss or Theft of Bill), and Article 59 (Law of Place of Payment of Checks); and

(ix) Chapter IX (Maritime Commerce) comprising Article 60 (Maritime Commerce), Article 61 (Collision of Ships), and Article 62 (Salvage).

In the meantime, the revised bill of Korea's Act on Private International Law is as follows:

(i) Chapter I (General Provisions) comprises subchapters 1 to 3. The subchapter 1 (Purpose) of Chapter I constitutes Article 1 (Purpose). The subchapter 2 (International Jurisdiction) comprises Article 2 (General

Principle), Article 3 (General Jurisdiction), Article 4 (Special Jurisdiction over the Place of Office or of Business, etc.), Article 5 (Special Jurisdiction over the Place where Property Is Located), Article 6 (Jurisdiction over Related Actions), Article 7 (Jurisdiction over Counterclaim), Article 8 (Choice of Court), Article 9 (Jurisdiction Based on Appearance of Defendant), Article 10 (Exclusive Jurisdiction), Article 11 (*lis pendens*), Article 12 (Failure to Exercise of International Jurisdiction), Article 13 (Exception to Application), Article 14 (Jurisdiction over Interim Measures), and Article 15 (Jurisdiction over Non-contentious Cases). The subchapter 3 (Applicable Law) of Chapter I consists of Article 16 (Law of Nationality), Article 17 (Law of Habitual Residence), Article 18 (Application of Foreign Law), Article 19 (Scope of Applicable Law), Article 20 (Mandatory Application of Acts of Republic of Korea), Article 21 (Exception to Designation of Applicable Law), Article 22 (Renvoi in Case of Designation of Applicable Law), and Article 23 (Provisions of Foreign Law Contrary to Social Order).

(ⅱ) Chapter II (Person) comprises subchapters 1 and 2. The subchapter 1 of Chapter II consists of special international jurisdiction over adjudication of disappearance (Article 24) and company employee, etc (Article 25). The subchapter 2 of Chapter II consists of Article 26 (Legal Capacity), Article 27 (Judicial Declaration of Disappearance), Article 28 (Capacity for Legal Acts), Article 29 (Protection of Business Transaction), and Article 30 (Corporations and Other Organizations).

(ⅲ) Chapter III (Juristic Act) comprises Article 31 (Method of Juristic Act) and Article 32 (Agency in Fact).

(ⅳ) Chapter IV (Real Property Rights) comprises 2 subchapters. The subchapter 1 of Chapter 4 governs international jurisdiction in real property cases (Article 33). The subchapter 2 of Chapter 4 consists of Article 34 (Applicable Law of Real Property Rights), Article 35 (Means of Transportation), Article 36 (Bearer Securities), Article 37 (Things in Transit), and Article 38 (Stipulated Security Interests on Bonds, etc.).

(ⅴ) Chapter V (Intellectual Property Rights) consists of 2 subchapters. The subchapter 1 of Chapter V comprises Article 39 (Special Jurisdiction in

Contract Cases Relating to Intellectual Property Rights) and Article 40 (Special Jurisdiction over Infringement of Intellectual Property Rights). The subchapter 2 of Chapter V is Article 41 governing the applicable law concerning protection of intellectual property laws.

(vi) Chapter VI (Claims) comprises two subchapters. The subchapter 1 of Chapter VI covers international jurisdiction over claims, ranging from Article 42 to Article 45. Article 42 governs special jurisdiction over contract cases. Article 43 prescribes international jurisdiction in consumer contracts. Article 44 provides international jurisdiction in employment contracts. Article 45 stipulates special jurisdiction in torts cases. The subchapter 2 of Chapter VI consists of Article 46 (Party's Autonomy), Article 47 (Objective Connection at Time of Decision of Applicable Law), Article 48 (Consumer Contract), Article 49 (Employment Contract), Article 50 (Formation and Validity of Contract), Article 51 (Management of Affairs), Article 52 (Unjust Enrichment), Article 53 (Torts), Article 54 (Ex Post Facto Agreement on Applicable Law), Article 55 (Assignment of Claim and Acceptance of Obligation), and Article 56 (Transfer of Claim by Act).

(vii) Chapter VII (Family) comprises two subchapters. The subchapter 1 of Chapter VII covers special jurisdiction in marriage-related cases (Article 57), cases related to establishment or dissolution of a legitimate child (Article 58), adoption-related cases (Article 59), cases related to parental rights (Article 60), child custody (Article 61), or visitation rights for a minor child (or minor children) (Article 62), cases related to duty to support (Article 63), guardianship cases (Article 64), and family conciliation cases (Article 65). The subchapter 2 of Chapter VII comprises Article 64 (Establishment of Marriage), Article 65 (General Validity of Marriage), Article 66 (Marital Property System), Article 67 (Divorce), Article 68 (Children in Wedlock), Article 69 (Children out of Wedlock), Article 70 (Legitimation of Children Born out of Wedlock), Article 71 (Adoption and Its Dissolution), Article 72 (Consent), Article 73 (Legal Relations between Parents and Children), Article 74 (Duty to Support), and

Article 75 (Other Kinship), and Article 76 (Guardianship).

(viii) Chapter VIII (Inheritance) comprises two subchapters. The subchapter 1 of Chapter VIII covers international jurisdiction over inheritance and will (Article 77). The subchapter 2 of Chapter VIII consists of Article 78 (Inheritance) and Article 79 (Will).

(ix) Chapter IX (Note and Check) comprises two subchapters. The subchapter 1 of Chapter IX covers special jurisdiction over cases related to notes or checks (Article 80). The subchapter 2 of Chapter IX covers Article 81 (Capacity for Legal Act), Article 82 (Qualification for Drawee of Check), Article 83 (Method), Article 84 (Validity), Article 85 (Acquisition of Underlying Claim), Article 86 (Partial Acceptance and Partial Payment), Article 87 (Method of Action for Exercise and Preservation of Rights), Article 88 (Loss or Theft of Bill), and Article 89 (Law of Place of Payment of Checks).

(x) Chapter X (Maritime Commerce) comprises two subchapters. The subchapter 1 of Chapter X consists of international jurisdiction in cases related to limitation to liability of ship-owners, etc. (Article 90), in cases related to ship's navigation (Article 91), cases related to general average (Article 92), cases related to collision of ships (Article 93), salvage cases (Article 94). The subchapter 2 of Chapter XI covers Article 95 (Maritime Commerce), Article 96 (Collision of Ships), and Article 97 (Salvage).

2-2. CONTENTS

On one hand, this bill has adopted general and special provisions on international jurisdiction intensively to promote legal certainty and predictability of courts and parties about international jurisdiction. On the other hand, it has inserted *forum non conveniens* doctrine subject to strict requirements to secure specific flexibility in certain cases. In addition, it has adopted *lis pendens* provision. However, it failed to adopt rules of international jurisdiction in non-contentious family cases due to poor precedent researches.[3]

Notes

1. Sang Hyun Kim, *Current Development in the Revisions of Private International Law in Korea*, at Public Hearing for Comprehensively Revised Bill of Korea's Act on Private International Law held on February 27, 2018, p. 6.
2. *Id.* at p. 7.
3. Hyun Suk Kwang, *Introduction to the Revised Bill of Korea's Act on Private International Law,* at Public Hearing for Comprehensively Revised Bill of Korea's Act on Private International Law held on February 27, 2018, p. 98.

The National Assembly's Role in Negotiations for KORUS FTA Amendment: The Legal Dimension

CHUNG Min-Jung
Legislative Research Officer
National Assembly Research Service, Seoul, Korea

1. INTRODUCTION

On November 7, 2017, President Moon Jae-in and the U.S. President Trump announced the process for amending the *Free Trade Agreement between the Republic of Korea and the United States of America* (hereinafter referred to as "*KORUS FTA*") would be expedited.[1] The domestic procedure of the Republic of Korea (hereinafter referred to as "Korea") concerning commercial treaty actions is dictated by what is known as the *Act on the Conclusion Procedure and Implementation of Commercial Treaties* (hereinafter referred to as "*Commercial Treaties Act*"), which is Korea's Trade Promotion Authority (TPA)[2] equivalent. So, Korea completed, after the summit announcement, an economic feasibility assessment outlining potential amendment areas in the KORUS FTA under the Article 9 of the *Commercial Treaties Act*.[3]

Then, Korea and the U.S., on March 27, 2018, settled on an agreement in principle on several amendments and modifications[4] to the KORUS FTA and a quota arrangement that serves as an alternative to the global 25 percent tariff on steel the U.S. administration imposed via Section 232 of the Trade Act of 1962. Those changes to the KORUS FTA included arrangements on U.S. truck tariffs and auto exports, environmental standards, pharmaceutical reimbursements, customs facilitation, investor-state dispute settlement, the harmonization of emissions test requirements and a currency side deal.[5]

Since then, the two countries have been working out the details in the final pact. The final text containing the KORUS FTA amendments and modifications is reported to be released by the end of May 2018.[6] The final text to be released will be subject to domestic review procedures in Korea. Modifications to the U.S. tariff schedule (delaying the U.S. tariff cuts on Korean trucks) will undergo consultation and layover procedures provided under the Article 12 of the *Commercial Treaties Act*. Whether or not the changes will be subject to a vote for consent to ratification is yet to be determined and depends on the legal interpretation of the amendments by the Ministry of Government Legislation under the Article 60, paragraph 1 of the Constitution of the Republic of Korea and Article 13 of the *Commercial Treaties Act*.

The idea that cross-border trade policies are not only the domain of the executive and but also that of the legislature is at least as old as the emergence of Korea's initiation of the FTA drive in 2003. In 2011, the *Report of Reviewing the Act on the Conclusion Procedure and Implementation of Commercial Treaties* (hereinafter referred to as "*Commercial Treaties Act Review Report*")[7] informed the Foreign Affairs, Trade and Reunification Committee that the increasing influence that commerce treaties were having on legislation in Korea made it imperative that the National Assembly address its relationship to commerce treaty actions. Specifically, it urged the Committee that it must consider whether it should have a meaningful role in the legislative consent of commerce treaties. These arguments in favor of an expanded role of the National Assembly in the conduct of cross-border trade policy have driven material change in the legal and constitutional arrangements in Korea.

The reasons why there has been a substantial recent redistribution of the trade policy power in Korea may be found in (a) a perceived democratic deficit; (b) the legislative functions of commercial treaties; (c) the need to check the exercise and potential abuse of executive power; (d) the requirement to expose the conduct of commerce treaty-making to public scrutiny; and (e) the indirect impact of unincorporated side agreements.

2. DEMOCRATIC DEFICIT

The general argument in favor of greater legislative involvement in commercial treaty-making is the need to fill a democratic deficit. The *Commercial Treaties Act* provides the process of negotiating commercial treaties. According to the Act, the negotiations shall be conducted in conjunction with an extensive array of required notifications to and consultations with the National Assembly and other stakeholders. The purpose on which the present Act is founded is 'to enhance transparency in procedures for concluding commerce treaties and to promote efficient commercial negotiations with citizens' understanding and participation.'[8] The Act accepted the idea that the representative of a nation in his or her discourses with foreign Parties should, so far as practicable, act with the fullest possible democratic sanction behind him or her.

The notion of 'democratic deficit' has been coined to address another phenomenon that did not form a significant part of the sphere of international commercial relations until the FTAs emerged. It refers to the transfer of domestic decision-making power, including law-making power, from national polities to international commerce treaties. It originated in the paradox that although each of the Parties of the FTA is democratic, decision making has become increasingly removed from the control of citizens and their representative institutions as more domestic issues have been decided by the FTA. This kind of concern was also the subject of much debate in the National Assembly reviewing the KORUS FTA.[9]

When decision-making power over domestic issues passes from the Legislative Body to the commercial treaty, the National Assembly-men or women risk becoming increasingly unimportant, and increasingly isolated from influence over affairs that may be of direct concern to him or her.

The decline in the extent of legislative authority may mean that policy affecting the citizen may be determined at levels altogether too remote, in international forums by administrative officials somewhat immune to the sorts of pressures that the citizen can still exert over policy-making by the National Assembly.

But this concern has been balanced against the compelling need of our times to find bilateral solutions to sound development of both national economies. The *Commercial Treaties Act Review Report* summarized the dilemma: "To be democratic, the National Assembly must remain in control of the trade treaty making processes of the administration at every level. No sovereign democracy can be subject to foreign control over the kind of laws it must adopt. Yet many issues have to be dealt with at the international level."[10] Article 16 is dealing with the problem of the collision of values between the necessity of continued economic cooperation and ample policy space guarantees by providing that "no provision in commerce treaties shall be construed as justifying any infringement on the legitimate economic rights and interests of the Republic of Korea."

3. LEGISLATIVE FUNCTION OF TREATIES

The proposition that the exclusion of the National Assembly from commercial treaty-making leads to a democratic deficit has gained contemporary currency from the unprecedented increase in the volume and density of commercial treaty-making and its effect on domestic law-making. This in turn is a response to trade liberalization. The *Commercial Treaties Act Review Report* stated in 2011: "The trend toward forming bilateral or regional economic groups had implied a new interrelationship, not only for an economic nature, but with juridical, political, and social effects as well. Some of the most notable of these regional economic groups are the European Union (EU) and the North American Free Trade Agreement (NAFTA). As the regional trade governance continued its rapid expansion since the early 1990s, Korea must have remained competitive by keeping up with its new partners by making bilateral or regional commercial treaties."[11]

But bilateral or regional commercial treaty making only increases the challenge for democratic institutions. The National Assembly proposed changes to the commercial treaty-making process on the following premise: "Our economy and way of life are dependent on decisions and events remote from our shores concerning bilateral or regional commercial agreements. As yet our institutions have failed to adapt to these changes."[12]

The contemporary impact of commercial treaty obligations on the legislative function is not to be underestimated. In Korea, partial amendments of at least 28 statutes[13] have implemented the KORUS FTA obligations. The figure was significantly higher for statutes amended to implement other FTAs that had been concluded by Korea.

If the National Assembly has no effective role in the commerce treaty-making process, it can be placed in the position of simply ratifying a *fait accompli* when it is asked to enact implementing legislation. If the government decides that it will enter into a particular commerce treaty, it is saying to the world that we are, as a nation, prepared to commit ourselves to this. That has the effect, whether deliberate or unintended, that the National Assembly is put in a situation where they have to toe the government's line or risk jeopardizing Korea's international reputation.[14]

For example, if the standstill and ratchet mechanisms apply to certain sectors or activities, the National Assembly cannot pass subsequent amendments that fall within the scope of areas and that return to a lower degree of conformity with the FTA into law. Almost all FTA Trade in Services and Investment Chapters include schedules wherein parties make their market access commitments to which the substantive commitments in the Trade in Services and Investment Chapters apply. There are two main approaches for listing market access commitments in an FTA, namely through use of a positive[15] or a negative list of commitments.[16]

The negative list approach also normally consists of two annexes;

reservations for future measures listed in Annex II and reservations for current measures listed in Annex I.[17] Under Annex I, States list those non-conforming measures that they agree not to make any more non-conforming or restrictive. This is often referred to as a standstill commitment that maintains *status quo* rather than liberalizes trade.

Some FTA Trade in Services and Investment Chapters, such as KORUS FTA and Korea – Singapore FTA, also subject measures listed in Annex I to a 'ratchet mechanism,' whereby any future amendment to a measure in that Annex that brings it into greater conformity with the FTA automatically becomes an international commitment or binding. The measure cannot then be returned by legislation to its original non-conforming state without being in breach of the FTA.[18] The National Assembly is prohibited from introducing new non-conforming legislation beyond the level of those included in the negative list. Standstill commitments effectively freeze the degrees of legislation in particular sectors, and the National Assembly are no longer free to implement more stringent regulatory provisions.[19] The point here is that the assumption of commercial treaty obligations will nevertheless bind, and therefore limit the freedom of operation of future National Assembly, even though the existing law is already in conformity with the proposed international obligation.

4. EXECUTIVE ACCOUNTABILITY

A third strand in the case for legislative involvement in the commerce treaty-making is the application of the guiding idea behind the distribution of powers within a constitutional democracy: that of checks and balances. In this context, the fact that the executive's foreign trade policy-making power continues to find its origins in the presidential prerogative has tended to limit its real accountability to the National Assembly. As the *Commercial Treaties Act Review Report* put it, "The presidential prerogative has been used as a smoke-screen by Ministers to obfuscate the use of power for which they are sufficiently accountable."[20] This concern has been central to the commercial treaty-making practice reforms. The National Assembly passed the *Commercial Treaties Act* to tame the presidential prerogative and to strengthen ministerial accountability to the National Assembly. In relation to commercial treaty-making, the point, as *Commercial Treaties Act Review Report* pointed out in 2011, is that the fact that the executive has the power to negotiate and ratify a commercial treaty does not necessarily qualify the existence or extent of the National Assembly's power to express consent or dissent of or otherwise to supervise the executive's commerce treaty actions.

5. PUBLIC SCRUTINY

The need for effective legislative supervision in foreign trade policy may be particularly acute precisely because of the secrecy of negotiations. The processes that lead to the conclusion of multilateral commercial treaties, such as the World Trade Organization,[21] which are open to all states are themselves frequently exposed to wide public view and participation.[22] By contrast, however, bilateral commercial treaties such as FTAs are typically negotiated on a confidential basis.[23] The practice has persisted despite expression of discontent from members of the National Assembly and civil society until the KORUS amendment negotiations.

At the time when Korea and the U.S. were participating in the negotiations of a proposed KORUS Amendment Protocol, the negotiating documents were held subject to a confidentiality agreement between the parties. The position taken by the executive in both states, responding from members of the Legislature for greater disclosure to the National Assembly and Congress has been that this will not take place until the final text is agreed. At this point, it will not be easy for the National Assembly to revisit particular decision taken in the course of negotiations.

6. UNINCORPORATED SIDE AGREEMENTS

Finally, an unincorporated side agreement sometimes imposes non-binding, recommendatory and discretionary obligations on the executive. Once it is recognized that these obligations, even if not incorporated into the FTA, may bear on administrative decisions for which the executive is answerable, the potential impact of unincorporated side agreements within the domestic polity becomes unmistakable.

Related to the KORUS FTA amendment, this controversy was unleashed as a result of a currency agreement being negotiated by the U.S. Treasury Department and Korea's Ministry of Strategy and Finance.[24] It was reported that KORUS currency deal would include commitments on transparency as well as a commitment not to devalue currency for competitive advantages, but would fall short of demand that those obligations be binding.[25]

The currency deal would not be subject to the KORUS FTA dispute settlement rules. Instead, the currency deal would serve as an adequate foundation for a legitimate expectation, absent statutory or executive indications to the contrary, so that Korean administrative decision-makers would act in conformity with the deal and Trump administration could rely on Korea being a serious partner that abides by its currency commitments. A bill expressly designed to reverse the effect of such expectation, if any, to be introduced in the National Assembly will hardly be passed into law.

7. CONCLUSION

The Korean constitutional system accepts commercial treaties as a directly applicable source of law even if the administration usually submits to the National Assembly a draft implementing bill. A spur to greater legislative involvement in commercial treaty actions has been the recognition of the potential impact of commerce treaty obligations on legislation by the National Assembly as well as on administrative decision-making by the executive.

As the National Assembly recognized in the *KORUS FTA Review Report*, the case for its involvement depends on the operation of commerce treaties as laws of indefinite duration unless or until the Parties of the commercial treaty agree otherwise. The fact that the consent procedure of the KORUS FTA in 2011 was extremely costly compared to that of other FTAs demonstrated the increasing impact that the KORUS FTA had in Korea. This increasing impact of the KORUS FTA is, in itself, reason for greater legislative involvement in the KORUS FTA amendment negotiations prior to the ratification of the treaties.

In conclusion, given the significant status which the KORUS FTA has attained in our domestic legal system, it is particularly important that the National Assembly be more involved in scrutinizing treaties which incur international obligations on behalf of Korea, before the ratification by the Executive, in order to enhance their democratic democracy.

Notes

1. "Trump, Moon agree to 'expedite' KORUS Process; withdrawal still possible," *Inside U.S. Trade,* Vol. 35, No. 10, November 10, 2017, at 1.

2. As to the U.S.'s TPA, *see* Ian F. Fergusson and Christopher M. Davis, *Trade Promotion Authority (TPA): Frequently Asked Questions,* CRS Report, R43491, November 14, 2017.

3. "South Korea set to publish report outlining KORUS amendment scenarios," *Inside U.S. Trade,* Vol. 35, No. 10, November 10, 2017, at 15.

4. The terminology for how to frame the process was highly political for Seoul. Both side have shied away from calling it a "renegotiation" for amendment and instead had described it as a process within the FTA to consider modifications.

5. "Lawmakers view KORUS changes as a re-commitment to Asia-Pacific," *Inside U.S. Trade,* Vol. 36, No. 13, March 30, 2018, at 16.

6. "Sources: Final KORUS text to be released by the end of May," *Inside U.S. Trade,* Vol. 36, No. 19, May 11, 2018, at 18.

7. Foreign Affairs, Trade and Reunification Committee, *A Report of Reviewing the Act on the Conclusion Procedure and Implementation of Commercial Treaties,* 2011.11., *available at* http://likms.assembly.go.kr/bill/billDetail.do?billId=PRC_V0C8K0Q6T3O0O1F6W3I1T5H6Q6E8Q2 [Accessed on May 3, 2018].

8. *See* Art. 1 of the Commercial Treaties Act.

9. *See* Foreign Affairs, Trade and Reunification Committee, *A Report of Reviewing the Free Trade Agreement between the Republic of Korea and the United States of America,* 2011.8., at 17-19 (hereinafter referred to as "*KORUS FTA Review Report*"), *available at* http://likms.assembly.go.kr/bill/billDetail.do?billId=PRC_R1C1W0Y6Q0U3N1E7O5S7D2Z8S6O5D6 [Accessed on April 29, 2018].

10. *Commercial Treaties Act Review Report,* at 13-15.

11. *Commercial Treaties Act Review Report,* at 1.

12. *Ibid.*

13. As to the subsequent legislation in Korea after the conclusion of the KORUS FTA, *see Customs Act; Act on the Investigation of Unfair International Trade Practices and Remedy against Injury to Industry; Act on Regulation and Punishment of Criminal Proceeds Concealment; Enforcement Decree of the Foreign Trade Act; Radio Waves Act; Individual Consumption Tax Act; Enforcement Decree of the Local Subsidy Act; Postal Service Act; Administrative Procedures Act; Patent Act; Design Protection Act; Enforcement Decree of the Monopoly Regulation and Fair Trade Act; Unfair Competition Prevention and Trade Secret Protection Act; Act on Special Cases of the Customs Act for the Implementation of Free Trade Agreements; Postal Savings and Insurance Act;*

Trademark Act; Utility Model Act; Copyright Act; Certified Public Accountant Act; Telecommunications Business Act; Pharmaceutical Affairs Act; Certified Tax Accountant Act; Foreign Legal Consultant Act; Broadcasting Act; Act on Agricultural Cooperatives; Act on Fisheries Cooperatives; Community Credit Cooperatives Act; Credit Unions Act.

14. *See KORUS FTA Review Report,* at 15.

15. The positive list is a GATS-style approach, whereby member States list those sectors which they are prepared to subject to the FTA Trade in Services and Investment Chapters commitments. For example, the *Free Trade Agreement between the Republic of Korea, of the One Part, and the European Union and its Member States, of the Other Part (Korea - EU FTA)* has adopted a positive list approach to scheduling commitments on service and investment. Ministry of Foreign Affairs and Trade, *Materials Containing Detailed Explanation as to Korea - EU FTA,* Oct. 6, 2010, p. 94.

16. Under the negative list approach to scheduling FTA Trade in Services and Investment Chapters commitments, all measures affecting trade in services and investment in all sectors of the economy are required to be in conformity with the FTA Trade in Services and Investment Chapters unless otherwise specified in a list of reservations to the FTA. Numerous FTA Trade in Services and Investment Chapters have adopted the negative list approach to scheduling commitments, including the KORUS FTA, the *Free Trade Agreement between the Government of the Republic of Korea and the Government of the Republic of Singapore (Korea – Singapore FTA),* the *Free Trade Agreement between the Government of the Republic of Korea and the Government of Australia (Korea – Australia FTA),* and the *Free Trade Agreement between the Government of the Republic of Korea and New Zealand (Korea – New Zealand FTA). See* Ministry of Trade, Industry and Energy, *Materials Containing Detailed Explanation as to Korea - Peru FTA,* 2011, p. 53, available at http://fta.go.kr/webmodule/_PSD_FTA/pe/1/peru1.pdf [Accessed on May 8, 2018]; Ministry of Trade, Industry and Energy, *Materials Containing Detailed Explanation as to Korea – Australia FTA,* 2014, p. 53, available at http://fta.go.kr/webmodule/_PSD_FTA/au/1/3_description.pdf [Accessed on May 8, 2018]; Ministry of Trade, Industry and Energy, *Materials Containing Detailed Explanation as to Korea – Canada FTA,* 2014, pp. 65-66, available at http://fta.go.kr/webmodule/_PSD_FTA/ca/2/2_ko_ca.pdf [Accessed on May 8, 2018]; Ministry of Trade, Industry and Energy, *Materials Containing Detailed Explanation as to Korea – New Zealand FTA,* 2014, p. 49, available at http://fta.go.kr/webmodule/_PSD_FTA/nz/2/specific.pdf [Accessed on May 8, 2018].

17. Joshua P. Meltzer, "Investment," *in* Simon Lester and Bryan Mercurio (*eds.*), *Bilateral and Regional Trade Agreements: Commentary and Analysis,* Cambridge: Cambridge Univ. Press, 2009, at 269.

18. *KORUS FTA Review Report*, at 15.

19. *See* Rodrigo Manardes V., "Challenges for Countries in Trade in Services' Negotiations with the NAFTA Approach: The Experience of Chile in the Free Trade Agreement with the United States," 5 *Brit. J. Am. Legal Stud.* 371, 378 (2016); Tae Jung Park, "Reservation List in International Investment Law: An Alternative Flexibility Device for Securing Policy Space," 43 *N. C. J. Int'l L.* 83, 93 (2018).

20. *Commercial Treaties Act Review Report*, at 2.

21. *See* Art. 2.1. (a) of the Commercial Treaties Act.

22. Steve Charnovitz, "WTO Cosmopolitics," 34 *N. Y. U. J. Int'l L. & Pol.* 299, 313 (2002).

23. *KORUS FTA Review Report*, at 17-19.

24. "KORUS currency deal will non-binding, lays 'groundwork' for NAFTA," *Inside U.S. Trade,* Vol. 36, No. 13, March 30, 2018, at 1.

25. "KORUS currency deal to be model for future pacts," *Inside U.S. Trade,* Vol. 36, No. 13, March 30, 2018, at 15.

REFERENCES

1. Books
Campbell McLachlan, *Foreign Relations Law* (UK: Cambridge University Press, 2014).

2. Articles
Rodrigo Manardes V., "Challenges for Countries in Trade in Services' Negotiations with the NAFTA Approach: The Experience of Chile in the Free Trade Agreement with the United States," 5 *Brit. J. Am. Legal Stud.* 371 (2016).

Steve Charnovitz, "WTO Cosmopolitics," 34 *N. Y. U. J. Int'l L. & Pol.* 299 (2002).

Tae Jung Park, "Reservation List in International Investment Law: An Alternative Flexibility Device for Securing Policy Space," 43 *N. C. J. Int'l L.* 83 (2018).

Tania Voon, "Balancing Regulatory Autonomy with Liberalization of Trade in Services: An Analytical Assessment of Australia's Obligations under Preferential Trade Agreements," 18 *Melb. J. Int'l L.* 373 (2017).

Yong-Shik Lee, Jamin Lee and Kyung-Han Sohn, "The United States – Korea Free Trade Agreement: Path to Common Economic Prosperity or False Promise?," 6 *E. Asia L. Rev.* 111 (2016).

3. Articles in Collections
Joshua P. Meltzer, "Investment," *in Bilateral and Regional Trade Agreements: Commentary and Analysis* (Simon Lester and Bryan Mercurio *eds.*, UK: Cambridge University Press, 2009).

I. M. Destler, "American Trade Policymaking: A Unique Process," *in The Domestic Sources of American Foreign Policy: Insights and Evidence* (James M. McCormick *ed.*, UK: Rowman & Littlefield Publishers, Inc., 2012).

4. Articles in Newspaper
"Trump, Moon agree to 'expedite' KORUS Process; withdrawal still possible," *Inside U.S. Trade,* Vol. 35, No. 10, November 10, 2017.

"South Korea set to publish report outlining KORUS amendment scenarios," *Inside U.S. Trade,* Vol. 35, No. 10, November 10, 2017.

"Lawmakers view KORUS changes as a re-commitment to Asia-Pacific," *Inside U.S. Trade,* Vol. 36, No. 13, March 30, 2018.

"Sources: Final KORUS text to be released by the end of May," *Inside U.S. Trade,* Vol. 36, No. 19, May 11, 2018.

"KORUS currency deal will non-binding, lays 'groundwork' for NAFTA," *Inside U.S. Trade,* Vol. 36, No. 13, March 30, 2018.

5. Working Papers and Reports

Ian F. Fergusson and Christopher M. Davis, *Trade Promotion Authority (TPA): Frequently Asked Questions,* CRS Report, R43491, November 14, 2017.

6. Internet Sources

Foreign Affairs, Trade and Reunification Committee, *A Report of Reviewing the Free Trade Agreement between the Republic of Korea and the United States of America,* 2011.8, *available at* http://likms.assembly.go.kr/bill/billDetail.do?billId=PRC_R1C1W0Y6Q0U3N1E7O5S7D2Z8S6O5D6 [Accessed on April 29, 2018].

Foreign Affairs, Trade and Reunification Committee, *A Report of Reviewing the Act on the Conclusion Procedure and Implementation of Commercial Treaties,* November, 2011, *available at* http://likms.assembly.go.kr/bill/billDetail.do?billId=PRC_V0C8K0Q6T3O0O1F6W3I1T5H6Q6E8Q2 [Accessed on May 3, 2018].

CONTEMPORARY PRACTICE
AND JUDICIAL DECISIONS

Judicial Decisions in
Public International Law (2017)*

LEE Keun-Gwan
Professor
Seoul National University, School of Law, Seoul, Korea

CONSTITUTIONAL COURT DECISION No. 2016HEONBA388
RENDERED ON MAY 25, 2017

Main Issue

Whether an Ordinance promulgated by the United States Military Government in Korea [hereinafter, "USAMGIK"] can be impugned as violative of international law before the Korean courts

Facts

On liberation from the Japanese colonial rule in August 1945, the Korean peninsula was placed under military occupation by the United States of America and the former Soviet Union. Governmental powers over the area south of 38° North Latitude were exercised by the USAMGIK until the establishment of the Government of the Republic of Korea

* The cases presented in this section are selected and translated from "Korean Judicial Decisions Related to Public International Law" edited by Professor Chung In-Seop (School of Law, Seoul National University) as printed in *Seoul International Law Journal*, volume 24 no. 2 and volume 25 no. 1. The editor of this section sincerely appreciates Prof. Chung's great efforts at systematically documenting Korean judicial practice in public international law.

in August 1948. On February 23, 1946, the USAMGIK promulgated Ordinance 57 ("Deposit of Notes of Bank of Japan and Bank of Taiwan"). This ordinance ordered all natural and juridical persons within Korea south of 38° North Latitude to deposit in the designated financial institutions all notes of the Bank of Japan and all notes of the Bank of Taiwan owned or possessed by them. It also prohibited them from "importing, exporting, receiving, paying out, knowingly owning or possessing, giving or otherwise transferring or dealing in or engaging in any transaction with respect to any such currency." As ordered by the ordinance, a Mr. Jeong deposited notes of the Bank of Japan in the amount of 3,100 yen in the Chosen Industrial Bank [the predecessor of the Korean Industrial Bank] and later died without receiving any compensation for this deposit. His successor filed a claim for compensatory damages, arguing that the ordinance in question was unconstitutional because it encroached on the right to property and that the [legislative] act taken by the United States Government was in violation of international law. After this claim was rejected by the Korean courts, the plaintiff lodged a constitutional petition with the Korean Constitutional Court.

Decision

It is an established rule of customary international law that *acta jure gestionis* which do not fall under sovereign authority of a state are not immune from the jurisdiction of another state, while *acta jure imperii* are immune from it (Judgment, Korean Supreme Court, rendered on December 17, 1998, 97DA39216, Full Court). The Office of the Military Governor, falling under the jurisdiction of the United States of America, promulgated the ordinance impugned in this case with a view to abolishing the old monetary order based on the notes of the Bank of Japan and introducing a new monetary order within Korea south of 38° North Latitude. As an act undertaken in the exercise of a high degree of sovereign authority, it falls under the category of *acta jure imperii*. Even assuming that an economic motive was considered by the United States of America in reaching the decision to introduce a new monetary order and that as a result the economic interests of those who possessed the notes of the Bank of Japan were affected, these circumstances alone cannot lead to the conclusion that the promulgation of the ordinance impugned in this case should be regarded as falling under the category of *acta jure gestionis*, constituting an exception from sovereign immunity. Therefore, to put forth claims *vis-à-vis* the United States of America for compensatory damages or the restitution of unjust enrichment by reason of the unconstitutionality of the ordinance impugned in this case is violative of the rule of customary international law and, as a result, is not admissible. In consequence, claims *vis-à-vis* the United States of America for compensatory damages or the restitution of unjust enrichment by reason of the unconstitutionality of the ordinance impugned in this case are illegal *per se* and should be dismissed without the need to consider the unconstitutionality of the ordinance impugned in this case.

Notes

This decision rendered by the Korean Constitutional Court proceeds from the premise that the USAMGIK was legally entitled, under the international law of military occupation, to exercise governmental powers in Korea south of 38° North Latitude. According to the Constitutional Court, the measure impugned in this case, that is, the promulgation of the USAMGIK Ordinance 57 falls within the category of *acta jure imperii*, ie, acts taken in the exercise of sovereign authority, thus attracting sovereign immunity.

Concerning the reasoning of the Court, the following comment is in order. The Korean courts had subscribed to the theory of absolute sovereignty until the 1990s when the theory of restrictive immunity was finally adopted by the Korean judiciary. For this reason, the reasoning of the Court based on the theory of restrictive immunity is not quite correct in terms of inter-temporal law in the absence of any other compelling reasons. It would be better if the Court considered the measure taken by the USAMGIK in 1946 on the basis of absolute immunity.

SUPREME COURT JUDGMENT No. 2016DU56080
RENDERED ON JULY 11, 2017

Main Issue

Whether homosexuality, as sexual orientation, fits the definition of 'membership of a particular social group' as provided for in Article 1 of the Refugee Convention

Judgment

Taking into account Article 1 and Article 2(i) of the Act on Refugees, Article 1 of the Convention relating to the Status of Refugees [hereinafter, 'Refugee Convention'] and Article 1 of the Protocol relating to the Status of Refugees, the [Korean] Minister of Justice, as defendant, is under a legal obligation to recognize as a refugee under the Refugee Convention a foreigner within Korea who 'owing to well-founded fear of being persecuted for reasons of race, religion, nationality, membership of a particular social group or political opinion, is outside the country of his nationality and is unable or, owing to such fear, is unwilling to avail himself or herself of the protection of that country' and submits application for the status of refugee.

In this definition, 'a particular social group' obtains when the members of a certain group share a common characteristic which they should not be compelled to forsake (the characteristic which is innate, unchangeable, or which is otherwise fundamental to identity, conscience) and, in the given social environment, they are recognized as distinct from the other groups. Homosexuality, as sexual orientation, can be regarded as fitting the definition of a particular social group if it conflicts with the moral or legal norms of the country from which the refugee applicant originates, the person engaging in homosexuality, if found out, is likely to be persecuted, and the person's government is either unwilling or unable to provide protection for the person.

The 'persecution' directed to the foreigner in question means the 'act that causes a grave violation or discrimination of the essential dignity of human beings, including the threat to life, person or liberty.' (Refer to, among others, Supreme Court judgment 2007du3930, rendered on July 24, 2008) A person can decide to hide his or her own sexual orientation because, if his or her homosexuality, as sexual orientation or sexual identity, is revealed, he or she is likely to subjected to social hostility and censure. Such cases may be regarded as undue social constraints, but do not amount to persecutions as provided for in the Refugee Convention, that is, persecutions from which the refugee applicant requires international protection. However, if the refugee applicant suffers, beyond the conventional degree of social denunciation, a grave violation or discrimination of the essential dignity of human beings, including the threat to life, person or liberty by reason of his or her sexual orientation, then it amounts to persecution as provided for in the Refugee Convention. Therefore, for homosexual persons to be recognized as refugees, it is required that, their sexual orientation having been revealed in their countries of origin and, for that reason, having been subjected to specific persecutions there, they have a well-founded fear of being persecuted by their government or certain social factions when they leave Korea and return to their countries of origin. The existence of 'well-founded fear' is to be proven by the foreigner submitting the application.

[After discussing whether the plaintiff meets the requirements of a refugee as provided for in the [Korean] Act on Refugees, the Refugee Convention and the Protocol relating to the Status of Refugees, the Court concludes as follows]

It is difficult to recognize that the plaintiff has a well-founded fear of persecution by, among others, the Egyptian Government, comprehensively taking into account the following circumstances: the statements made by the plaintiff is lacking in consistency and persuasiveness; overall, his statements have a low degree of credibility; and the Court does not have sufficient materials with which to ascertain whether his statements comport with the objective situation obtaining in Egypt. ... Therefore, it is unanimously decided to reverse the original judgement and remand it to the original court for retrial.

Notes

Recently, the Korean courts have been confronted with an avalanche of cases relating to refugees. A number of these cases turn on the question of whether a certain circumstance or situation falls within the purview of the five Refugee Convention grounds, that is, race, religion, nationality, membership of a particular social group and political opinion. In this case, the Korean Supreme Court discusses whether homosexuality, as sexual orientation, fits the definition of 'membership of a particular social group' and answers in the positive if the refugee applicant suffers, beyond the conventional degree of social denunciation, a grave violation or discrimination of the essential dignity of human beings, including the threat to life, person or liberty by reason of his or her sexual orientation.

Such a conclusion is largely consistent with Guidelines on International Protection No. 9: Claims to Refugee Status based on Sexual Orientation and/or Gender Identity within the context of Article 1A(2) of the 1951 Convention and/or its 1967 Protocol relating to the Status of Refugees issued by the UNHCR on October 23, 2012 (HCR/GIP/12/09). The differences of the judgment from the Guidelines are as follows. First, the Guidelines, pointing out that "the five Convention grounds ... are not mutually exclusive and may overlap," (para. 40) It goes on to discuss homosexuality not only under the heading of 'membership of a particular social group', but also under the categories of religion and political opinion. Secondly, the Guidelines are wider in its coverage. The document considers not only lesbians and gay men, but also bisexual, transgender and intersex people. (para. 10)

The Korean Supreme Court, in its judgment No. 2016du42913 (rendered on December 5, 2017), recognized female genital mutilation as falling within the Convention grounds. The Court again discussed female genital mutilation under the category of 'membership of a particular social group.'

Seoul Administrative Court Judgment No. 2017A12095
Rendered on August 14, 2017

Main Issue

Whether an assembly and march that effectively encircles a diplomatic mission violates Article 22 of the Vienna Convention on Diplomatic Relations that provides for the receiving state's 'special duty to take all appropriate steps to protect the premises of the mission against any intrusion or damage and to prevent any disturbance of the peace of the mission or impairment of its dignity.'

Facts

In August 2017, the applicant, a civic body called 'All the Citizens' Action Committee for the National Liberation Day,' notified the respondent, Head of the Seoul Municipal Police, of its plan to organize an 'All the Citizens' Action on the National Liberation Day for the Recovery of Sovereignty and the Accomplishment of Peace on the Korean Peninsula.' The police, in its reply, prohibited assembly and march in certain areas near the United States and the Japanese Embassies. The civic body lodged an application of provisional measure, requesting the court to issue a temporary restraining order.

Decision

1) In connection with the Notice of Prohibition, let us begin by looking at the part relating to the prohibition of assembly and demonstration at the back streets of the United States Embassy and the Japanese Embassy.

   A) Considering the content and form of Subparagraph 4 of Article 11 of the Act on Assembly and Demonstration, outdoor assembly or demonstration within a 100-meter radius from the boundary of the diplomatic office buildings or residences is prohibited in principle.

It is permitted on an exceptional basis when the assembly or demonstration, falling under one of the three items enumerated in Subparagraph 4, "is recognized as causing no concern of interfering with the functions or security of diplomatic offices or residences of heads of diplomatic missions."

B) The Court can ascertain the following circumstances from the notification of assembly and march submitted by the Applicant, the contents of the Notice of Prohibition, the explanation provided by the Respondent and the overall purports of courtroom examinations.

(i) Taking into account the fact that the title of assembly and march in this case mentions 'the Recovery of Sovereignty and the Accomplishment of Peace on the Korean Peninsula,' the fact that according to the notification submitted by the Applicant the assembly and march in this case aims to encircle both the United States and the Japanese Embassies, the fact that the Applicant made public the intention to 'encircle both the United States and the Japanese Embassies by forming a human chain around them,' and the international tension brought about by the recent missile launch tests by North Korea and the reactions of the United States of America and Japan to those tests, it appears that the assembly and march in this case has the United States of America and Japan within its sights and that, therefore, the assembly and march is aimed against the United States and the Japanese Embassies.

(ii) If 3,000 participants keep marching around the United States and the Japanese Embassies, it is tantamount to holding an assembly that encircles the diplomatic missions in question for the duration of the assembly.

(iii) The persons concerned of the United States and the Japanese Embassies clarify that "although the National Liberation Day [which falls on August 15] is a public holiday, a small number of staff will come to work at the embassy premises because of international tension caused by the North Korean nuclear situation and the sensitive nature of the National Liberation Day itself."

(iv) [...] If the assembly and march takes place in accordance with the notification submitted by the Applicant and, as a result, both Embassy buildings end up being encircled by the participants, access by the staff members of both Embassies to the diplomatic premises can be restricted. The staff members within the Embassy buildings can also develop a sense of being locked up. Such a circumstance contravenes Article 22 of the Vienna Convention [on Diplomatic Relations] that provides for the receiving state's 'special duty to take all appropriate steps to protect the premises of the mission against any intrusion or damage and to prevent any disturbance of the peace of the mission or impairment of its dignity.' [...]

(v) The back streets of the United States and the Japanese Embassies are narrow, forming a space where the field of vision is substantially closed. Those streets are not appropriate for the purpose of assembly or march unless the assembly or march is intended to 'encircle the United States and the Japanese Embassies.' Furthermore, it appears that the purpose of the assembly and march in this case can be mostly achieved even when it is organized on the front streets of the United States and the Japanese Embassies.

C) Taking into consideration all these circumstances, it cannot be definitively excluded that the assembly and march in this case will 'cause no concern of disturbing the function or the peace of the diplomatic missions.' To permit an assembly or march that purports to encircle a diplomatic mission violates the relevant provision of the Vienna Convention that provides for the duty of the receiving state to protect the diplomatic mission. The Applicant can achieve most of its objective by holding an assembly or march on the front streets of the United States and the Japanese Embassies. Therefore, the measure taken in this case by the Respondent to prohibit an assembly and march on the back streets of the United States and the Japanese Embassies accords with the legislative purpose as provided for in Article 1 of the Act on Assembly and Demonstration, that is, 'achiev[ing] an appropriate balance between the guarantees of the right to assemble and demonstrate and public peace and order.'

Notes

As is pointed out in a leading textbook on the international law of diplomatic relations (Eileen Denza, *Diplomatic Law: Commentary on the Vienna Convention on Diplomatic Relations*, 4th ed. (Oxford University Press, 2016), pp. 140), "politically motivated demonstrations in front of foreign embassies have become a highly favoured method of public protest at the policies of the sending State." In case of Korea, such demonstrations not infrequently take place in the vicinity of the United States and the Japanese Embassies. In such cases, a tricky question of striking a proper balance between the fundamental rights of assembly and demonstration, on the one hand, and the receiving state's duty to prevent disturbance of the peace of the mission or impairment of its dignity, on the other, arises. In the relations between Korea and Japan, there is the festering diplomatic question of statues of 'comfort women' forced into sexual servitude for Japanese soldiers during World War II (one in front of the Japanese Embassy in Seoul, the other in front of the Japanese Consulate General in Busan). The question boils down to how to interpret the relevant part of Article 22(2), that is, the receiving state's 'special duty to take all appropriate steps … to prevent any disturbance of the peace of the mission or impairment of its dignity.' For a related case decided by the General Division of the Federal Court in Australia in 1992, see *Re Minister of Foreign Affairs and Trade; the Commissioner of the Australian Federal Police and the Commonwealth of Australia v Geraldo Magno and Ines Almeida* [1992] FCA 566 [(1992) 37 FCR 298; (1992) 112 ALR 529].

SEOUL CENTRAL DISTRICT COURT JUDGMENT NO. 2017GADAN25114
RENDERED ON DECEMBER 12, 2017

Main Issue

Whether a foreign national who is arrested or committed to prison or to custody pending trial or detained in any other manner has the right of consular notification and access within Korea.

Facts

The plaintiff, a Nigerian national, lent his Foreign National Registration card to his acquaintance, another Nigerian. When the latter was arrested for the charge of theft, the same person showed the police the plaintiff's registration card. When the plaintiff's acquaintance did not appear for court proceedings, the police arrested the plaintiff under the mistaken belief that the plaintiff had committed the crime of theft. When the police arrested him, they notified him of the right to remain silent and the right to be assisted by an attorney. However, they did not notify the Nigerian Embassy of his arrest or notify the plaintiff of the right of consular access.

Judgment

Concerning the question whether the Respondent is under an obligation to notify the Plaintiff of the right of consular notification and the right of consular access, the Court needs to consider the following circumstances.

(i) According to Subparagraphs (a) and (b) of Article 36(1) of the Vienna Convention on Consular Relations that has the same effects as the domestic laws of Korea in accordance with Article 6(1), nationals of the sending state shall be free to communicate with consular officers of the sending state and to have access to them. Under the same provisions, a national of the sending state can request the competent authorities of the receiving state to inform the consular post of the sending state if he or she is arrested or committed to prison or to custody pending trial or detained in any other manner. The competent authorities of the receiving state shall inform the person concerned without delay his or her rights of consular notification and access.

(ii) According to Subparagraph (c) of Article 36(1) of the Vienna Convention on Consular Relations, consular officers of the sending state are to decide whether to take certain measures for him or her ["to visit a national of the sending state who is in prison, custody or detention, to converse and correspond with him and to arrange for his legal representation"] in accordance with his or her wish. Therefore, it would be correct to regard the right of consular notification and access as a personal right held by the individual in question.

(iii) For the implementation of the Vienna Convention, Article 241 of the Rules on Crime Investigation, Article 74 of the Rules on Duties of Police Officers to Protect Human Rights (both Rules are applicable to the police) and Article 57 of the Rules on the Protection of Human Rights in Criminal Investigations (applicable to public prosecutors and other officials engaged in criminal investigations) have been adopted. All these provisions provide for the right of consular notification and the right of consular access in case of arrest, committal to prison or custody pending trial, or detention in any other manner of foreigners.

Notes

The issue of consular notification and access frequently forms the subject of judicial investigation, as is demonstrated by the long list of relevant cases before the International Court of Justice (such *LaGrand*, *Avena* and *Breard*) and national courts (for instance, before the United States Supreme Court, *Bustillo v. Johnson*, *Sanchez-Llams v Oregon* and *Medellin v. Texas*). This judgment makes clear that the Korean Government is under a legal obligation to guarantee the right of foreigners for consular notification and access. It enlists the legal documents that have been adopted for the domestic implementation of the Vienna Convention on Consular Relations.

Judicial Decisions in Private International Law (2017)

JANG Jiyong
Research Fellow (Judge)
Judicial Policy Research Institute, Seoul, Korea

1. RECOGNITION AND ENFORCEMENT

1-1. Reciprocity (Mutual Guarantee)

Supreme Court Decision 2012DA23832
Decided on May 30, 2017 [Decision on the Recognition and Enforcement of a Foreign Judgment]

Main Issues and Holdings

[1] Standard of determining whether the requirements are met for mutual guarantee under Article 217(1)4 of the Civil Procedure Act

[2] Purpose of the enforcement judgment under Article 26(1) of the Civil Execution Act, and the meaning of "final and conclusive judgment of a foreign court, etc."

[3] Measures to be taken by a court in Korea as the country where the judgment is to be enforced, in cases where either or both the form and mode in which a specific performance decree is stated in a final and conclusive judgment of a foreign court, etc. are different from the form of disposition or the mode of statement in Korean judgments

Whether a Korean court may grant compulsory execution in cases where the terms of an agreement, as the object of a specific performance decree, are not sufficiently certain to make the precise act which is to be executed clearly ascertainable, so that their enforcement is difficult to be immediately compelled even in the United States of America, the country where the judgment was rendered (negative)

[4] In cases where a foreign court entered a decree of payment of attorneys' fees and legal costs of the suit, in addition to a decree of specific performance of obligation, the standard of determining whether to grant a judgment of execution on the decree of payment of attorneys' fees and costs

Facts

[1] Defendant Ringfree Co., Ltd. (hereinafter "Defendant Company") holds a patent in connection with the method and equipment generating ringback tones in voice, text, and image during the call waiting time on telephony or cell phone services. On December 7, 2002, Defendant Company entered into an exclusive license agreement with Plaintiff Ringfree USA Corp. (hereinafter "Plaintiff Ringfree USA"), under which Plaintiff Ringfree USA would be granted the exclusive and transferrable right to exploit, lease, and sublease Defendant Company's patent in the United States of America and Canada (hereinafter the "instant Exclusive License Agreement").

[2] On December 9, 2002, Defendant Company, Defendant Company's Managing Director Defendant 2, Plaintiff Ringfree USA, and Plaintiff Ringfree USA's Managing Director Nonparty 1 executed the instant Memorandum of Agreement. Under the said Memorandum: (a) the counterparties would establish Plaintiff Ringfree International Corporation (hereinafter "Plaintiff Ringfree International"), as a joint venture; (b) Defendant Company would transfer, assign, and deliver to Plaintiff Ringfree International all domestic and foreign patent application and patent rights that it owns or controls in connection with the method and equipment to generate ringfree tones in voice, text, and image during call waiting.

[3] However, when Defendant Company failed to perform according to its agreement with Plaintiff Ringfree International, but instead notified the Plaintiffs, etc. to the effect that the instant Memorandum of Agreement and the Exclusive License Agreement were null and void, the Plaintiffs brought a lawsuit against the Defendants before the United States District Court for the Central District of California Western Division (hereinafter the "instant U.S. court") on the ground that the Defendants defaulted on their obligations under the instant Memorandum of Agreement and the Exclusive License Agreement and sought both specific performance and payment of attorneys' fees and costs.

[4] The instant U.S. court held a jury trial from August 19 to 22, 2008, and from August 26 to 28, 2008. On August 28, 2008, the jury returned a verdict finding that the Defendants breached their obligation under the instant Memorandum of Agreement and the Exclusive License Agreement, thereby incurring loss to the Plaintiffs. The instant U.S. court granted the Plaintiffs' motion to enter a decree of specific performance on October 21, 2008 and granted the Plaintiffs' motion for attorneys' fees and costs on January 12, 2009.

[5] On January 15, 2009, the instant U.S. court rendered a judgment holding that the Plaintiffs were entitled to a decree of specific performance of the parties' Memorandum of Agreement and the Exclusive License Agreement against defendants Ringfree Company, Limited, and Defendant 2, and ordered the Defendants to jointly and severally pay to the Plaintiffs USD 940,378.32 in attorneys' fees and costs (hereinafter the "instant judgment"), which became final and conclusive as is.

Summary of Decision

[1] For a final and conclusive judgment of a foreign court to be recognized, Article 217(1)4 of the Civil Procedure Act requires that "mutual guarantee exists or the respective requirements for recognition of final judgment, etc. in the Republic of Korea and the foreign country to which the foreign court belongs are not disproportionately off balance

and are not substantially different in important points." Accordingly, the requirements for mutual guarantee of the recognition of judgments under Article 217(1)4 of the Civil Procedure Act shall be deemed fulfilled inasmuch as the respective requirements for recognition of like judgments in Korea and the other country are not disproportionately off balance, the foreign requirements are not unduly more burdensome overall than those in Korea, and the two sets of requirements are not substantially different in important points. It is sufficient to find mutual guarantee by comparing the requirements for recognition based on the relevant foreign laws and regulations, case law, and customs and practices. A treaty with the other country is not necessarily required. Even in the absence of a specific precedent, it is sufficient insofar as the foreign court is expected to recognize a similar judgment rendered by a Korean court in a real case.

[2] Article 26(1) of the Civil Execution Act provides, "Compulsory execution based on a final and conclusive judgment of a foreign court or an adjudication recognized to have the same effect (hereinafter "final and conclusive judgment, etc.") may only be conducted if a court of the Republic of Korea approves of the compulsory execution by a judgment of execution." The purport of the system of judgment of execution as stipulated in this provision is as follows: (a) in cases of compelling enforcement in Korea of the rights of the parties concerned as ascertained in a judgment rendered in a competent foreign court; (b) enforcement may be grounded in the foreign judgment without having to compel redundant proceedings in Korea, such as by bringing a new action; (c) rather the parties shall obtain a judgment of execution in Korea based on the deliberation and approval of whether compulsory enforcement of the judgment shall be granted; ultimately (d) leading to a result that reconciles the parties' demand for facilitation of enforcement of their rights with the state's exercise of its exclusive prerogatives over coercive enforcement and thereby striking an appropriate balance. From this perspective, a "final and conclusive judgment of a foreign court, etc." under the foregoing provision means a final judgment on a juristic relationship rendered by a

competent judicial organ of a foreign country based on its authority under an adversarial system, the content of which is appropriate for compulsory enforcement, such as specific performance of an obligation.

[3] At equity, courts of the United States may, at its discretion, enter a decree of specific performance ordering the performance of the terms of the contract, in cases where damages cannot appropriately provide remedy to the obligee. To enforce a specific performance decree, the terms of an agreement, as the object of specific performance, must be sufficiently certain to make the precise act which is to be done clearly ascertainable (California Civil Code Section 3390 subdivision (e)). In view of the legal nature of a specific performance decree, combined with the legislative purport of the provisions on the recognition and enforcement of foreign judgments under the Korean Civil Procedure Act and the Civil Execution Act, as a matter of principle, a court of Korea, as the country where the judgment is to be enforced, shall offer a legal remedy under the Civil Execution Act, which is the same as or similar to enforcement under the final and conclusive judgment of a foreign court, etc., even when the form and mode in which the specific performance decree is stated in a final and conclusive judgment of a foreign court or adjudication recognized to have the same effect (hereinafter the "final and conclusive judgment, etc.") are different from the form of disposition or mode of statement in Korean judgments.

However, a Korean court must not grant compulsory execution in cases where the terms of an agreement, as the object of a specific performance decree, are not sufficiently certain to make the precise act which is to be executed clearly ascertainable, so that their enforcement is difficult to be immediately compelled even in the United States of America, the country where the judgment in the instant case was rendered.

As the object of a specific performance is neither sufficiently specific nor clear, a coercive enforcement of the instant specific performance decree is unlikely to be immediately feasible even in the U.S., the country where the judgment was rendered. Therefore, its compulsory execution cannot be granted by a Korean court either.

[4] In cases where a foreign court entered a decree of payment of attorneys' fees and legal costs of the suit, in addition to a decree of specific performance of obligation, determination whether to grant a judgment of execution on a decree of payment of attorneys' fees and costs shall be made separately and apart from the decree of specific performance and based on an examination of whether that part, by itself, meets the requirements under Article 27(2) of the Civil Execution Act.

According to the above legal doctrine and the provisions of the California Civil Code and Code of Civil Procedure, the part of the instant judgment on attorneys' fees and costs is a separate subject matter of litigation apart from the part seeking specific performance and cannot be deemed subordinate to the judgment on the specific performance decree. Therefore, whether enforcement judgment may be granted on said part shall be determined separately from the part on the specific performance decree, by examining whether the requirements under Article 27(2) of the Civil Execution Act are met.

1-2. Recognition and Enforcement of Foreign Arbitral Award (New York Convention)

Supreme Court Decision 2017DA238837
Decided on December 22, 2017 【Decision on Enforcement】

Main Issues and Holdings

[1] Legislative purpose of Article 5(1)(d) of the United Nations Convention on the Recognition and Enforcement of Foreign Arbitral Awards

[2] Whether the degree of violation of a party's procedural right due to an arbitral procedure must be obvious and intolerable to constitute grounds for refusal of recognition and enforcement of arbitral awards as stipulated under the aforementioned Convention (affirmative)

[3] In a case where a party participated in an arbitral procedure without raising any timely objection to a defect in the procedure that serves to protect the party's rights and interests, whether the party may contest during the procedure for recognition and enforcement of arbitral rewards (negative)

Facts

[1] Apart from the agreement for the resolution of dispute through arbitration by the International Chamber of Commerce (ICC), the Plaintiff applied for arbitration with the Ireland Branch of the Chartered Institute of Arbitration (hereinafter "the instant arbitral agency"), and subsequently, the arbitral procedure commenced and an arbitrator selected. However, without raising any particular objection, the Defendant participated in the arbitral procedure commenced by the instant arbitral agency that implemented the procedure, and thereafter, the relevant arbitral award was handed down.

[2] The Plaintiff sought the recognition and enforcement of the instant arbitral award according to the United Nations Convention on the Recognition and Enforcement of Foreign Arbitral Awards (hereinafter "New York Convention").

Summary of Decision

[1] Article 5(1)(d) of the New York Convention provides that recognition and enforcement of arbitral awards may be refused in cases where "the composition of the arbitral authority or the arbitral procedure was not in accordance with the agreement of the parties, or, failing such agreement, was not in accordance with the law of the country where the arbitration took place." This stems from the contractual nature of arbitral procedures, which, as a matter of principle, are based on the parties' autonomy and agreement, but, as a supplementary method, an arbitration procedure takes place by a discretionary provision if there is no agreement by the parties.

[2] However, the simple fact that there was either a breach of the

parties' agreement or the discretionary provision alone is insufficient to constitute grounds for refusal of recognition and enforcement of arbitral rewards as stipulated under the New York Convention. Additionally, it required is that the extent to which a party's procedural right was violated due to the arbitral procedure should be obvious and intolerable. Also, when determining the violation of either an arbitral authority or an arbitral procedure, a court of the country where the arbitration was recognized or enforced (i) should strongly consider whether "a timely objection was made during the arbitral procedure," and, on that conclusive basis, (ii) may deem the right to object having been waivered in a case where, even if there was a procedural violation, a party failed to raise a timely objection thereto during the arbitration procedure, and such violation was to protect the party's procedural rights and interests, rather than the public interest. Although the New York Convention does not have an express provision regarding the waiver of the right to object, if a party participated in an arbitral procedure without raising any timely objection to a defect in the procedure that serves to protect the party's rights and interests, it is tenable to construe that the party may not object during the procedure for recognition and enforcement of arbitral rewards.

[3] We find it difficult to deem such procedure, which was undertaken by the arbitrator selected by another arbitral agency other than what was agreed upon, as constituting a fundamental and grave procedural defect of an irreparable nature (such as violation of a mandatory provision), and there is no evidence supporting that the Defendant was unaware of the procedural defect. Moreover, the matter of selecting an arbitral agency and an arbitrator pertains to the protection of a party's rights and interests, rather than the public interest, and therefore, may be the subject of a waiver.

In view of the instant arbitral agency's progression of the arbitral procedure and the extent of the Defendant's procedural participation, etc., it should be deemed that the Defendant: (a) waivered the procedural right, i.e., arbitration via ICC that was previously agreed upon; and (b) made a new agreement for the instant arbitral agency to undergo the arbitral procedure.

2. GOVERNING LAW

2-1. Applicable Law of a Direct Claim Between an Insurer and a Third Party (Applicable Law of the Insurance Contract: English Third Party Rights Act)

Supreme Court Decision 2015DA42599
Decided on October 26, 2017 【Damages (Etc.)】

Main Issues and Holdings

[1] Legal nature of a direct claim between an insurer and a third party in a liability insurance contract (i.e., cumulative acceptance of an obligation for compensation)

[2] Whether the legal basis of Articles 34 and 35 of the Act on Private International Law, which provides for the acceptance of an obligation or the transfer of a claim to be governed by the applicable law surrounding the legal relationship of the obligation or claim to be transferred shall be referenced in cases involving the acceptance of an obligation under law (affirmative)

In regards to a liability insurance contract involving a foreign element, the governing law applicable to a legal relationship surrounding a third party's exercise of a direct claim (i.e., a country's law applicable to a liability insurance contract)

Facts

[1] The Plaintiffs, along with a subrogation insurance claim, selectively sought a third party claim against the Defendant by asserting to the effect that "Bright Shipping neglected, despite its obligation, to safely

deliver cargo to the intended destination and caused damage to the cargo, and therefore is liable to compensate for damages."

[2] The liability insurance contract on marine cargo (hereinafter "the instant insurance contract") concluded between Bright Shipping Co., Ltd. (the insured; hereinafter "Bright Shipping") and the Defendant (the insurer) contains a clause stating that U.K. law will be applied as the governing law regarding the Defendant's liability.

Summary of Decision

[1] There is no direct provision under the Act on Private International Law as to the criteria for determining the governing law in cases where a third party, who has the right to seek compensation for damages under the laws of the Republic of Korea against an insured party to a liability insurance contract that is governed by a foreign law, exercises a direct claim against an insurer in Korea.

In a liability insurance contract, the legal nature of a direct claim between an insurer and a third party pertains to a legal relationship whereby the insurer concurrently accepts an obligation for compensation against a victimized party (the insured's third party) under law.

[2] Article 34 of the Act on Private International Law equally treats the legal relationship surrounding the acceptance of an obligation and the transfer of a claim by providing that "[…] the assignability of the claim and the effect of the assignment of the claim against a debtor and a third party shall be governed by the applicable law of the claim to be assigned" (para. 1) and "[t]he provision of paragraph (1) shall be applied *mutatis mutandis* to the acceptance of obligations" (para. 2). Also, Article 35 of the same Act stipulates, "[t]he transfer of a claim by Act shall be governed by the applicable law of the legal relations between the old creditor and the new creditor, which are the cause of the transfer" (para. 1) and "[i]n case the legal relations of paragraph (1) do not exist, the applicable law of the claim transferred shall govern" (para. 2). As can be seen, it is tenable to take under consideration the legal basis of Articles 34 and 35 thereof that provides for

the acceptance of an obligation or the transfer of a claim to be governed by the applicable law surrounding the legal relationship of the obligation or claim to be transferred in cases involving the acceptance of an obligation under law.

Yet, the cause for an insurer's cumulative acceptance of an insured's compensation obligation is separate from that of the insured's assumption of the liability for compensation against a third party, given that there exists a statutory provision acknowledging a third party's right of a direct claim against an insurer regarding a liability insurance contract between the insurer and the insured. Furthermore, where a third party's right of a direct claim is acknowledged, there is no mechanism other than by a liability insurance contract to set the details of the scope of liability to be assumed by the insurer against the third party, and the rights and obligations assumed by the insurer and the insured are subject to change according to the liability insurance contract.

In full view of the above circumstances, as to the matter of a liability insurance contract involving a foreign element, the law of the country applicable to a legal relationship surrounding a third party's exercise of a direct claim is deemed the most closely connected with the contract. Therefore, it is deemed tenable to construe that country's law to be the governing law.

As the instant insurance contract between Bright Shipping (the insured) and the Defendant (the insurer) contains a clause stating that U.K. law will be applied as the governing law regarding the Defendant's liability, that country's law shall be the applicable governing law as to the insurer's liability; and the U.K. law is applicable with regard to the Primary Plaintiff (the victim in the instant case)'s direct claim against the Defendant, given that the victimized party's exercise of direct claim against the insurer should abide by the governing law of the relevant insurance contract.

[3] According to U.K.'s Third Parties (Rights against Insurers) Act 1930 (hereinafter "Third Party Rights Act"), in order for a third party, the victimized party of liability insurance, to be transferred the insured party's right and

subsequently exercise the right of direct claim against the insurer, the insured shall be in a default state, such as having entered into bankruptcy, as prescribed under Article 1(1) of the Third Party Rights Act; if the insured is an entity, a winding-up order or resolution for a voluntary winding-up should have been undertaken, a receiver or manager should have been appointed to that entity's business or assets, or ownership of the entity's asset as a whole should have been transferred to a floating security rights-holder.

As the aforesaid provision narrowly and exhaustively construed cases of permitting direct claim by taking under consideration the legislative purpose, regulatory method, etc. of Article 1 of the Third Party Rights Act, inasmuch as Bright Shipping had not yet commenced legal proceedings for filing bankruptcy or rehabilitation, but had shut down and was merely in a "*de facto*" state of bankruptcy, the company did not satisfy the requirements mentioned in the aforesaid provision. Accordingly, the Primary Plaintiff, the victimized party of the instant case, could not exercise the right of direct claim against the Defendant, the insurer.

2-2. Repudiation under English Contract Law

Supreme Court Decision 2014DA233176, 233183
Decided on May 30, 2017 【Damages (Etc.); Sales Payment Return】

Main Issues and Holdings

Meaning of "repudiation" under English contract law and method of determination of whether intent to repudiate was expressed / In the event a party exhibits a negative or passive attitude toward a contractual performance, such an act should not be readily concluded as clearly and definitively expressing intent to repudiate

Facts

[1] 21st Century Shipbuilding Co., Ltd. (hereinafter "21st Century Shipbuilding"), a Korean shipbuilder, and C-Wing Holdings Limited (hereinafter "C-Wing"), Co-Defendant of the original trial, concluded an agreement for the construction of vessels (hereinafter "the instant agreement"); the intervenor joining the Plaintiff (Counterclaim Defendant) issued a refund guarantee (hereinafter "R/G") as to each vessel of the instant case; and the Defendant (Counterclaim Plaintiff; hereinafter "Defendant") and C-Wing entered into a loan agreement and a collateral transfer agreement related to the first installment payment (amounting to USD 2.5 million per vessel) under the instant agreement, and was accordingly granted exclusive status with respect to exercising C-Wing's rights over 21st Century Shipbuilding incurring thereunder.

[2] C-Wing, following the payment of the first installment, planned to transfer the instant agreement to a would-be acquirer, a fact that 21st Century Shipbuilding was well aware of. However, in the wake of the global financial crisis that erupted in the second half of 2008, C-Wing had difficulty in procuring funds due to the lack of potential buyers arising from the decline in shipbuilding orders. Against this backdrop, on November 10, 2009, 21st Century Shipbuilding and C-Wing mutually agreed on the change of the sales amount and delivery date.

[3] On December 28, 2009, immediately after the aforementioned agreement on change, a creditor financial institution conducted a joint administrative proceeding (hereinafter "workout process"), under the former Corporate Restructuring Promotion Act, against 21st Century Shipbuilding. Under the measures for business normalization in a due diligence report prepared by an accounting firm during the workout process, the construction of each vessel of the instant case was excluded on the ground that C-Wing was facing difficulties procuring funds.

[4] 21st Century Shipbuilding: (i) on July 15, 2010, notified C-Wing that it would start cutting steel for the ship's hull (hull number: CSN-267); (ii) on July 30 of the same year, performed the steel cutting process without

C-Wing's participation, and subsequently, notified C-Wing of such fact by attaching a letter of confirmation with the signature of a vessel inspector from the American Bureau of Shipping ("ABS"); and (iii) thereafter, notified C-Wing after having performed the steel cutting process on several occasions related to each vessel of the instant case.

[5] On August 25, 2010, the Defendant notified 21st Century Shipbuilding that: (i) it did not undergo construction of the vessels despite the delivery date under the instant agreement either having lapsed or nearing lapse because 21st Century Shipbuilding refused to perform the obligation thereunder; and (ii) it was rescinding the instant agreement on the ground that anticipating contractual performance from 21st Century Shipbuilding was difficult.

Summary of Decision

[1] Given that there is a foreign element regarding the instant agreement, a governing law needs to be established pursuant to the Act on Private International Law that provides, "A contract shall be governed by the law which the parties choose explicitly or implicitly" (Article 25). In this case, English law was stipulated as the governing law of the instant agreement.

[2] The doctrine of anticipatory breach of contract is acknowledged under English contract law. If one party to a contract unlawfully repudiates it and that repudiation is accepted by the other party thereof, then the other party is discharged without delay from further performance and may seek claim for damages arising from contractual breach, but the contract itself is not rescinded (of note, "rescission" encompasses the concepts "cancellation" and "termination" under Korean civil law) (*see, e.g.,* Hochster v. De la Tour [1853] 118 E.R. 922; Heyman v. Darwins Ltd. [1942] A.C. 356).

"Repudiation" means an act by a party to a contract who, either through verbal or non-verbal behavior, expresses intent to not perform and/or inability to perform an important contractual obligation, thereby causing the other party to no longer anticipate performance of obligations under the contract (*see* Heyman v. Darwins Ltd., *supra*).

Inasmuch as whether intent of repudiation is a matter of fact-finding that should be objectively determined, "If one of the parties to a contract, either in express terms or by conduct, leads the other party to the reasonable conclusion that [he/she] does not mean to carry out the contract, this amounts to a repudiation which will justify the other in treating the contract as at an end" (*see* Forslind v. Bechely-Crundall [1922] S.L.T. 496). The intent to repudiate does not always have to be explicit, nor does it have to be expressed through specific words or actions, and can be implicit through a series of acts or conduct; however, repudiation must be expressed clearly, absolutely, and definitively (*see, e.g.,* Chilean Nitrate Sales Corp. v. Marine Transportation Co. [1982] 1 Lloyd's Rep. 570; SK Shipping (S) PTE Ltd. v. Petroexport Ltd. [2009] EWHC 2974 (Comm)). Even if a party to a contract exhibits a negative or passive attitude toward performing obligations under the contract, such an act should not be readily concluded as clearly and definitively expressing intent to repudiate without considering overall circumstances (*see, e.g.,* Mersey Steel and Iron Co. v. Naylor, Benzon & Co. [1884] 9 App. Cas. 434; Woodar Investment Development Ltd. v. Wimpey Construction UK Ltd. [1980] 1 W.L.R. 277).

There was no basis to deem that the right to rescind following anticipatory repudiation — acknowledged under English common law — took effect.

2-3. Negotiation of L/C and Beneficiary's Fraud under UCP 600

Supreme Court Decision 2017DA216776
Decided on November 14, 2017 [L/C Payment Claim]

Main Issues and Holdings

[1] Meaning and method of "negotiation" under Article 2 of the Uniform Customs and Practice for Documentary Credits, 2007 Revision, ICC Publication No. 600 ("UCP 600"), and in cases where a merchant trader's bank, in issuing a so-called back-to-back letter of credit (L/C),

enters into an agreement on the negotiation of a master letter of credit (L/C), whether it constitutes a "definite undertaking of an unconditional obligation to pay funds in lieu of a real payment of funds," which is one of the ways to negotiate a letter of credit (negative)

[2] Point at which the negotiating bank of a sight irrevocable documentary credit must pay the L/C negotiating funds to the beneficiary (held: on or before five banking days following the date on which the documents reached the issuing bank)

[3] In cases where a bank's L/C negotiation was unlawful, whether the issuing bank may refuse to pay the presenting bank upon L/C maturity on the ground that the beneficiary's fraud was revealed in a documentary credit transaction (affirmative)

Facts

[1] Notwithstanding its direct negotiation and agreement with a Japanese scrap metal dealer on matters pertaining to the importation of the instant scrap metals, SteelM Co. Ltd. (hereinafter "SteelM") decided to import the instant scrap metals instead by having United Metals purchase them from the Japanese scrap metal dealer, which in turn would be imported by SteelM from United Metals.

[2] SteelM had United Metals open a back-to-back L/C as the importer, through which it had the Japanese scrap metal dealer ship and deliver the instant scrap metals to Korea.

[3] Upon the arrival of the instant scrap metals in Korea, instead of obtaining and using a genuine bill of lading as required under each of the instant L/C through a normal process of settling the import price, SteelM removed and sold the instant scrap metals in advance, using the bill of lading separately drawn up for customs purposes.

[4] Since the instant scrap metals were already removed and sold, the Defendants, as the issuing bank of each of the instant L/C, could not acquire security interest therein, even if they were to be presented with complying documents for their L/C reimbursement.

[5] As the beneficiary of each of the instant L/C, United Metals knew or could have sufficiently anticipated the fact that SteelM was abusing each of the instant L/C as a means for the aforementioned illegal, fraudulent transaction, in light of the previous transactions with SteelM, as well as the purpose of, and developments leading up to, its involvement in the instant scrap metal import.

Summary of Decision

[1] Article 2 of the Uniform Customs and Practice for Documentary Credits, 2007 Revision, ICC Publication No. 600 ("UCP 600") defines "negotiation" as "the purchase by the nominated bank of drafts (drawn on a bank other than the nominated bank) and/or documents under a complying presentation, by advancing or agreeing to advance funds to the beneficiary on or before the banking day on which reimbursement is due to the nominated bank." A nominated bank can negotiate documents as defined in the said provision by either immediately advancing or undertaking to advance a real payment in cash or by wire transfer to the beneficiary. Negotiation by the latter method requires the negotiating bank to give a definite undertaking of an unconditional obligation to pay funds to the beneficiary on a specific date, in lieu of a real payment.

The so-called back-to-back letter of credit (L/C) means an L/C issued by the bank of a merchant trader to the order of the actual exporter, secured by a master letter of credit (L/C) to the order of the merchant trader itself. Even where, in issuing a back-to-back L/C, the bank of a merchant trader signed an agreement regarding the master L/C negotiation, it cannot be deemed an agreement to definitely pay funds to the beneficiary on a specific date. Thus, it does not constitute a definite undertaking of an unconditional obligation to pay funds, in lieu of a real payment of funds.

[2] The nominated bank must advance or agree to advance funds to the beneficiary on or before the banking day on which reimbursement is due to the nominated bank, and has a maximum of five banking

days following the day of presentation to determine if a presentation is complying (Article 14(b) of UCP 600). Therefore, in case of a sight irrevocable documentary credit, the negotiating bank must advance funds to the beneficiary on or before five banking days following the date on which the documents reached the issuing bank.

[3] Even where a documentary credit transaction only turns out to be fraudulent after a lawful L/C negotiation, the negotiating bank may still claim against the issuing bank for reimbursement of funds, unless the negotiating bank is found to have been involved as a party to the fraud, or was aware of or had good reasons to suspect the fraud at the time of advancement or negotiation of funds. However, a bank's L/C negotiation is not a "negotiation" as defined in UCP 600 unless it is lawful, even with the advancement of funds. In the event of an unlawful negotiation, the issuing bank can stand up against the presenting bank upon L/C maturity on all the grounds on which it can stand up against the beneficiary. Therefore, where the beneficiary's fraud was revealed in a documentary credit transaction, it constitutes a ground for the issuing bank to refuse to advance funds to the presenting bank.

[4] Beneficiary United Metals colluded with SteelM, the applicant for each of the instant L/C, and claimed the L/C payment against the Defendants, as the issuing banks of each of the instant L/C, by abusing the independence and abstraction of documentary credit transaction even when all the instant scrap metals have already been removed and sold. In light of the structure and nature of documentary credit transaction, this is impermissible as a fraudulent transaction under the pretext of documentary credit. Therefore, as seen above, the Defendants may, on the ground of the beneficiary's fraudulent transaction, refuse to pay the Plaintiff for its failure to lawfully negotiate each of the instant L/C. The Defendants, as the issuing banks of each of the instant L/C, do not owe L/C payment to the beneficiary United Metals, and thus, can stand up against the Plaintiff seeking the payment on each of the instant L/C as the presenter of the instant documentary credit, or as the transferee of the

rights of beneficiary United Metals.

3. INTERNATIONAL PATENT

SUPREME COURT DECISION 2014DU42490
DECIDED ON APRIL 28, 2017 [CLAIM FOR REVOCATION OF DISPOSITION OF REJECTION]

Main Issues and Holdings

[1] In the event an applicant, when filing an international patent application, claims priority over an earlier application, whether the "priority date" under the text of Article 201(1) of the former Patent Act is the filing date of the earlier application whose priority is so claimed (affirmative)

[2] Whether an international patent applicant is required to follow the procedures specified under the Patent Cooperation Treaty and the former Patent Act based on the date of claiming priority (affirmative in principle), and in such case, whether it can be viewed differently depending on the existence or absence of substantive validity (negative)

Facts

The Plaintiff (a) on May 18, 2009, filed an international patent application for the invention called "Flash X-Ray Irradiator" in the Republic of Korea, which is a designated Contracting State of the PCT, (b) but prior to filing such international application, on May 16, 2008, claimed priority pursuant to Article 8 of the PCT over an earlier application filed in the United States, which is a country party to the Paris Convention, and (c) thereafter, on December 16, 2011, submitted to the Defendant a Korean translation of the international patent application for national phase entry.

The Defendant (Commissioner of the Korea Intellectual Property Office), on November 12, 2012, rejected the Korean translation of the international patent application (hereinafter "the instant disposition") on the ground that the Plaintiff did not submit the translation within two years and seven months from the date of claiming priority (May 16, 2008), and as such, the international application was deemed to have been withdrawn based on Article 201(2) of the former Patent Act.

Summary of Decision

[1] According to the provisions of Article 201(1) and (2) of the former Patent Act and Articles 2(xi) and 8 of the Patent Cooperation Treaty (hereinafter "PCT"), if an applicant, when filing an international patent application, were to have claimed priority over an earlier application filed in a Contracting State of the Paris Convention for the Protection of Industrial Property, the "priority date" under the text of Article 20(1) of the former Patent Act shall be the filing date of the earlier application whose priority is so claimed, not the filing date of the international patent application.

[2] Moreover, the "priority date" is based on: (i) the date of various procedures comprising the international phase, such as the publication, search, and request for preliminary examination of an international patent application, under the PCT and the Regulations established thereunder; and (ii) the date of submission of a translation of a patent specification, including the claims, under the former Patent Act. As can be seen, there is a need to uniformly set the "priority date" inasmuch as it considerably affects the duties of relevant agencies and interested persons. Therefore, unless an international patent applicant made an obvious error in claiming priority, the date of claiming priority shall be deemed the priority date and the procedures under the PCT and the former Patent Act shall be undertaken based on the date thereof, and such conclusion shall not change depending on the existence or absence of substantive validity of such priority claim.

[3] Inasmuch as the Plaintiff has claimed priority over an earlier application while filing an international patent application, May 16,

2008, the filing date of the earlier application, shall be deemed the priority date. Furthermore, there is no need to consider the existence or absence of substantive validity of such priority claim.Notwithstanding that the Plaintiff was required to submit a Korean translation within two years and seven months from the aforementioned priority date as specified in the text of Article 201(1) of the former Patent Act, the Plaintiff did not meet the specified deadline by submitting the Korean translation on December 16, 2011.

Accordingly, the Defendant was correct to have issued the instant disposition on the ground that the international patent application was deemed as having been withdrawn pursuant to Article 201(2) of the former Patent Act. Moreover, the Court cannot accept the Plaintiff's argument purporting that the Defendant, when determining the compliance of the period for submission of a Korean translation, should consider "the conditions for, and the effect of, any priority claim" under Article 8(2) of the PCT, that is, whether a priority claim satisfies the requirements of Article 4(h) of the Paris Convention.

International Law-Related Resolutions of the 20th National Assembly with a Focus on Free Trade Agreement, Armistice Agreement and Fisheries Agreement

CHUNG Min-Jung
Legislative Research Officer
National Assembly Research Service, Seoul, Korea

The resolution adopted by the National Assembly (hereinafter referred to as "legislative resolution") of the Republic of Korea (hereinafter referred to as "Korea") is an expression of legislative will. Legislative resolutions do not comply with procedural formalities necessary to give them legal status yet nonetheless influence the behavior of the domestic and foreign administrations and of the public. Legislative resolutions affect behavior by informing the public and domestic and foreign political institutions about the intentions and foreign policy preferences of the National Assembly, which are informative about the National Assembly's view of the international affairs, relevant to the decision making of various political agents as well as that of the public and thus influential in the direction of foreign policy initiatives.

Periodically, proposals surface to pay more attention to the legislative resolution as a mechanism for influencing foreign policy. Total 23 legislative resolutions were adopted at the plenary assembly, after the deliberation of various standing or select committees, in the first half of the 20th Session (May 30, 2016 - May 29, 2018).[1] The legislative resolutions related to foreign relations are three; the first one is the legislative resolution against the People's Republic of China (herein after referred to as "China") primarily under the auspices of the Foreign Affairs and Reunification Committee (standing committee);[2] the second legislative resolution was brought against the Democratic People's Republic of Korea (hereinafter referred to as "North Korea") under the purview of the Defense Committee (standing committee);[3] and the last one is the legislative resolution against China under the authority of the Agriculture, Food, Rural Affairs, Oceans and Fisheries Committee (standing committee).[4]

The National Assembly uses the rhetoric of international law as practical art of persuasive discourse because international law is considered shared logic and common understanding. For example, firstly, *the Free Trade Agreement Between the Government of the Republic of Korea and the Government of the People's Republic of China* (hereinafter referred to as the "Korea - China FTA")[5] was referred to in the *Legislative resolution urging China to suspend trade retaliations Allegedly Related to Korea's Deployments of the Terminal High Altitude Area Defense (hereinafter referred to as "THAAD")*. Secondly, the *Agreement Between the Commander-in-Chief, U.N. Command and the Supreme Commander, Korean People's Army, and the Commander of the Chinese People's Volunteers, Concerning a Military Armistice in Korea* (hereinafter referred to as "Armistice Agreement")[6] was mentioned in the *Legislative resolution condemning North Korea's missile launch and its violation of the Armistice Agreement*. Lastly, the *Agreement Concerning Fisheries between the Republic of Korea and the People's Republic of China* (hereinafter referred to as "Korea – China Fisheries Agreement")[7] was referred to in the *Legislative resolution calling for taking all necessary measures to tackle illegal fishing by the Chinese vessels*.

The 20th National Assembly invoked, as the grounds of accusing China of violating international norms, bilateral treaties such as the free trade agreement and the fisheries agreement which had been concluded between Korea and China rather than multilateral treaties because referring to bilateral treaties had advantages. Bilateral treaties dealt with arrangements that were more coherent in that they tailored their arrangements to the specific needs and circumstances of the particular dyadic associated with cultural diversity and competing values. In addition, the lack of uniformity allowed the Parties of bilateral treaties greater room for creativity, flexibility, and political expediency in solving foreign affairs concerns. A tailored agreement also endowed its Parties with a sense of ownership over its provisions, thereby increasing their propensity to comply.

This paper sets forth selected legislative resolutions related to the free trade agreement, the armistice agreement and the fisheries agreement. The legislative resolutions introduced here are primarily geared towards urging the country complained against by the National Assembly to implement specific measures regarding the issue, encouraging the Korean government to use active diplomacy to its end, and promoting alliance with the international community for its purpose.

1. LEGISLATIVE RESOLUTION URGING CHINA TO SUSPEND TRADE RETALIATIONS ALLEGEDLY RELATED TO KOREA'S DEPLOYMENTS OF THE THAAD

The Korean government and the Chinese government got themselves ready and prepared to construct trust relationship in the political and economic field since 1992, in which Korea established diplomatic relations with China and cut official ties with Taiwan. However, as the United States deployed THAAD to Korea in March 2017 to address growing concerns over North Korea's quickly progressing missile programs, China had seen the THAAD deployments as a sign of escalating tensions between the United State and China.

Therefore, the Chinese government decided to impose massive retaliatory measures of one variety or another, i.e., from levying of unauthorized trade sanctions on the Korean enterprises to a complete ban of cultural and human resources exchange between Korea and China, which, the National Assembly deemed, were not directly related to the THAAD deployment. Specifically,

China's Department of Recreation had imposed restrictions on tourism service supplies and suppliers from Korea for retaliation. They became a barrier that stood between Korea and China that would prevent both countries from maintaining inter-dependent and reciprocal relations and realizing common goods.

On March 30, 2017, the National Assembly adopted a legislative resolution expressing deep concerns over the imposition of suspension upon Korean-invested enterprises in Chinese territory by the Chinese government and urging the Chinese government to realize that its policies and practices must comport with the rules of the international trading system.

The National Assembly alleged that China was acting contrary to international law and international trade principles because it obligated itself to non-discriminatory treatment and market access in its WTO General Agreement on Trade in Services (GATS) schedule for both cross-border (Mode 1) and commercial presence (Mode 3) tourism service providers. From an international economic law standpoint, China's retaliatory actions were the violations of its WTO and FTA obligations to respect freedom, rule of law and non-discriminatory treatment in international service trade as well as its failure to follows its own rhetoric on international trade of "resisting any kind of protectionism."

Next, this Legislative resolution proposed that the Chinese government provide Korean entrepreneurs and tourists with full protection and security. Then the National Assembly called for strong support and cooperative alliance from the Chinese government with the international community for stopping North Korea's progressing nuclear missile programs and for achieving the goal of a denuclearized Korean Peninsula. Lastly, the National Assembly urged the Korean government to make best efforts to discuss North Korea's nuclear weapons program with China.

2. LEGISLATIVE RESOLUTION CONDEMNING NORTH KOREA'S MISSILE LAUNCH AND ITS VIOLATION OF THE ARMISTICE AGREEMENT

On December 2, 2017, the National Assembly adopted a resolution condemning North Korea's launch of an intercontinental ballistic missile (ICBM), defining it as severely and sufficiently provocative acts contrary to the Armistice Agreement. The National Assembly warned the North Korea that all responsibility for threats to international peace and security lied on it.

In 1950, North Korea invaded Korea with the support of China and Russia. After three years of fighting, the war came to an end, and the representatives of the UN, the Korean People's Army, and the Chinese People's Volunteers signed a Military Armistice Agreement in 1953 agreeing to a cessation of hostilities on the Korean peninsula and the separation of the two Koreas along the 38th parallel.

The Armistice Agreement requires a closer look at its purpose because it remains, more or less, the sole document responsible for ending the hostilities of the Korea war. Specifically, Section 62 of the Agreement stated that the armistice would remain in effect "until expressly superseded either by mutually acceptable amendments and additions or by provision in an appropriate agreement for a peaceful settlement at a political level between both sides." However, in the 65 years since the Armistice Agreement came into force, there has been no such "peaceful settlement" to replace the Armistice Agreement.

When applying traditional international law theory *mutatis mutandis* to a ceasefire agreement, a violation of the agreement would only entitle the parties to the agreement to resume hostilities. However, the 1953 armistice agreement in Korea is part of a contemporary trend in armistices which completely divest the parties of the right to renew military operations under any circumstances whatever. An armistice of this nature puts an end to the war, and does not merely suspend the combat.[8]

Therefore, the National Assembly could urge the North Korea that it should still comply with the Armistice Agreement, discontinuing military provocation like missile launch that would have a severely negative impact on peace and security of the world. Furthermore, the National Assembly indicated that the continuous violation of the armistice agreement by North Korea involved the inhumane treatment of the shooting at a North Korean soldier fleeing into Korea in the Joint Security Area (JSA).

The National Assembly urged the Korean government, respectful of the resolution of the National Assembly, to take a firm stance against North Korea and to further the Administration's efforts to prevent North Korea from advancing its nuclear and missile programs. The National Assembly had previously adopted a similar resolution vehemently declining the slightest possibility of nuclear-armed North Korea on July 18, 2017.

3. LEGISLATIVE RESOLUTION CALLING FOR TAKING ALL NECESSARY MEASURES TO TACKLE ILLEGAL FISHING BY THE CHINESE VESSELS

The Chinese government started to eliminate some of the most destructive fishing practices in its own waters, while using a double standard in the territorial sea and the Exclusive Economic Zone (EEZ) of Korea. Therefore, Chinese fishing vessels had a history of illegal fishing activities near the coast of Korea, which had jeopardized the food supply and source of income of Korean fishermen. They were forced to travel further to catch fish and often had to compete for space with Chinese vessels near dangerous waters such as the Northern Limit Line (NLL), increasing the risk of deaths at sea and abductions by the North Korean authorities. And also the Chinese Vessels had continuously threatened to infringe upon sovereign rights of Korea over its sea. Sometimes the violent conflict would occur while the Korean Coast Guard exercised regulatory authority over the Chinese vessels engaging in illegal fishing activities.

On November 3, 2016, the National Assembly adopted a resolution recognizing that the Chinese fishing activities violated the Fisheries Agreement concluded between Korea and China and also urging the Chinese government to take all new steps to combat illegal fishing by its nationals. A critical point in the legislative resolution's allegations was that the Chinese government had been condoning and even subsidizing the illegal practices and had insufficient willingness to implement strong enforcement measures effectively. In other words, budgetary shortfalls and lack of know-how or the infrastructure were not the determining factor to contribute to the lack of implementation and enforcement of its fisheries laws.

Therefore, the National Agreement vehemently called on the Chinese government to enforce its fisheries management regulation in order to prevent Chinese flagged vessels from engaging in plundering marine resources in the foreign sea. And also the National Assembly recognized that it was time both governments strengthen governance and close all loopholes in the Fisheries Agreement by consolidating enforcement cooperation.

Notes

1. The National Assembly of the Republic of Korea, *Bill Information* (2018), *available at* http://likms.assembly.go.kr/bill/stat/statFinishBillSearch.do [Accessed on April 23, 2018].

2. *Legislative resolution urging China to suspend trade retaliations allegedly related to South Korea's deployments of the Terminal High Altitude Area Defense*, Submitted by Foreign Affairs and Reunification Committee Chairman, 2006509, (March 30, 2017) [adopted as submitted].

3. *Legislative resolution condemning North Korea's missile launch and its violation of the Armistice Agreement,* Submitted by Defense Committee Chairman, 2010577, (December 2, 2017) [adopted as submitted].

4. *Legislative resolution calling for taking all necessary measures to tackle illegal fishing by the Chinese vessels,* Submitted by Agriculture, Food, Rural Affairs, Oceans and Fisheries Committee Chairman, 2002644, (November 3, 2016) [adopted as submitted].

5. *Free Trade Agreement Between the Government of the Republic of Korea and the Government of the People's Republic of China* (June 1, 2015), *available at* http://fta.go.kr/webmodule/_PSD_FTA/cn/1/2_ko_cn_eng_151220.pdf [Accessed on April 23, 2018].

6. *Military Armistice in Korea and Temporary Supplementary Agreement,* T.I.A.S. No.2782, 4 U.S.T. 234 (July 27, 1953), *available at* https://1.next.westlaw.com/Link/Document/FullText?findType=Y&serNum=1953048169&pubNum=0006792&originatingDoc=Ie401d083d8d811d9bf60c1d57ebc853e&refType=CA&originationContext=document&transitionType=DocumentItem&contextData=(sc.Search) [Accessed on April 23, 2018].

7. *Agreement Concerning Fisheries between the Republic of Korea and the People's Republic of China*, UN Treaty NO. 14839 (August 3, 2000), *available at* http://treatyweb.mofa.go.kr/JobGuide.do [Accessed on April 23, 2018].

8. Yoram Dinstein, "The Initiation, Suspension, and Termination of War," *in International Law across the Spectrum of Conflict,* 140-142 (Michael N. Schmitt ed., Naval War College, 2000).

Act on the Exclusive Economic Zone and Continental Shelf

[Enforcement Date Mar. 21, 2017]
[Act No.14605, Mar. 21, 2017, Partial Amendment]

The Editorial Board
ILA Korean Branch

1. REASONS FOR THE AMENDMENT
[Partial Amendment]

◇ REASONS

The purpose of the amendment is to include the provisions on the exclusive economic zone and the continental shelf that actively reflect the United Nations Convention on the Law of the Sea (hereinafter referred to as the "Convention") in order to reaffirm the rights and interests of the Republic of Korea in the sea and the continental shelf and to contribute to the establishment of international maritime order. For this purpose, the amendment has changed the title of the Act to the "Act on the Exclusive Economic Zone and Continental Shelf" and added provisions on the continental shelf.

◇ KEY AMENDMENT POINTS

A. The title of the Act has changed to the "Act on the Exclusive Economic Zone and Continental Shelf."

B. The provision that specifies that this Act prescribes the sovereign right exercised by the Republic of Korea and jurisdiction thereof regarding its exclusive economic zone and continental shelf in accordance with the Convention was newly included to clarify the purpose of the enactment of this Act (Article 1).

C. The continental shelf of the Republic of Korea was defined as "the seabed and subsoil of the submarine areas that extend beyond its territorial sea throughout the natural prolongation of its land territory to the outer edge of the continental margin" (Article 2).

D. A provision was newly inserted to provide grounds for the exercise of the sovereign rights of the Republic of Korea in the continental shelf as well as in the exclusive economic zone for the exploration and development of natural resources and other rights in the continental shelf in accordance with the Convention (Article 3).

E. The rights and duties of foreign states or foreigners in the continental shelf of the Republic of Korea were prescribed (Article 4).

F. It was prescribed that the statutes of the Republic of Korea apply to the exercise of its rights in the continental shelf referred to in Article 3 and that the relevant agency may take necessary measures, including the exercise of the right of hot pursuit referred to in Article 111 of the Convention, stopping or boarding vessels, inspection, arrest, and judicial proceedings against the person who infringes the rights or violates the statutes of the Republic of Korea (Article 5).

* English Translation provided by the Ministry of Government Legislation

2. AMENDMENT

The Partial Amendment to the Act on the Exclusive Economic Zone, which was passed by the National Assembly, is promulgated as set forth herein.

Acting President and Prime Minister of the Republic of Korea Hwang Kyo-ahn

March 21, 2017

Prime Minister   Hwang Kyo-ahn

Cabinet Member and Minister of Foreign Affairs   Yun Byung-se

⊙ Aᴄᴛ Nᴏ. 14605

The Partial Amendment to the Act on the Exclusive Economic Zone

The part of the Act on the Exclusive Economic Zone has been amended as follows.

The title of the Act has been changed to the "Act on the Exclusive Economic Zone and Continental Shelf."

Article 1 has been amended as follows.

Article 1 (Purpose) The purpose of this Act is to protect the rights and interests of the Republic of Korea in the sea and contribute to establishing international maritime order by prescribing the sovereign right exercised by the Republic of Korea and jurisdiction thereof regarding its exclusive economic zone and continental shelf in accordance with the United Nations Convention on the Law of the Sea (hereinafter referred to as the "Convention").

Article 2 has been retitled from the "Scope of Exclusive Economic Zone" to the "Scope of Exclusive Economic Zone and Continental Shelf." The"baseline" in Clause 1 has been maintained as the "baseline"; while "Notwithstanding paragraphs (1), the delimitation of the exclusive economic zone and continental shelf" in Clause 2 has been replaced by "Notwithstanding paragraphs (1) and (2), the delimitation of the exclusive economic zone and continental shelf." Clause 2 has been renumbered as Clause 3 and with the insertion of the following new

Clause 2.

(2) Under the Convention, the continental shelf of the Republic of Korea comprises the seabed and subsoil of the submarine areas that extend beyond its territorial sea throughout the natural prolongation of its land territory to the outer edge of the continental margin, or to a distance of 200 nautical miles from the baselines from which the breadth of the territorial sea is measured where the outer edge of the continental margin does not extend up to that distance: Provided that the area where the continental margin extends beyond 200 nautical miles from the baselines, the outer edge thereof shall be established pursuant to the Convention.

Article 3 has been retitled from "Rights in Exclusive Economic Zone" to "Rights in Exclusive Economic Zone and Continental Shelf." "The exclusive economic zone" in the part other than each clause of Article 3 has been changed to "the exclusive economic zone under the Convention" while the part, with the exception of the title, has been re-established as Clause 1 with Clause 2 newly inserted in Article 3 as follow.

(2) The Republic of Korea shall have the following rights in the continental shelf under the Convention:

1. Sovereign rights to explore its continental shelf;

2. Sovereign rights to exploit minerals of the seabed and subsoil, other non-living resources, and sedentary species (referred to in Article 77(4) of the Convention);

3. Other rights as provided for in the Convention.

"The exclusive economic zone" in Article 4 Clauses 1 and 2 has been changed to "the exclusive economic zone and continental shelf."

"The exclusive economic zone" in the former part of Article 5 Clause 1 has been changed to "the exclusive economic zone and continental shelf";

"Article 3.2(1)" in the latter part of the same clause to "the exclusive economic zone and continental shelf"; and "the exclusive economic zone" in Clause 3 to "the exclusive economic zone and continental shelf."

3. ADDENDA

Article 1 (Enforcement Date) This Act shall enter into force on the date of its promulgation. However, Article 2.12 of Addenda comes into force on June 28, 2017.

Article 2 (Amendments to Other Acts) (1) The part of the Aggregate Extraction Act has been amended as follows.

The "Act on the Exclusive Economic Zone" in the part other than each clause of Article 22.1 has been changed to the "Act on the Exclusive Economic Zone and Continental Shelf."

(2) The part of the Public Waters Management and Reclamation Act has been amended as follows.

The "Act on the Exclusive Economic Zone" in Article 2.1(1), Article 4.2(1), and in the part other than the individual items of Article 13.3 has been changed to the "Act on the Exclusive Economic Zone and Continental Shelf," respectively.

(3) The part of the Act on Special Accounts for Traffic Facilities has been amended as follows.

The "Act on the Exclusive Economic Zone" in Article 7.1(4) has been changed to the "Act on the Exclusive Economic Zone and Continental Shelf."

(4) The part of the Act on the Preservation, Management, and Use of Agro-Fishery Bio-Resources has been amended as follows.

The "Act on the Exclusive Economic Zone" in Article 2.9(2) has been changed to the "Act on the Exclusive Economic Zone and Continental Shelf."

(5) The part of the Act on Protection and Inspection of Buried Cultural Heritage has been amended as follows.

"Exclusive economic zones, as defined in Article 2 of the Act on the Exclusive Economic Zone" in Article 3.1 have been changed to "exclusive economic zones, as defined in Article 2 of the Act on the Exclusive Economic Zone and Continental Shelf."

(6) The part of the Act on the Exercise of Sovereign Rights on Foreigners' Fishing, etc. within the Exclusive Economic Zone has been amended as follows.

The "Act on the Exclusive Economic Zone" in Article 2.1 and Article 3.3 has been changed to the "Act on the Exclusive Economic Zone and Continental Shelf," respectively.

(7) The part of the Ballast Water Management Act has been amended as follows.

The "Act on the Exclusive Economic Zone" in Article 2.11(3) has been changed to the "Act on the Exclusive Economic Zone and Continental Shelf."

(8) The part of the Framework Act on Fishers and Fishing Villages Development has been amended as follows.

The "Act on the Exclusive Economic Zone" in Article 47.1(8) has been changed to the "Act on the Exclusive Economic Zone and Continental Shelf."

(9) The part of the Act on the Search and Rescue, etc. in Waters has been amended as follows.

The "Act on the Exclusive Economic Zone" in Article 19.1(2) has been changed to the "Act on the Exclusive Economic Zone and Continental Shelf."

(10) The part of the Marine Scientific Research Act has been amended as follows.

The "Act on the Exclusive Economic Zone" in Article 2.4(2) has been changed to the "Act on the Exclusive Economic Zone and Continental Shelf."

(11) The part of the Act on Securing, Management, Use, etc. of Marine Bio-Resources has been amended as follows.

The "Act on the Exclusive Economic Zone" in Article 2.3(2) has been changed to the "Act on the Exclusive Economic Zone and Continental Shelf."

(12) The part of the Act on Securing, Management, Use, etc. of Marine Bio-Resources (Act No. 14513, New Enactment) has been amended as follows.

The "Act on the Exclusive Economic Zone" in Article 2.5(2) has been changed to the "Act on the Exclusive Economic Zone and Continental Shelf."

(13) The part of the Marine Environment Management Act has been amended as follows.

"Exclusive economic zones, as defined in Article 2 of the Act on the Exclusive Economic Zone" in Article 2.20(1) and Article 3.1(2) have been changed to "exclusive economic zones, as defined in Article 2 of the Act on the Exclusive Economic Zone and Continental Shelf," respectively.

4. FULL TEXT[*]

ACT ON THE EXCLUSIVE ECONOMIC ZONE AND CONTINENTAL SHELF
[Enforcement Date Mar. 21, 2017]
[Act No.14605, Mar. 21, 2017, Partial Amendment]

Article 1 (Purpose)
The purpose of this Act is to protect rights and interests of the Republic of Korea in the sea and contribute to establishing international

---

[*] This English translation is not the official translation.

maritime order by prescribing the sovereign right exercised by the Republic of Korea and jurisdiction thereof regarding its exclusive economic zone and continental shelf in accordance with the United Nations Convention on the Law of the Sea (hereinafter referred to as the "Convention").

[This Article Wholly Amended by Act No. 14605, Mar. 21, 2017]

Article 2 (Scope of Exclusive Economic Zone and Continental Shelf) (1) The exclusive economic zone of the Republic of Korea shall be the zone, excluding the territorial sea of the Republic of Korea, stretching up to 200 nautical miles outwards from the baseline referred to in Article 2 of the Territorial Sea and Contiguous Zone Act (hereinafter referred to as the "baseline") in accordance with the Convention. <Amended by Act No. 14605, Mar. 21, 2017>

(2) Under the Convention, the continental shelf of the Republic of Korea comprises the seabed and subsoil of the submarine areas that extend beyond its territorial sea throughout the natural prolongation of its land territory to the outer edge of the continental margin, or to a distance of 200 nautical miles from the baselines from which the breadth of the territorial sea is measured where the outer edge of the continental margin does not extend up to that distance: Provided, That where the continental margin extends beyond 200 nautical miles from the baselines, the outer edge thereof shall be established pursuant to the Convention. <Newly Inserted by Act No. 14605, Mar. 21, 2017>

(3) Notwithstanding paragraphs (1) and (2), the delimitation of the exclusive economic zone and continental shelf between the Republic of Korea and states with opposite or adjacent coasts (hereinafter referred to as the "relevant states") shall be established by agreement with the relevant states on the basis of international laws. <Amended by Act No. 14605, Mar. 21, 2017>

[This Article Wholly Amended by Act No. 10523, Apr. 4, 2011]

Article 3 (Rights in Exclusive Economic Zone and Continental Shelf) (1) The Republic of Korea shall have the following rights in the exclusive economic zone under the Convention: <Amended by Act No. 14605, Mar. 21, 2017>

1. Sovereign rights for the purpose of exploring and exploiting, conserving and managing the natural resources, whether living or non-living, of the waters superjacent to the sea-bed and of the sea-bed and its subsoil, and the sovereign rights with regard to other activities for the economic exploitation and exploration of the zone, such as the production of energy from the water, currents and winds;

2. Jurisdiction as provided for in the Convention with regard to the following:

    (a) The establishment and use of artificial islands, installations and structures;

    (b) marine scientific research;

    (c) The protection and conservation of the marine environment.

3. Other rights as provided for in the Convention.

(2) The Republic of Korea shall have the following rights in the continental shelf under the Convention: <Newly Inserted by Act No. 14605, Mar. 21, 2017>

1. Sovereign rights to explore its continental shelf;

2. Sovereign rights to exploit mineral of the seabed and subsoil, other non-living resources and sedentary species (referred to in Article 77(4) of the Convention);

3. Other rights as provided for in the Convention.

[This Article Wholly Amended by Act No. 10523, Apr. 4, 2011]

Article 4 (Rights and Duties of Foreign States or Foreigners) (1) In the exclusive economic zone and continental shelf of the Republic of Korea, foreign states or foreigners may, on condition that they shall comply with the relevant provisions of the Convention, enjoy the freedom of navigation, overflight, the laying of submarine cables or pipelines, and other internationally recognized lawful uses of the sea in relation to the freedom. <Amended by Act No. 14605, Mar. 21, 2017>

(2) In exercising the rights and performing the duties in the exclusive economic zone and continental shelf of the Republic of Korea, foreign states or foreigners shall have due regard as to the rights and duties of the Republic of Korea and shall comply with its statutes. <Amended by Act No. 14605, Mar. 21, 2017>

[This Article Wholly Amended by Act No. 10523, Apr. 4, 2011]

Article 5 (Exercise etc. of Rights by the Republic of Korea) (1) Except as otherwise provided for in the agreement with foreign states, the statutes of the Republic of Korea shall govern in the exclusive economic zone and continental shelf of the Republic of Korea, in order to exercise or protect the rights referred to in Article 3. The same shall also apply to the legal relations in respect of artificial islands, installations and structures in the exclusive economic zone and continental shelf. <Amended by Act No. 14605, Mar. 21, 2017>

(2) The Republic of Korea shall not exercise its rights in its exclusive economic zone under Article 3 in the area beyond the median line between the Republic of Korea and relevant states unless agreed separately between the relevant states and the Republic of Korea. In this case, the term "median line" means the line in respect of which the lineal distance from each point on such line to the nearest point on the baseline of the Republic of Korea is equivalent to the lineal distance to the nearest point on the baseline of the relevant states.

(3) The relevant agency may take necessary measures including the exercise of the right of hot pursuit referred to in Article 111 of the Convention, stopping or boarding vessels, inspection, arrest and judicial proceedings against the persons who infringe the rights referred to in Article 3 in the exclusive economic zone and continental shelf of the Republic of Korea or who are deemed to be under suspicion of violating the statutes of the Republic of Korea applied in relation to the relevant exclusive economic zone and continental shelf. <Amended by Act No. 14605, Mar. 21, 2017>

[This Article Wholly Amended by Act No. 10523, Apr. 4, 2011]

ADDENDA
<Act No. 10523, Apr. 4, 2011>

This Act shall enter into force on the date of its promulgation.

ADDENDA
<Act No. 14605, Mar. 21, 2017>

This Act shall enter into force on the date of its promulgation. (Proviso Omitted.)

Territorial Sea and Contiguous Zone Act

[Enforcement Date Mar. 21, 2017]
[Act No.14607, Mar. 21, 2017, Partial Amendment]

The Editorial Board
ILA Korean Branch

1. REASONS FOR THE AMENDMENT
[Partial Amendment]

◇ REASONS AND KEY AMENDMENT POINTS

The purpose of this amendment is to newly insert a provision that prescribes the inclusive acceptance of the provisions of treaties, etc. in the statutes of the Republic of Korea in order to reaffirm the spirit of the nation's Constitution with regard to the effect of treaties, etc. and declare its firm will to protect its territorial sovereignty.

* English Translation provided by the Ministry of Government Legislation

2. AMENDMENT

The Partial Amendment to the Territorial Sea and Contiguous Zone Act, which was passed by the National Assembly, is promulgated as set forth herein.

Acting President and Prime Minister of the Republic of Korea Hwang Kyo-ahn

March 21, 2017
　　Prime Minister　　　Hwang Kyo-ahn
　　Cabinet Member and Minister of Foreign Affairs　　　Yun Byung-se

⊙ Act No. 14607

The Partial Amendment to the Territorial Sea and Contiguous Zone Act

The part of the Territorial Sea and Contiguous Zone Act has been
amended as follows.

Articles 7 and 8 have been renumbered as Articles 8 and 9, respectively,
with the new insertion of Article 7 as follows.

Article 7 (Relationship with Treaties, etc.) Matters not provided for in this Act
with regard to the territorial sea and contiguous zone of the Republic
of Korea shall be governed by treaties concluded and promulgated
in accordance with the Constitution of the Republic of Korea or by
generally accepted international laws.

3. ADDENDA

This Act shall enter into force on the date of its promulgation.

4. FULL TEXT*

TERRITORIAL SEA AND CONTIGUOUS ZONE ACT
[Enforcement Date Mar. 21, 2017]
[Act No.14607, Mar. 21, 2017, Partial Amendment]

Article 1 (Breadth of Territorial Sea)

The territorial sea of the Republic of Korea shall be the zone not extending beyond 12 nautical miles measured from the baseline: Provided, That in cases of specified areas, the breadth of the territorial sea may be otherwise determined within the breadth of 12 nautical miles, as prescribed by Presidential Decree.

[This Article Wholly Amended by Act No. 10524, Apr. 4, 2011]

Article 2 (Baseline) (1) The ordinary baseline for measuring the breadth of the territorial sea shall be the low-water line along the coasts as marked on large-scale charts officially recognized by the Republic of Korea.

(2) In cases of the area of the sea where special geographical circumstances exist, straight lines joining points as prescribed by Presidential Decree may be employed.

[This Article Wholly Amended by Act No. 10524, Apr. 4, 2011]

Article 3 (Internal Waters)

Waters on the landward side of the baseline for measuring the breadth of the territorial sea shall be the internal waters.

[This Article Wholly Amended by Act No. 10524, Apr. 4, 2011]

Article 3-2 (Breadth of Contiguous Zone)

The contiguous zone of the Republic of Korea shall be the zone, excluding the territorial sea of the Republic of Korea, not extending beyond 24 nautical miles outwards measured from the baselines: Provided, That in specified areas, the breath of the contiguous zone may be otherwise determined within 24 nautical miles from the baseline, as

---

* This English translation is not the official translation.

prescribed by Presidential Decree.

[This Article Wholly Amended by Act No. 10524, Apr. 4, 2011]

Article 4 (Delimitation between States with Adjacent or Opposite Coasts)

The delimitation of the territorial sea and contiguous zone between the Republic of Korea and states with adjacent or opposite coasts shall, unless otherwise agreed between the states concerned, be the median line joining every point of which is equidistant from the nearest points on the baselines from which the breadth of the territorial sea of each of the two states is measured.

[This Article Wholly Amended by Act No. 10524, Apr. 4, 2011]

Article 5 (Passage of Foreign Vessels) (1) Foreign ships may enjoy the right of innocent passage through the territorial sea of the Republic of Korea so long as it is not prejudicial to peace, public order, or security of the Republic of Korea. When a foreign warship or government ship operated for non-commercial purposes intends to pass through the territorial sea, it shall give prior notice to the authorities concerned as prescribed by Presidential Decree.

(2) Passage of a foreign ship shall be considered to be prejudicial to peace, public order, or security of the Republic of Korea, if the ship engages in any of the following activities in the territorial sea: Provided, That this shall not apply to cases where the activities prescribed in subparagraphs 2 through 5, 11 and 13 have been permitted, approved, or given consent by the authorities concerned:

1. Any threat or use of force against the sovereignty, territorial integrity, or independence of the Republic of Korea, or in any other manner in violation of the principles of international law embodied in the Charter of the United Nations;

2. Any exercise or practice with weapons;

3. The launching, landing, or taking on board of any aircraft;

4. The launching, landing, or taking on board of any military device;

5. Underwater navigation;

6. The collection of information prejudicial to the security of the

Republic of Korea;

7. The propaganda or instigation prejudicial to the security of the Republic of Korea;

8. The loading or unloading of any commodity, currency, or person which violates the statutes of the Republic of Korea concerning customs, finances, immigration, or health and hygiene;

9. The discharge of pollutants exceeding the standards prescribed by Presidential Decree;

10. Any fishing activities;

11. Conduct of research or survey activities;

12. Any act of interfering with any communications system, or any other facilities or installations of the Republic of Korea;

13. Any other activity prescribed by Presidential Decree not having a direct bearing on passage.

(3) The innocent passage of foreign ships may be temporarily suspended in specified areas of the territorial sea as prescribed by Presidential Decree if such suspension is essential for security of the Republic of Korea.

[This Article Wholly Amended by Act No. 10524, Apr. 4, 2011]

Article 6 (Stopping of Vessels, etc.)

If a foreign ship (excluding foreign warships and government ships operated for non-commercial purposes; hereinafter the same shall apply) is deemed to have violated Article 5, the authorities concerned may stop, search, or seize the ship, or issue other necessary orders or take other necessary measures.

[This Article Wholly Amended by Act No. 10524, Apr. 4, 2011]

Article 6-2 (Power of Competent Authorities in Contiguous Zones)

In the contiguous zone of the Republic of Korea, the competent authorities may exercise their official authority within the extent required for the following purposes, as prescribed by the statutes:

1. Preventing infringement of the sstatutes of the Republic of Korea concerning customs, finances, immigration, or health and hygiene

within the territory or territorial sea of the Republic of Korea;

2. unishing violations of the statutes of the Republic of Korea concerning customs, finances, immigration, or health and hygiene within the territory or territorial sea of the Republic of Korea.

[This Article Wholly Amended by Act No. 10524, Apr. 4, 2011]

Article 7 (Relationship with Treaties, etc.)

Matters not provided for in this Act with regard to the territorial sea and contiguous zone of the Republic of Korea shall be governed by treaties concluded and promulgated in accordance with the Constitution of the Republic of Korea or by generally accepted international laws.

[This Article Newly Inserted by Act No. 14607, Mar. 21, 2017]

Article 8 (Penalty Provisions) (1) Crew or other passengers on board of a foreign ship who have violated Article 5 (2) or (3) shall be punished by imprisonment for not more than five years or a fine not exceeding 200 million won, and when necessary in consideration of the circumstances, the relevant ship, its equipment, its catches, or other articles in violation may be confiscated.

(2) Crew or other passengers on board of a foreign ship who have disobeyed, hindered, or evaded any order issued or measure taken in accordance with Article 6 shall be punished by imprisonment for not more than two years or a fine not exceeding 10 million won.

(3) In cases of paragraph (1) or (2), imprisonment and fines may be imposed concurrently.

(4) In applying this Article, if the act referred to in this Article concurrently constitutes a crime under other Acts other than this Act, it shall be punished by the severest punishment among the penalty provisions of each Act.

[This Article Wholly Amended by Act No. 10524, Apr. 4, 2011]

Article 9 (Special Cases concerning Warships, etc.)

If a foreign warship or government ship operated for non-commercial purposes or its crew or passengers on board violate this Act or other relevant statutes, such ship may be required to remedy the violation or to leave the territorial sea.

[This Article Wholly Amended by Act No. 10524, Apr. 4, 2011]

ADDENDA
<Act No. 4986, Dec. 6, 1995>

This Act shall enter into force on the date as prescribed by the Presidential Decree within the limit of one year from the date of its promulgation.

ADDENDA
<Act No. 10524, Apr. 4, 2011>
This Act shall enter into force on the date of its promulgation.

ADDENDA
<Act No. 14607, Mar. 21, 2017>
This Act shall enter into force on the date of its promulgation.

Act on Conservation and Utilization of the Marine Environment

[Enforcement Date Sept. 22, 2017]
[Act No.14746, Mar. 21, 2017, New Enactment]

The Editorial Board
ILA Korean Branch

1. REASONS FOR THE AMENDMENT

[ENACTMENT]

◇ **Reasons for the Enactment**

The ocean is the base for the survival of human beings that occupies a dominant part of Earth. Therefore, the international community has proactively responded to changes in the marine environment due to climate change, marine pollution, and the deterioration of marine ecosystems. Despite the endeavors of the international community, Korea faces a unique situation. In Korea, there has been no law that systematically establishes superior law and order concerning the marine environmental policies encompassing the basic principles and policy directions suitable for the characteristics of the marine environment. Within the same environment, however, various laws and ordinances regarding the development and use of the oceans, including the promotion of the marine industry, has quite actively been enacted and amended.

The current Marine Environment Management Act was enacted on January 19, 2007, and has established a comprehensive management system for the marine environment. However, it has been faced with the following limitations: difficulty in identifying the causal relationship of pollution and its effects due to the wide range of physical space, which is a characteristic unique to the marine environment; long-term accumulation of polluting effects and the subsequent manifestation of pollution; the lack of a spatial perspective based on the overall circulation process through media; and the failure to enforce the observance of regulations based on international conventions and participation in international cooperation.

Therefore, there has been a wide consensus on the need to recognize that sustainable utilization of the oceans can be achieved through the harmonization of development and the active conservation of the marine environment. It is also necessary to change the regulatory paradigm centered on the land environment in order to reflect the inherent characteristics of the marine environment for the establishment of a legal system. The legal system would address relevant issues, including the prevention of marine pollution, the conservation and management of the marine environment, the recovery of the destroyed marine environment, and the harmonization of the protection of marine ecosystems, and the eco-friendly development and utilization of marine resources. There is also the need to systematize various laws and regulations related to the marine environment based on the mother law.

Therefore, the enactment of the Act on Conservation and Utilization of the Marine Environment has been sought to re-establish policy directions suitable for the marine environment as a foundation for the development of the marine environmental law system. The establishment of this system can form a complementary relationship with the land-centered environmental law system in consideration of the problems that have been arisen from the enforcement of laws and regulations related to the marine environment, including the Marine Environment Management Act. The Act on Conservation and Utilization of the Marine Environment also intends to provide various measures necessary for the establishment of comprehensive and systematic marine environmental policies.

◇ **KEY PROVISION OUTLINE**

A. The purpose of this Act is to prescribe matters concerning the basic direction-setting for marine environment policies and the establishment and implementation system for such policies. The objective would be to manage the sea in a systematic and sustainable manner, thereby contributing to the enhancement of the quality of life of citizens as well as to continuous national development (Article 1).

B. Under the Act, the State and local governments shall have the duty of formulating and implementing plans and policies necessary to properly conserve, manage, and utilize the marine environment. Moreover, all citizens shall cooperate with the State and local governments in their policies to preserve and utilize the marine environment (Articles 3 and 4).

C. In accordance with the Act, the State and local governments shall control activities regarding the use or development of the sea. This to ensure that such activities are performed in a manner that does not damage marine health and is acceptable by the marine environment. For regulation of the activities, the Minister of Oceans and Fisheries shall establish a marine health assessment system (Article 5).

D. The Act prescribes the basic principles of marine environmental conservation policies that the State and local governments shall formulate. These include the principles of the conservation and management of marine ecosystems and the management of the inflows, discharges, and disposal of pollutants into the sea, as well as the polluter pays principle (Articles 6 to 8).

E. The Act specifies, with respect to the comprehensive plans for the marine environment established by Minister of Oceans and

Fisheries and the implementation of the plans, that the marine environmental standards should be taken into account during the formulation of a plan or the execution of a project (Articles 10 to 14).

F. The major policies to be established and implemented are provided by the Act as follow: the designation of marine environmental management sea areas, response to marine climate change, comprehensive marine environmental surveys, marine environmental quality assessment, sea area utilization impact assessment, etc. (Articles 15 to 20).

G. The Act also stipulates that the foundations to be established for the implementation of marine environmental policies are as follow: integrated management system for marine environment information, accuracy control of marine environment information, science and technology related to marine environment, international cooperation, promotion of and support for marine environmental education, etc. (Articles 21 to 25).

H. The Act specifies the basis for the establishment of the Marine Environment Preservation Association, measures for the promotion of private organizations' activities, and the delegation and entrustment of duties (Articles 26 to 28).

* English Translation provided by the Ministry of Government Legislation

2. ENACTMENT

The Act on Conservation and Utilization of the Marine Environment, which was passed by the National Assembly, is promulgated as set forth herein.

Acting President and Prime Minister of the Republic of Korea Hwang Kyo-ahn

March 21, 2017
    Prime Minister   Hwang Kyo-ahn
    Cabinet Member and Minister of Oceans and Fisheries
                                    Kim Yeong-seok

⊙ **ACT NO. 14746**

The Act on Conservation and Utilization of the Marine Environment

[The body of the Act is omitted]

3. ADDENDA

Article 1 (Enforcement Date) The Act enters into force six months after the date of its promulgation.

Article 2 (General Interim Measures) The acts of or related to the administrative agencies under the former Marine Environment Management Act that are being performed at the time of the enforcement of this Act shall be deemed to be the acts of or related to the administrative agencies pursuant to this Act, which correspond to the former Act.

Article 3 (Interim Measures for Comprehensive Plans for the Marine Environment) The comprehensive plans for the marine environment that have been established and are being implemented pursuant to Article 14 of the former Marine Environment Management Act at the time of the enforcement of this Act shall be deemed to be the comprehensive plans for the marine environment that were established in accordance with Article 10 of this Act.

Article 4 (Amendments to Other Acts) (1) The part of the Coast Management Act has been amended as follows.

"Article 14 of the Marine Environment Management Act" in Article

13.1(3) has been changed to "Article 10 of the Act on Conservation and Utilization of the Marine Environment."

(2) The part of the Environmental Education Promotion Act has been amended as follows.

Article 125 of the Marine Environment Management Act" in Article 18.3 has been changed to "Article 26 of the Act on Conservation and Utilization of the Marine Environment."

4. FULL TEXT*

ACT ON CONSERVATION AND UTILIZATION OF THE MARINE ENVIRONMENT
[Enforcement Date Sept. 22, 2017]
[Act No.14746, Mar. 21, 2017, New Enactment]

CHAPTER I. GENERAL PROVISIONS

Article 1 (Purpose)

The purpose of this Act is to prescribe matters concerning basic direction-setting for policies to conserve and utilize the marine environment and concerning the establishment and implementation system for such policies, so as to manage the sea in a systematic and sustainable manner, thereby improving marine health and contributing to the enhancement of quality of life of citizens as well as to continuous national development.

Article 2 (Definitions)

The terms used in this Act shall be defined as follows:

1. The term "marine environment" means the natural and living

---

* This English translation is not the official translation.

conditions at sea, including organisms inhabiting the sea, abiological environments surrounding the organisms, such as seawater, land at sea, and marine atmosphere, and human behavioral patterns at sea;

2. The term "conservation and utilization of the marine environment" means acts of preserving, managing and utilizing the sea, while maintaining marine health by preventing marine pollution and deterioration of marine ecosystems, improving polluted or deteriorating sea and restoring and maintaining its original state through the elimination, etc. of pollutants, and by appropriately utilizing and using spatial resources, bioresources, food resources, etc. in the marine environment;

3. The term "marine pollution" means a state in which substances or energy flowing into the sea or generated at sea adversely affects or is likely to adversely affect the marine environment;

4. The term "deterioration of marine ecosystems" means a state in which such activities as overfishing of marine organisms, etc., destruction of their habitats, and disturbance of marine order seriously damage the original functions of marine ecosystems;

5. The term "marine health" means a state of the marine environment contributing to the welfare of present and future generations and the national economy, which includes production of fishery products, marine tourism, job creation, pollution cleanup, response to climate change, and coastal protection, as well as the sustainability of such state;

6. The term "marine environmental standards" means marine environmental levels which it is desirable for the State to achieve and meet in order to protect citizens' health and the marine environment;

7. The term "accuracy control of marine environment information" means management activities which pursue the appropriateness of production, management, utilization, etc. of data through marine environment surveys;

8. The term "sea area management authority" means any of the following administrative agencies that perform the duties of marine environment management, such as activities to improve the marine environment and prevent marine pollution for the waters under its jurisdiction:

(a) The competent Metropolitan City Mayor, Do Governor, and Special Self-Governing Province Governor (hereinafter referred to as "Mayor/Do Governor"), in cases of the territorial sea and internal waters specified in the Territorial Sea and Contiguous Zone Act and sea areas prescribed by Presidential Decree;

(b) The Minister of Oceans and Fisheries, in cases of an exclusive economic zone defined in Article 2 of the Act on the Exclusive Economic Zone and Continental Shelf, sea areas prescribed by Presidential Decree, and a sea area inside a harbor.

Article 3 (Duty of State and Local Governments) (1) The State shall have the duty to formulate and implement plans and policies necessary to prevent marine pollution and deterioration of marine ecosystems and to properly conserve, manage and utilize the marine environment in consideration of the characteristics of the Korean marine environment, while observing international agreements on the marine environment.

(2) Each local government shall have the duty to formulate and implement plans and policies necessary to conserve and utilize the marine environment of the waters under its jurisdiction in consideration of the local characteristics and conditions, in accordance with national plans and policies necessary to conserve and utilize the marine environment.

Article 4 (Responsibilities of Citizens and Business Entities) (1) All citizens shall endeavor to prevent marine pollution and deterioration of marine ecosystems in their daily lives, and cooperate with the State and local governments in their policies to preserve and utilize the marine environment.

(2) Any person who engages in an activity or a business which affects

the marine environment, such as development or usage at sea, shall take measures necessary to minimize marine pollution and deterioration of marine ecosystems.

Article 5 (Assessment of Marine Health) (1) The State and local governments shall control activities to use or develop the sea to ensure that such activities are performed to the extent not damaging marine health and are acceptable by the marine environment.

(2) The Minister of Oceans and Fisheries shall establish a marine health assessment system and reflect the results of assessments therefrom in the comprehensive plan for the marine environment referred to in Article 10, as prescribed by Presidential Decree.

Article 6 (Conservation and Management of Marine Ecosystems)

The State and local governments shall prevent deterioration of marine ecosystems in advance, improve systems for preserving marine biodiversity and sustainably using marine living resources; and shall formulate plans and policies to protect marine assets.

Article 7 (Control of Flow, Discharge and Disposal of Pollutants into Sea)

(1) The State and local governments shall prepare policies to prevent pollutants from flowing into the sea in advance, and to minimize impacts that discharge, disposal, etc. of pollutants into the sea will have on the marine environment.

(2) The State and local governments shall prepare measures necessary to control the creation of contaminated sediments, waste, other substances, etc. in the sea, to promptly restore and recover damage to the marine environment, to improve the marine environment, and to perform environmentally-friendly control of pollutants.

Article 8 (Polluter-Pays Principle)

A person whose use or development of sea results in marine pollution or deterioration of marine ecosystems (hereinafter referred to as "polluter"), shall be liable to prevent such pollution or deterioration and restore the polluted or deteriorating marine environment, and in principle, shall bear expenses incurred in restoring the marine environment and rectifying damage caused by such pollution or deterioration.

Article 9 (Relationship with other Acts) (1) Any other Acts relating to the conservation and utilization of the marine environment shall be enacted or amended in compliance with this Act.

(2) Except as otherwise expressly provided for in other Acts, this Act shall apply to the conservation and utilization of the marine environment.

CHAPTER II. FORMULATION, ETC. OF COMPREHENSIVE PLANS FOR MARINE ENVIRONMENT

Article 10 (Formulation of Comprehensive Plans for Marine Environment)
(1) The Minister of Oceans and Fisheries shall formulate and implement a comprehensive plan for conservation and utilization of the marine environment (hereinafter referred to as "comprehensive plan for the marine environment") every ten years, as prescribed by Presidential Decree.

(2) Where the Minister of Oceans and Fisheries intends to formulate or amend a comprehensive plan for the marine environment, he/she shall consult with the heads of relevant central administrative agencies after hearing the opinions of Mayors/Do Governors; and shall finalize the plan after deliberation by the Maritime Affairs and Fisheries Development Committee established under Article 7 of the Framework Act on Marine Fishery Development: Provided, That the same shall not apply to any amendment of minor matters prescribed by Presidential Decree.

(3) Where deemed necessary to formulate or amend a comprehensive plan for the marine environment, the Minister of Oceans and Fisheries may hold a hearing, etc. to gather consensus from citizens, relevant experts, etc.

(4) Where the Minister of Oceans and Fisheries formulates or amends a comprehensive plan for the marine environment, he/she may request

the heads of relevant central administrative agencies or the Mayors/Do Governors to submit necessary data.

Article 11 (Details of Comprehensive Plans for Marine Environment)

Each comprehensive plan for the marine environment shall include the following:

1. Current status of the marine environment and changes in conditions;

2. Target-setting and step-by-step strategies for conserving and utilizing the marine environment;

3. Assessment of marine health and marine environmental quality, and the marine environmental standards;

4. Comprehensive space management for the marine environment;

5. Managing the marine environment to respond to climate change;

6. Promoting and supporting marine environmental education;

7. Promoting marine environmental technology and the marine environmental industry;

8. International cooperation for conservation and utilization of the marine environment;

9. Securing finances for conservation and utilization of the marine environment;

10. Other matters relating to conservation and utilization of the marine environment.

Article 12 (Implementation of Comprehensive Plans for Marine Environment, etc.) (1) Where a comprehensive plan for the marine environment is formulated or amended under Article 10, the Minister of Oceans and Fisheries shall notify the heads of relevant central administrative agencies and the Mayors/Do Governors thereof.

(2) Upon receipt of the notification under paragraph (1), the heads of relevant central administrative agencies and the Mayors/Do Governors shall take measures necessary to implement the comprehensive plan for the marine environment.

Article 13 (Establishment of Marine Environmental Standards) (1) After hearing opinions of the heads of relevant central administrative agencies, the Minister of Oceans and Fisheries shall establish and publicly notify marine environmental standards by sea area and purpose of use, which are required to implement policies for preserving the marine environment and marine ecosystems under Articles 13 and 14 of the Framework Act on Marine Fishery Development, taking into account the environmental standards referred to in Article 12 of the Framework Act on Environmental Policy; and shall ensure that the appropriateness of such marine environmental standards is maintained according to changes in the marine environment.

(2) Where deemed necessary based on the particular conditions of the waters under his/her jurisdiction, a Mayor/Do Governor may establish or amend separate local marine environmental standards, which are stricter than the marine environmental standards referred to in paragraph (1), and publicly notify the standards. In such cases, the Mayor/Do Governor shall obtain prior approval from the Minister of Oceans and Fisheries.

(3) Necessary matters, such as the methods of establishing or amending the marine environmental standards under paragraph (1) and the local marine environmental standards under paragraph (2), shall be prescribed by Presidential Decree.

Article 14 (Meeting Marine Environmental Standards)

Where the State or a local government formulates a plan, or executes a project, in relation to the marine environment, it shall take account of the following matters to meet the marine environmental standards referred to in Article 13:

1. Eliminating the causes of marine pollution or minimizing marine pollution;

2. Eliminating the causes of deterioration of the marine ecosystem and restoring the marine ecosystem;

3. Properly distributing finances for conservation and utilization of the marine environment.

Article 15 (Comprehensive Space Management of Marine Environment) (1) To systematically manage and sustainably use the marine environment, the Minister of Oceans and Fisheries shall manage the marine environment by classifying it into spaces by zone and purpose of use.

(2) In order to manage spaces of the marine environment under paragraph (1), the Minister of Oceans and Fisheries shall prepare necessary measures, such as formulating a plan for ocean spaces.

(3) The space management of the marine environment under paragraph (1), formulation of a plan for ocean spaces under paragraph (2), and other necessary matters shall be prescribed by Presidential Decree.

Article 16 (Designation, etc. of Marine Environmental Management Sea Areas) The Minister of Oceans and Fisheries shall prepare policies to systematically preserve and manage the marine environment and to sustainably develop and use it by classifying the waters into a sea area which has a desirable marine environment and requires continuous conservation; a sea area in which it is impracticable to meet the marine environmental standards; or a sea area in which substantial problems have occurred or are likely to occur in relation to the preservation of the marine environment.

Article 17 (Response to Marine Climate Change) (1) In order to respond to climate change defined in subparagraph 12 of Article 2 of the Framework Act on Low Carbon, Green Growth in the marine and fisheries sector, the State and local governments shall prepare policies necessary for matters prescribed by Presidential Decree, such as surveys on the sea, impact prediction, and adaptation.

(2) The Minister of Oceans and Fisheries may provide technical or administrative support for local governments, citizens, business entities, etc. in connection with their activities to respond to marine climate change.

Article 18 (Comprehensive Marine Environmental Surveys) (1) The Minister of Oceans and Fisheries shall regularly conduct a comprehensive survey on the status of, and changes in, the marine environment.

(2) A Mayor/Do Governor may conduct a survey on the marine environment for the waters under his/her jurisdiction, and shall report plans for, and finding from, the survey to the Minister of Oceans and Fisheries.

(3) Matters concerning the surveys referred to in paragraphs (1) and (2) shall be prescribed by Presidential Decree.

Article 19 (Marine Environmental Quality Assessment) (1) To efficiently preserve the marine environment and use the sea in an environmentally friendly manner, the Minister of Oceans and Fisheries shall conduct an assessment of the environmental value of the sea (hereinafter referred to as "marine environmental quality assessment").

(2) The criteria and method for conducting marine environmental quality assessments and other necessary matters shall be prescribed by Presidential Decree.

(3) The Minister of Oceans and Fisheries shall ensure that the results of marine environmental quality assessments will be reflected in the marine and fisheries-related plans prescribed by Presidential Decree, in cooperation with the heads of relevant central administrative agencies.

Article 20 (Sea Area Utilization Impact Assessment, etc.)

Any person who intends to engage in activities to develop or use the sea shall consult with the Minister of Oceans and Fisheries as to the appropriateness, etc. of the use of the relevant sea area in order to ensure that such activities influencing the marine environment can be performed in an environmentally sustainable manner; and the Minister of Oceans and Fisheries may assess the impacts of developing or using the sea on the marine environment.

CHAPTER III. ESTABLISHMENT OF FOUNDATION FOR MARINE ENVIRONMENTAL POLICIES

Article 21 (Integrated Management of Marine Environment Information)

(1) The Minister of Oceans and Fisheries shall prepare an integrated management system for marine environment information, such as building an integrated marine environmental information network, in order to disseminate knowledge and information about the marine environment, establish standards related to the marine environment, formulate relevant plans, and conduct assessments.

(2) Matters necessary for the integrated management system for marine environment information referred to in paragraph (1), shall be prescribed by Presidential Decree.

Article 22 (Accuracy Control of Marine Environment Information)

To enhance the reliability and utilization of data, information, etc. gathered through comprehensive marine environmental surveys, etc., the Minister of Oceans and Fisheries shall determine the standards for acquisition, processing and management of the data, information, etc., and take measures necessary for the implementation thereof, such as technical guidance and ability certification.

Article 23 (Development, etc. of Science and Technology related to Marine Environment) (1) The State and local governments shall promote research, technology development, and relevant industries necessary to prevent or respond to marine pollution and deterioration of marine ecosystems, to restore and improve the sea and marine ecosystems, or to enhance ship energy efficiency.

(2) In order to promote research, technology development, and relevant industries under paragraph (1), the Minister of Oceans and Fisheries shall prepare and implement policies necessary for nurturing professional manpower for marine environmental technology.

Article 24 (Facilitating International Cooperation) (1) The State and local governments shall recognize the seriousness of impacts of climate change on the marine environment, such as rising sea levels and ocean acidification; engage in exchanges of marine environment information and relevant technology; nurture professional manpower through international cooperation; and cooperate with foreign governments and international bodies relating to the marine environment, such as mutual cooperation on conserving and managing the marine environment at a global level in relation to climate change, marine pollution, etc.

(2) In order to promote cooperation under paragraph (1), the Minister of Oceans and Fisheries may implement projects prescribed by Presidential Decree, such as joint surveys of the marine environment and the development of science and technology related to the marine environment, in cooperation with foreign governments, international bodies, etc. relating to the marine environment. In such cases, the Minister of Oceans and Fisheries may require relevant Korean research institutes, academic institutions, etc. to jointly participate in relevant projects; and may grant necessary subsidies thereto, within budgetary limits, as prescribed by Presidential Decree.

Article 25 (Promotion of and Support for Marine Environmental Education)

(1) The State and local governments shall formulate policies to promote marine environmental education in order to raise awareness of the significance of conserving and utilizing the marine environment and to cultivate knowledge, functions, attitudes, values, etc. necessary for the sustainable conservation, management and utilization of the marine environment.

(2) The Minister of Oceans and Fisheries shall formulate and implement a promotion plan for marine environmental education, which includes the following matters, every five years pursuant to paragraph (1):

1. Objectives and development strategies for marine environmental education;

2. Nurturing and supporting professional manpower for marine environmental education;

3. Developing and disseminating teaching materials and programs relating to the marine environment;

4. Measures to subsidize marine environmental education implemented by marine-related private institutions, organizations, etc.;

5. Any other matters necessary to promote marine environmental education.

(3) The Minister of Oceans and Fisheries may fully or partially subsidize, within budgetary limits, necessary expenses incurred by institutions, organizations, etc. in conducting marine environmental education.

CHAPTER IV. SUPPLEMENTARY PROVISIONS

Article 26 (Marine Environment Preservation Association) (1) The Marine Environment Preservation Association (hereinafter referred to as the "Association") shall be established to conduct surveys, research, education, public relations, etc. for the conservation and utilization of the marine environment.

(2) The Association shall be a juristic person.

(3) The composition and operation of the Association and other necessary matters shall be prescribed by Presidential Decree.

(4) Except as otherwise expressly provided for in this Act, the provisions of the Civil Act governing incorporated associations shall apply mutatis mutandis to the Association.

Article 27 (Promotion of and Support for Activities by Private Organizations) (1) The State and local governments shall prepare policies necessary to promote voluntary activities by private organizations for conservation of the marine environment.

(2) Where a private organization engages in such activities as surveys, improvements, education, public relations, etc. in relation to the marine environment, the Minister of Oceans and Fisheries may provide necessary administrative support for such organization.

Article 28 (Delegation and Entrustment) (1) Part of the authority of the Minister of Oceans and Fisheries bestowed under this Act, may be delegated to a Mayor/Do Governor or the administrator of a regional office of oceans and fisheries, as prescribed by Presidential Decree.

(2) Part of the duties of the Minister of Oceans and Fisheries imposed under this Act, may be entrusted to the head of a relevant specialized institution or public institution, as prescribed by Presidential Decree.

TREATIES/AGREEMENTS
CONCLUDED BY
THE REPUBLIC OF KOREA

Treaties/Agreements
Concluded by the Republic of Korea*

The Editorial Board
ILA Korean Branch

1. BILATERAL AGREEMENTS

1-1 SOCIAL SECURITY

Agreement on Social Security between the Government of the Republic of Korea and the Government of the Republic of Chile
[Adopted April 22, 2015, Entered into force February 1, 2017]**

Agreement on Social Security between the Government of the Republic of Korea and the Government of the Republic of Finland
[Adopted September 9, 2015, Entered into force February 1, 2017]

Understanding on Social Security between the Government of the Republic of Korea and the Gouvernement du Québec
[Adopted November 24, 2015, Entered into force September 1, 2017]

1-2 MILITARY/SECURITY

Agreement between the Government of the Republic of Korea and the Government of the Hashemite Kingdom of Jordan on the Exchange and Mutual Protection of Classified Military Information

---

* Treaties are found at the homepage of Ministry of Foreign Affairs, Republic of Korea, http:/www.mofa.go.kr/
** Entered into force the Republic of Korea

[Adopted May 30, 2015, Entered into force February 1, 2017]

Agreement between the Government of the Republic of Korea and the Government of the Republic of Chile on Cooperation in the Fields of the Defense Industry and Logistics Support
[Adopted April 22, 2015, Entered into force April 22, 2017]

1-3 COOPERATION FUND

Framework Arrangement between the Government of the Republic of Korea and the Government of the Plurinational State of Bolivia concerning Loans from the Economic Development Cooperation Fund for the Years 2015 through 2019
[Adopted March 27, 2015, Entered into force February 1, 2017]

Framework Agreement between the Government of the Republic of Korea and the Government of the Arab Republic of Egypt concerning Loans from the Economic Development Cooperation Fund
[Adopted March 3, 2016, Entered into force December 29, 2017]

Arrangement between the Government of the Republic of Korea and the Government of the Arab Republic of Egypt concerning a Loan from the Economic Development Cooperation Fund for the Project for the Modernization of the Railway Signaling System on Nagh Hamady and Luxor Corridor in Egypt
[Adopted March 3, 2016, Entered into force January 9, 2017]

Arrangement between the Government of the Republic of Korea and the Royal Government of Cambodia concerning a Loan from the Economic Development Cooperation Fund for Upgrading of National Road No. 48 Project
[Adopted January 31, 2017, Entered into force January 31, 2017]

Framework Arrangement between the Government of the Republic of Korea and the Royal Government of Cambodia concerning Loans from the Economic Development Cooperation Fund for the Years 2016 through 2018
[Adopted January 31, 2017, Entered into force January 31, 2017]

Framework Arrangement between the Government of the Republic of Korea and the Government of the Republic of Ghana concerning Loans from the Economic Development Cooperation Fund for the Years 2017 through 2019
[Adopted March 29, 2017, Entered into force March 29, 2017]

Arrangement between the Government of the Republic of Korea and the Government of the Republic of Nicaragua concerning a Loan from the Economic Development Cooperation Fund for the Construction of Bypass Managua Project
[Adopted March 30, 2017, Entered into force March 30, 2017]

Agreement between the Government of the Republic of Korea and the Government of the Republic of India concerning Loans from the Economic Development Cooperation Fund
[Adopted June 14, 2017, Entered into force June 14, 2017]

Framework Arrangement between the Government of the Republic of Korea and the Government of the Socialist Republic of Vietnam concerning Loans from the Economic Development Cooperation Fund for the Years 2016 through 2020
[Adopted November 8, 2017, Entered into force November 8, 2017]

Framework Arrangement between the Government of the Republic of Korea and the Government of the Republic of Uzbekistan concerning Loans from the Economic Development Cooperation Fund for the Years 2018 through 2020
[Adopted November 23, 2017, Entered into force November 23, 2017]

Framework Arrangement between the Government of the Republic of Korea and the Government of the Democratic Socialist Republic of Sri Lanka concerning Loans from the Economic Development Cooperation Fund for the Year 2017 through 2019
[Adopted November 29, 2017, Entered into force November 29, 2017]

Arrangement between the Government of the Republic of Korea and the Government of the People's Republic of Bangladesh concerning Activities of the Economic Development Cooperation Fund in the People's Republic of Bangladesh
[Adopted December 3, 2017, Entered into force December 3, 2017]

Arrangement between the Government of the Republic of Korea and the Government of the Republic of Kenya concerning a Loan from the Economic Development Cooperation Fund for the Establishment of Kenya Advanced Institute of Science and Technology Project
[Adopted November 20, 2017, Entered into force November 20, 2017]

1-4. CULTURE

Cultural Agreement between the Government of the Republic of Korea and the Government of the Republic of Turkey
[Adopted August 31, 2013, Entered into force March 31, 2017]

1-5. MUTUAL WAIVER OF VISA REQUIREMENTS FOR HOLDERS OF DIPLOMATIC AND OFFICIAL PASSPORTS

Agreement between the Government of the Republic of Korea and the Government of the Republic of Mozambique on the Mutual Waiver of Visa Requirements for Holders of Diplomatic and Official Passports
[Adopted November 5, 2015, Entered into force February 16, 2017]

1-6. RECIPROCAL RECOGNITION AND EXCHANGE OF DRIVER'S LICENSES

Agreement between the Government of the Republic of Korea and the Government of the Republic of Nicaragua on the Reciprocal Recognition and Exchange of Driver's Licenses
[Adopted November 4, 2016, Entered into force April 5, 2017]

1-7. INFORMATION RELATING TO TAX MATTERS

Agreement between the Government of the Republic of Korea and the Government of the Republic of Mauritius on the Exchange of Informantion relating to Tax Matters
[Adopted August 11, 2016, Entered into force April 13, 2017]

Agreement between the Government of the Republic of Korea and the Government of the Republic of Vanuatu for the Exchange of Information relating to Tax Matters
[Adopted March 14, 2012, Entered into force June 8, 2017]

1-8. Tax

Convention between the Government of the Republic of Korea and the Government of the Republic of Kenya for the Avoidance of Double Taxation and the Prevention of Fiscal Evasion with respect to Taxes on Income
[Adopted July 8, 2014, Entered into force April 3, 2017]

Convention between the Republic of Korea and the Federal Democratic Republic of Ethiopia for the Avoidance of Double Taxation and the Prevention of Fiscal Evasion with respect to Taxes on Income
[Adopted May 26, 2016, Entered into force October 31, 2017]

1-9. Promotion and Protection of Investments

Agreement between the Government of the Republic of Korea and the Government of the Republic of Kenya for the Promotion and Protection of Investments
[Adopted July 8, 2014, Entered into force May 3, 2017]

1-10. Criminal Matters

Treaty between the Republic of Korea and the State of the United Arab Emirates on Mutual Legal Assistance in Criminal Matters
[Adopted February 28, 2014, Entered into force May 17, 2017]

1-11. Extradition

Treaty on Extradition between the Republic of Korea and the State of the United Arab Emirates
[Adopted February 28, 2014, Entered into force May 17, 2017]

1-12. Economy/Science/Technology

Agreement on Economic Cooperation between the Government of the Republic of Korea and the Government of the Slovak Republic
[Adopted February 28, 2017, Entered into force June 1, 2017]

Agreement for Science, Technology and Innovation Cooperation between the Government of the Republic of Korea and the Government of Canada
[Adopted December 20, 2016, Entered into force May 17, 2017]

1-13. EXEMPTION FROM VISA REQUIREMENTS FOR HOLDERS OF DIPLOMATIC PASSPORTS

Agreement between the Government of the Republic of Korea and the Government of the Hashemite Kingdom of Jordan On the Exemption from Visa Requirements for Holders of Diplomatic Passports
[Adopted September 11, 2015, Entered into force May 22, 2017]

1-14. CUSTOMS

Agreement between the Government of the Republic of Korea and the Government of the Islamic Republic of Iran regarding Co-operation and Mutual Administration Assistance in Customs Matters
[Adopted May 2, 2015, Entered into force June 2, 2017]

Agreement between the Republic of Korea and the Oriental Republic of Uruguay on Cooperation and Mutual Assistance in Customs Matters
[Adopted November 15, 2016, Entered into force September 27, 2017]

1-15. FTA

Exchange of Notes Amending the Annex 4 of the Free Trade Agreement between the Government of the Republic of Korea and the Government of the Republic of Chile
[Adopted March 20, 2017, Entered into force July 1, 2017]

1-16. OTHERS

Agreement between the Government of the Republic of Korea and the Government of the Russian Federation on the Establishment of the Direct Secure Communication System
[Adopted September 6, 2017, Entered into force September 6, 2017]

1-17. Air

Agreement between the Government of the Republic of Korea and the Government of the Federal Democratic Republic of Ethiopia for Air Services between and beyond their Respective Territories
[Adopted May 26, 2017, Entered into force November 6, 2017]

1-18. Grant Aid

Framework Arrangement on Grant Aid for the Year 2017 between the Government of the Republic of Korea and the Government of the Republic of Kenya
[Adopted November 20, 2017, Entered into force November 20, 2017]

Framework Arrangement on Grant Aid for the Year 2017 Between the Government of the Republic of Korea and the Government of the Republic of Rwanda
[Adopted December 7, 2017, Entered into force December 7, 2017]

2. MULTILATERAL AGREEMENTS

2-1. Trade/Commerce/Industry

Protocol Amending the TRIPS Agreement
[Adopted December 6, 2005, Entered into force January 23, 2017]

Decision to Endorse the Transposed Lists of Goods for the Treatment for Certain Goods in the Rules of Origin, Annex 3 of the Agreement on Trade in Goods
[Adopted July 20, 2016, Entered into force November 1, 2017]

Protocol Amending the Marrakesh Agreement Establishing the World Trade Organization (Trade Facilitation Agreement, TFA)
[Adopted November 27, 2014, Entered into force February 22, 2017]

Amendments to Annex I to the Free Trade Agreement between the Republic of Korea and the EFTA States on Rules of Origin and Customs Procedures
[Adopted March 14, 2012, Entered into force December 1, 2017]

2-2. DISARMAMENT

The Arms Trade Treaty
[Adopted April 2, 2013, Entered into force February 26, 2017]

2-3. ENVIRONMENT

Nagoya Protocol on Access to Genetic Resources and the Fair and Equitable Sharing
of Benefits Arising from their Utilization to the Convention on Biological Diversity
[Adopted October 29, 2010, Entered into force August 17, 2017]

2-4. MARINE/LAW OF THE SEA

International Convention for the Control and Management of Ships' Ballast Water
and Sediments, 2004
[Adopted February 13, 2004, Entered into force September 8, 2017]

2-5. HUMAN RIGHTS

Withdrawal of a Reservation of Article 21 Paragraph of the Convention on the Rights
of the Child
[Adopted November 20, 1989, Entered into force August 11, 2017]

2-6. NUCLEAR

Regional Co-operative Agreement for Research, Development and Training related to
Nuclear Science and Technology, 2017
[Adopted May 18, 2016, Entered into force December 8, 2017]

2-7. SCIENCE/TECHNOLOGY

Agreement continuing the International Science and Technology Center
[Adopted December 9, 2015, Entered into force December 14, 2017]

INDEX

AUTHOR GUIDELINES AND STYLE SHEET

I. SUBMISSION

Manuscripts should be submitted in Microsoft Word and electronically sent to ilakoreanbranch@gmail.com.

II. GENERAL TERMS AND PEER-REVIEW SYSTEM OF PUBLICATION

All manuscripts are subject to initial evaluation by the KYIL Editorial Board and subsequently sent out to independent reviewers for a peer review. The Editorial Board accepts manuscripts on a rolling basis and will consider requests for an expedited review in appropriate cases.

III. FORMATING

1. ABSTRACT

Please include an abstract (no more than 150 words) at the beginning of an article.

2. TEXT

Main Text: Times New Roman, font size 12, 1.5 spacing
Endnotes: Times New Roman, font size 10, single spacing

3. Citing Reference

The KYIL requires endnotes with subsequent numbering; the initial endnote should be indicated with '*,' if it is necessary to provide explanatory information about the manuscript.

Please include a reference list for all works that are cited at the end of the manuscript.

IV. NOTES

1. Books

P. Malanczuk, *Akehurst's Modern Introduction to International Law*, 7th ed. (New York: Eoutledge, 1997), p. 1.

2. Articles

Chao Wang, *China's Preferential Trade Remedy Approaches: A New Haven School Perspective*, Vol.21 No.1, Asia Pacific Law Review, (2013), p. 103.

3. Articles in collections

J. Paulsson & Z. Douglas, *Indirect Expropriation in Investment Treaty Arbitrations, in* Arbitrating Foreign Investment Disputes 148 (N. Horn & S. Kroll eds., Kluwer Law International, 2004).

4. Articles in newspaper

YI Whan-Woo, *Korea, New Zealand embrace free trade pact*, Korea Times, November 14, 2014.

5. Unpublished materials

PARK Jung-Won, *Minority Rights Constraints on a State's Power to Regulate Citizenship under International Law*, Ph.D thesis (2006), on file with author.

6. Working papers and reports

OECD, *'Indirect Expropriation' and the 'Right to Regulate' in International Investment Law*, OECD Working Paper, 2014/09.

7. Internet sources

C. Schreuer, *The Concept of Expropriation under the ETC and Other Investment Protection Treaties* (2005), http://www.univie,ac,at/intlaw/pdf/csunpuybl paper_3pdf. [Accessed on September 22, 2015]

V. GUIDELINE FOR AUTHORS

1. Article

Manuscripts must be in the form of a regular paper including endnotes and references. The length for an article should not exceed 10,000 words in English excluding notes and/or a full length should be within 15 pages in A4- sized paper. (Letter Size: 8.5 x 11 inch).

2. Special Report

Manuscripts for Special Report must be in the form of a descriptive report which covers the International law issues related to Korea in the past 5 years. Special Report must include author's comments with less than 10 endnotes and 5 references. The length for an special report should be no more than 5,000 words or within 7 pages in A4-sized paper. (Letter Size, 8.5 x 11 inch).

3. RECENT DEVELOPMENT

Manuscripts must cover the trends in international law related to Korea in the preceding year. Recent Development must be in the form of a short report, including less than 5 endnotes. The length for Recent Development should be no more than 2,000 words or within 4 pages in A4-sized paper. (Letter Size: 8.5 x 11 inch).